The Law Commission
(LAW COM No 307)

COHABITATION: THE FINANCIAL CONSEQUENCES OF RELATIONSHIP BREAKDOWN

Presented to the Parliament of the United Kingdom by the Lord Chancellor and Secretary of State for Justice by Command of Her Majesty
July 2007

Cm 7182   £32.50

The Law Commission was set up by the Law Commissions Act 1965 for the purpose of promoting the reform of the law.

The Law Commissioners are:

    The Honourable Mr Justice Etherton, *Chairman*
    Mr Stuart Bridge
    Mr David Hertzell[1]
    Professor Jeremy Horder
    Mr Kenneth Parker QC

The Chief Executive of the Law Commission is Mr Steve Humphreys.

The Law Commission is located at Conquest House, 37-38 John Street, Theobalds Road, London WC1N 2BQ.

The terms of this report were agreed on 3 July 2007.

The text of this report is available on the Internet at:

http://www.lawcom.gov.uk

---

[1]   Mr David Hertzell was appointed a Law Commissioner with effect from 1 July 2007, in succession to Professor Hugh Beale QC, FBA. The terms of this report were agreed on 3 July 2007.

THE LAW COMMISSION

COHABITATION: THE FINANCIAL CONSEQUENCES OF RELATIONSHIP BREAKDOWN

TABLE OF CONTENTS

THE LAW COMMISSION

COHABITATION: THE FINANCIAL CONSEQUENCES OF RELATIONSHIP BREAKDOWN

To the Right Honourable Jack Straw MP, Lord Chancellor and Secretary of State for Justice

PART 1
INTRODUCTION

THIS REPORT

1.1 This Report makes recommendations to Parliament on certain aspects of the law relating to cohabitants. It considers the financial consequences of the ending of cohabiting relationships by separation or death. It follows two years of work by the Law Commission and builds on a Consultation Paper published on 31 May 2006.

1.2 In this Report, we conclude that reform is needed to address inadequacies in the current law. We recommend a new statutory scheme designed specifically for cohabitants on separation. The scheme would apply only to cohabitants who have had children together or who have lived together for a specified number of years.[1] The scheme would not equate cohabitants with married couples or give them equivalent rights. Nor would it provide a new status which cohabitants should sign up to in order to gain new rights. The scheme would apply to all cohabitants who satisfied the eligibility criteria. But it would respect the autonomy of couples by allowing them, subject to necessary protections, to disapply the scheme and make their own arrangements. It would not automatically require parties to share their property with their ex-partners and would not require them to pay maintenance. Instead, the scheme would address particular economic consequences of the contributions made by the parties during the relationship.

1.3 We recognise that these recommendations will be unwelcome to some who, for various reasons, consider that cohabitants should not be granted legal remedies of this sort. Others may feel that the recommendations do not go far enough and that in the twenty-first century cohabitants should be given the same status and the same rights as married couples. Others may disagree with aspects of the technical operation of our recommended scheme. All of these views were expressed during consultation and have been taken into account in forming our recommendations.

1.4 Recent results of the British Social Attitudes survey indicate that a substantial majority of people in this jurisdiction think cohabitants should have access to

---

[1] Referred to in this Report as a "minimum duration requirement".

financial relief on relationship breakdown.[2] However, this is not an issue on which it is possible to achieve consensus. We believe that our recommendations offer a workable system to deal with the separation of cohabitants which would be a considerable improvement on the current law. Such a system would help individual cohabitants and their children. It would provide economically vulnerable members of society with the private means to rebuild their lives and ensure a fairer division of assets on relationship breakdown.

1.5　England and Wales would not be alone if it introduced a statutory scheme for the adjustment of property rights or financial provision between cohabiting couples on separation.[3] For example, all Australian states and most Canadian provinces have such legislation. In 2001, New Zealand extended its remedies applicable to spouses on divorce to cohabitants of three years' standing and to those with a child. Prominent amongst European jurisdictions which provide specific schemes for cohabitants is Sweden. Nearer home, Scottish legislation empowers the court to make orders for financial provision when cohabitants separate. And there have recently been recommendations in Ireland for the introduction of a statutory scheme dealing with the separation of cohabiting couples.[4]

WHY IS THIS ISSUE IMPORTANT?

1.6　Cohabitation outside marriage in England and Wales has become increasingly common over recent decades, and is expected to become more prevalent in the future. Similar trends have been observed in many other European countries.[5]

1.7　There are difficulties, discussed in Part 2 of the Consultation Paper, with presenting statistical evidence about the prevalence and characteristics of cohabiting relationships. Cohabiting relationships are not formalised, and since "cohabitation" can be described and defined in different ways, it is difficult to collect entirely accurate data about it. However, demographers and other researchers have devised various mechanisms for mitigating these difficulties and there is now a vast research literature on this subject.[6]

---

[2]　This is a large-scale quantitative survey that has been fielded most years since 1983. The most recent survey covered nearly 4000 people, around 3000 of whom were asked questions relating to cohabitation. The results of the 2006 Survey will be published in January 2008: A Park et al, *British Social Attitudes. The 24th Report* (forthcoming, January 2008). For the last published survey results on this issue, see A Barlow, S Duncan, G James and A Park, "Just a piece of paper? Marriage and cohabitation", in A Park, J Curtice, K Thompson, L Jarvis and C Bromley (eds), *British Social Attitudes: Public policy, social ties. The 18th Report* (2001).

[3]　See Appendix C to the Consultation Paper for a list of jurisdictions which have already legislated.

[4]　See para 1.45.

[5]　See K Kiernan, "The Rise of Cohabitation and Childbearing Outside Marriage in Western Europe" (2001) 15 *International Journal of Law, Policy and the Family* 1.

[6]　See the Consultation Paper, para 2.4 for a description of the most important sources of evidence.

Demographic data and future projections

1.8 While the marriage rate has been declining[7] and marriage is being deferred until later in life,[8] the number of cohabiting couples has increased dramatically since the 1970s and is expected to continue to rise. The 2001 Census[9] recorded just over two million cohabiting couples in England and Wales,[10] a 67% increase on the figures from 1991.

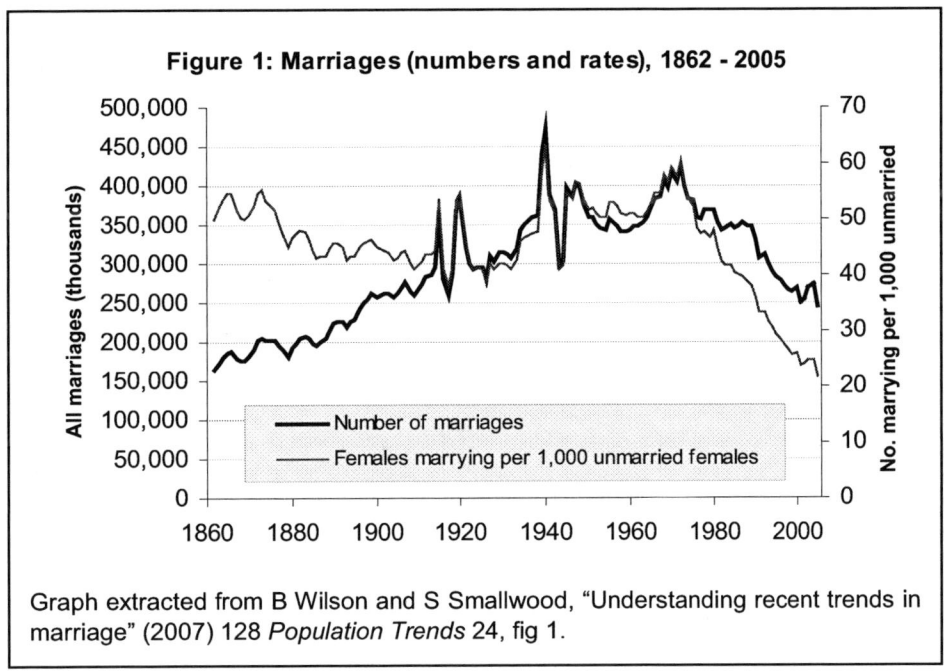

Figure 1: Marriages (numbers and rates), 1862 - 2005

Graph extracted from B Wilson and S Smallwood, "Understanding recent trends in marriage" (2007) 128 *Population Trends* 24, fig 1.

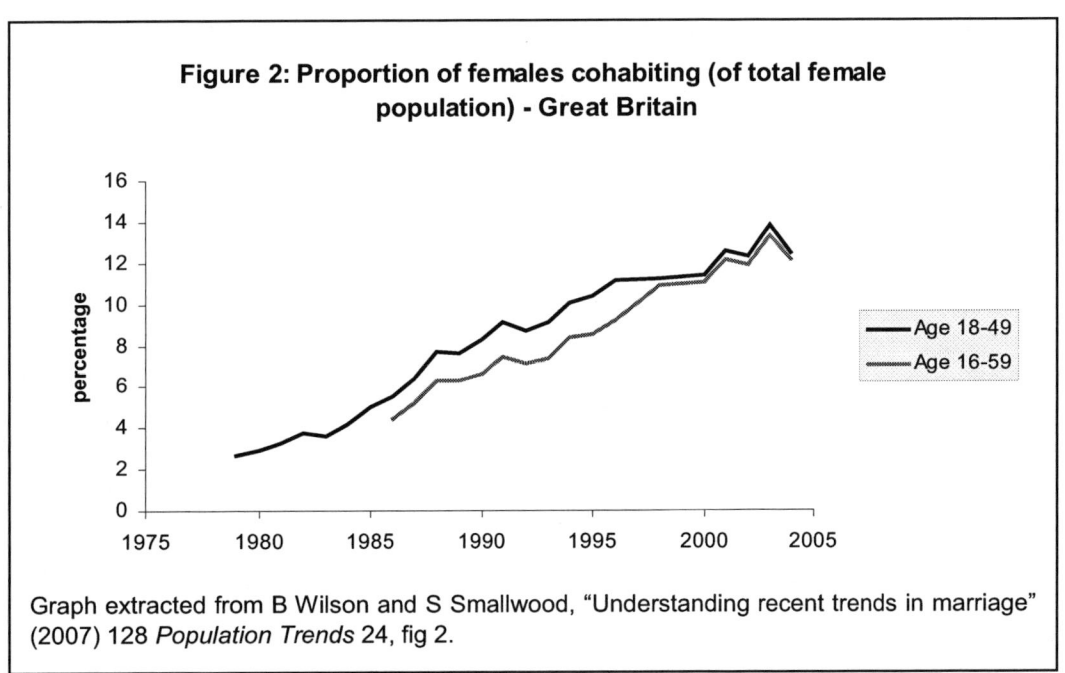

Figure 2: Proportion of females cohabiting (of total female population) - Great Britain

Graph extracted from B Wilson and S Smallwood, "Understanding recent trends in marriage" (2007) 128 *Population Trends* 24, fig 2.

---

7   Office for National Statistics ("ONS"), *Social Trends 37* (2007) p 18 and fig 2.9. See most recently, B Wilson and S Smallwood, "Understanding Recent Trends in Marriage" (2007) 128 *Population Trends* 24: see fig 1.

8   ONS, *Social Trends 37* (2007), p 18.

9   A survey of the population of England and Wales conducted by ONS once every ten years.

10 ONS, *Census 2001,* table S006; these figures include same-sex couples. See also fig 2.
.

1.9 The number of children being born to cohabiting couples in England and Wales has also risen. In 2001, over 740,000 cohabiting couples had dependent children,[11] between them supporting over 1.27 million children.[12] The number of cohabiting couple households with dependent children more than doubled between 1991 and 2001. This is reflected in the increasing rate of births in the UK to parents who are not married. In 1970, fewer than 10% of births were to unmarried parents.[13] By 2004, 42% of births fell in that category.[14] The increase in such births has been accompanied by a similar rise in the proportion of such births in England and Wales that are jointly registered by both parents. In 2004, 76.4% of those registrations were to parents recorded as living at the same address, who may reasonably be assumed to be cohabitants.[15]

1.10 Cohabitation is expected to become increasingly common and to spread across a wider range of the population in terms of age. The Government Actuary's Department has predicted that by 2031 the number of cohabiting couples in England and Wales will have increased to 3.8 million.[16] On this projection, over one in four couples will be cohabiting by 2031; 16% of adults[17] will be in cohabiting relationships and 41% married.[18] The elderly cohabiting population is expected to expand at a far greater rate than that of the cohabiting population as a whole. The population pyramid charts opposite (figures 3 and 4) are reproduced from the Government Actuary's Department website.[19] Other data suggest that the number of children dependent upon a cohabiting couple will also increase as more couples have children outside marriage and fewer parents subsequently marry.[20]

[11] See ONS, *Census 2001*, table S006.

[12] ONS, *Census 2001*, table T01; 27% of these children were aged 0 to 2. There were over 2.6 million children in lone parent families in 2001.

[13] K Kiernan, "Unmarried Cohabitation and Parenthood in Britain and Europe" (2004) 26 *Law and Policy* 33, at 40, fig 2.

[14] ONS, *Social Trends 36* (2006) p 30 and table 2.19, which provides comparisons with other EU countries; *Social Trends 35* (2005) pp 26 to 27 and fig 2.17, which shows the changes in jointly and solely registered non-marital births over time.

[15] ONS, *Birth Statistics* Series FM1 no 33 (2005) table 3.10. See also data from Millennium Cohort Study: K Kiernan and K Smith, "Unmarried parenthood: new insights from the Millennium Cohort Study" (2003) 114 *Population Trends* 26, fig 1: 25% of children were born to cohabiting couples.

[16] These are the principal projections from Government Actuary's Department, *Marital Status Projections for England and Wales* (2005), available at http://www.gad.gov.uk/marital_status_projections/background.htm (last visited 3 July 2007).

[17] "Adult" here refers to those over the age of 16.

[18] The current proportions are 10% and 53% respectively.

[19] http://www.gad.gov.uk/marital_status_projections/2003/results/pyramid/cohabitation.pps (last visited 3 July 2007).

[20] J Haskey, "Cohabitation in Great Britain: past, present and future trends – and attitudes" (2001) 103 *Population Trends* 4, at 18.

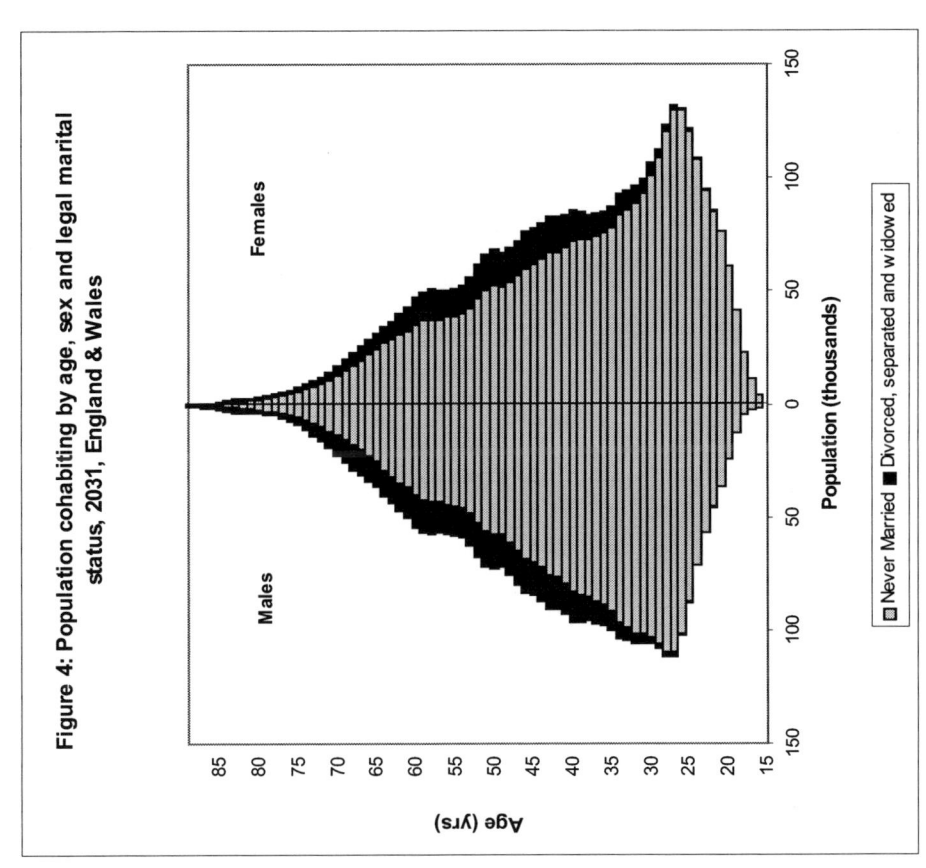

Figure 4: Population cohabiting by age, sex and legal marital status, 2031, England & Wales

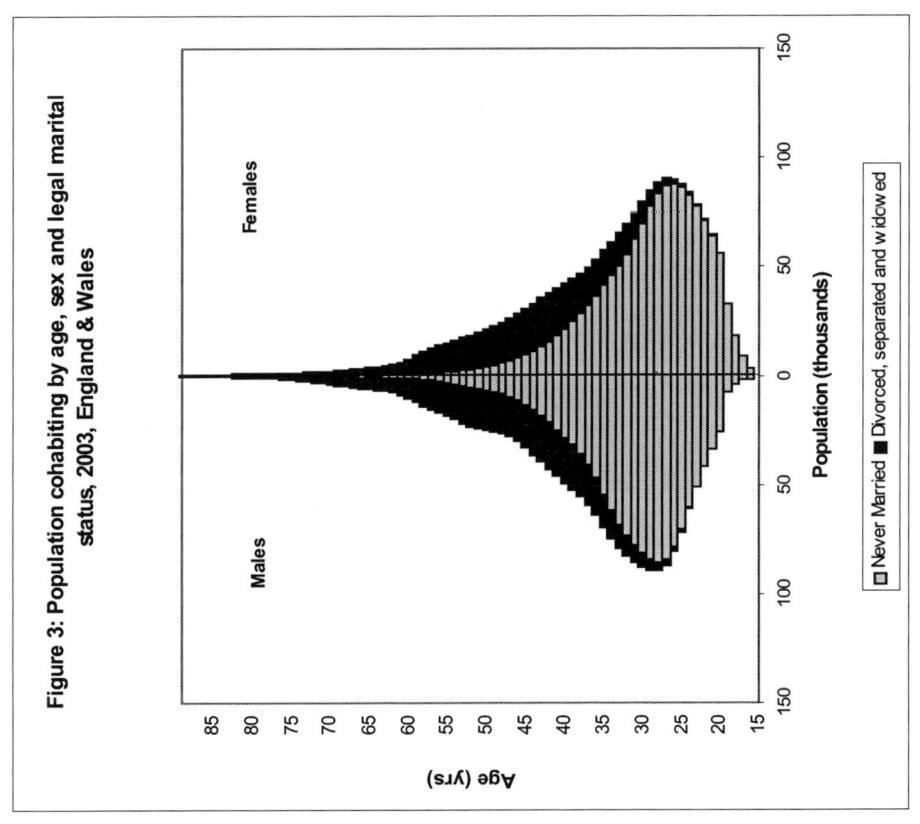

Figure 3: Population cohabiting by age, sex and legal marital status, 2003, England & Wales

Public attitudes towards cohabitation

1.11   Just as cohabitation has been increasing, so too has its public acceptance. The British Social Attitudes survey 2000 assessed public attitudes towards various aspects of cohabitation and marriage. 67% of respondents agreed that it was "all right for a couple to live together without intending to get married".[21]

1.12   Although responses varied markedly by age group (a higher proportion of those aged 18 to 24 (84%) agreed with the proposition compared with those aged over 65 (35%)), rates of agreement amongst different age groups are changing over time.[22] As today's older cohorts are gradually replaced by today's younger generations, the overall acceptance of cohabitation as a social practice seems likely to increase, along with the prevalence of cohabitation.

1.13   Cohabitation is therefore already a significant social practice. It is growing, and continued growth is forecast. This is, of course, not in itself a reason for law reform. But if it is accepted that the current law is inadequate and gives rise to unwelcome consequences, the fact that these consequences potentially affect a significant and increasing proportion of the population is highly relevant. The issues considered in this paper are therefore not issues that will go away. We urge Government to take the necessary steps to provide this increasingly significant section of society with legal remedies capable of dealing fairly with the financial consequences should they separate.

THE BACKGROUND TO THE PROJECT

1.14   In July 2002, the Law Commission published a Discussion Paper, Sharing Homes.[23] This paper considered the law relating to the property rights of home-sharers. It covered a broad range of relationships, including friends and relatives as well as married and unmarried couples. It focused on the complex legal principles which determine when, and to what extent, a person may claim an interest in property, and sought to formulate a straightforward, more certain scheme for ascertaining and quantifying property rights in the shared home.

1.15   The Commission concluded that it was not feasible to devise a scheme which could operate fairly and evenly across the diversity of contemporary domestic circumstances. It advocated that those who are living together should be encouraged to find out about the legal implications of doing so and to make express written arrangements setting out their intentions.[24]

1.16   However, the Commission also suggested:

---

[21]   A Barlow, S Duncan, G James and A Park, "Just a Piece of Paper? Marriage and Cohabitation", in A Park, J Curtice, K Thomson, L Jarvis and C Bromley (eds), *British Social Attitudes: Public policy, social ties. The 18th Report* (2001) table 2.2.

[22]   The agreement rate amongst all of the over-45 age groups had increased by more than 10% from the 1994 survey: A Barlow, S Duncan, G James and A Park, "Just a Piece of Paper? Marriage and Cohabitation", in A Park, J Curtice, K Thomson, L Jarvis and C Bromley (eds), *British Social Attitudes: Public policy, social ties. The 18th Report* (2001) table 2.5.

[23]   Sharing Homes: A Discussion Paper (2002) Law Com No 278, available at http://www.lawcom.gov.uk/docs/lc278(1).pdf.

[24]   Sharing Homes: A Discussion Paper (2002) Law Com No 278, para 1.31(2).

> ... that further consideration should be given to the adoption, necessarily by legislation, of new legal approaches to personal relationships outside marriage, following the lead given by other jurisdictions (such as France, Australia and New Zealand).
>
> These approaches may include such mechanisms as the formal registration of civil partnerships, or, less formally, a power for the court to adjust the legal rights and obligations of individuals who are or have been living together for a defined period or in defined circumstances.[25]

1.17 Since the publication of Sharing Homes, Parliament has offered same-sex couples the opportunity to register their relationships as civil partnerships and thereby to obtain broadly equivalent rights and obligations to those applying to married couples.

1.18 During the passage of the Civil Partnership Bill through Parliament, members of the House of Lords raised questions about the law's treatment of couples and others who live together but who neither marry nor (in the case of same-sex couples) register a civil partnership. Concerns were expressed, amongst other things, about the potential financial hardship suffered by cohabitants on the termination of their relationship owing to the current lack of any coherent legal remedies addressing their financial and property disputes. In a letter of 12 May 2004, Lord Filkin, then Parliamentary Secretary at the Department for Constitutional Affairs with responsibility for family justice, indicated to Peers that he had asked the Law Commission to undertake a review of cohabitation law.

TERMS OF REFERENCE

1.19 The Law Commission's Ninth Programme of Law Reform set out the terms of reference for the project, making it clear that the project was not to consider all those who live in the same home. Relationships between blood relatives or "caring" relationships and "commercial" relationships (such as landlord and tenant or lodger) were excluded.

1.20 We acknowledged in the Consultation Paper that some would contend that the law relating to these other categories of home-sharers is also in need of reform. We expressed no opinion on the merits of such arguments. However, we took the view that "[a]rguments for wider changes to the law should not prevent us from considering reform for those within our current remit".[26] That remains our position.

1.21 The home-sharers that this project has considered are those commonly referred to as "couples", both opposite-sex and same-sex, who live together in intimate relationships. As we noted in the Consultation Paper, this group comprises a highly diverse range of partners:

> At one extreme there are young couples who move in together to save rent, but who keep their finances entirely separate and have no

---

[25] Sharing Homes: A Discussion Paper (2002) Law Com No 278, Part 6, paras (7) and (8).

[26] Cohabitation: The Financial Consequences of Relationship Breakdown (2006) Law Commission Consultation Paper No 179, para 1.20, available at http://www.lawcom.gov.uk/docs/cp179.pdf.

longer term joint plans. At the other, there are established partners who have lived together for decades, bringing up children and intending to stay together forever. There are many different sorts of relationship in between.[27]

1.22 Just as the range of relationships to be addressed by the project was limited, so too was the range of issues relating to those relationships. A number of issues were specifically excluded from consideration: parental responsibility for children, next of kin rights, insolvency, tax and social security. The operation of the child support legislation and the role of the Child Support Agency were also outside the scope of the project.[28] The project was instead deliberately confined to the financial consequences of the termination of cohabiting relationships, whether by separation or by death, as the Ninth Programme described:

> The project will focus on the financial hardship suffered by cohabitants or their children on the termination of the relationship by breakdown or death. It will only consider opposite-sex or same-sex couples in clearly defined relationships. Particular attention will be given to:
>
> (1) capital provision where there is a dependent child or children;
>
> (2) capital and income provision on relationship breakdown;
>
> (3) intestate succession and family provision on death; and
>
> (4) the Inheritance (Provision for Family and Dependants) Act 1975.
>
> The project will also consider the place of cohabitation contracts and the extent to which cohabitants should be free to make and to enforce agreements concerning their respective liabilities to provide and to maintain following separation.[29]

1.23 The principal focus of the project has therefore been on financial relief between cohabiting couples on separation. The current law does not entirely ignore the position of cohabitants who separate, but there is no jurisdiction specifically designed to provide financial relief in such circumstances. By contrast, the Inheritance (Provision for Family and Dependants) Act 1975 already provides a specific set of remedies for certain cohabitants whose relationships end on death. As a consequence, there is less need for fundamental reform in that category of case.

1.24 It is important to emphasise that we have not been asked to consider, and our review has not considered, how the State generally deals with or recognises cohabitants. At no point have we proposed the creation of a new status of cohabitant conferring a broad range of rights and privileges. We have instead

---

[27] Consultation Paper, para 1.22.

[28] See the Law Commission: Ninth Programme of Law Reform (2005) Law Com No 293, para 3.7, n 4 for the list of excluded matters, available at http://www.lawcom.gov.uk/docs/9th_Prog_Final(2).pdf.

concentrated on whether, and if so on what basis, cohabitants should be able to claim financial remedies from each other when their relationship ends.

THE CONSULTATION PAPER

1.25 The Law Commission produced two versions of its consultation document. The full 373-page Consultation Paper (referred to in this Report as "the CP") contained a comprehensive examination of the issues and set out, in considerable detail, a provisionally proposed scheme of financial relief for cohabitants. A much shorter overview paper ("the Overview") summarised the main issues under consideration. Both papers contained consultation questions and provisional proposals, the full paper addressing a larger number of issues than the Overview.

The Consultation Paper's provisional proposals in outline

1.26 The CP examined the case for reform of the law as it applies to cohabitants on their separation. It started by making clear what the law does not do and drawing attention to the popular misconception about the legal status of cohabitants, centred on what is known as the "common law marriage myth". This myth[30] perpetuates the mistaken belief that the law of England and Wales recognises cohabitants as "common law spouses" once they have lived together for some period of time.

1.27 The paper went on to examine the law that does apply to cohabitants. It concluded that the law that is currently engaged when a cohabiting couple separate is unsatisfactory. There are specific statutory remedies available in certain limited circumstances. However, the court has no jurisdiction that is specifically designed to make orders between cohabitants addressing the financial consequences of relationship breakdown. Consequently, the general law of contract, property and trusts determines the outcome by reference to entitlement to particular items of property, notably the home which the parties shared during their relationship. The CP contended that those rules have proved to be:

> ... relatively rigid and extremely difficult to apply, and their application can lead to what many would regard as unfairness between the parties. The formulation of a claim based on these rules is time-consuming and expensive, and the nature of the inquiry before the court into the history of the relationship results in a protracted hearing for those disputes that are not compromised. The inherent uncertainty of the underlying principles makes effective bargaining difficult to achieve as parties will find it hard to predict the outcome of contested litigation.[31]

---

[29] The Law Commission: Ninth Programme of Law Reform (2005) Law Com No 293, paras 3.6 to 3.7.

[30] Subscribed to by 56% of respondents to the 2000 British Social Attitudes survey; 2006 BSA data shows that a majority still hold this belief: A Park et al, *British Social Attitudes. The 24th Report* (forthcoming, January 2008).

[31] CP, para 1.28.

1.28 Having explained the deficiencies of the current law, the CP examined the possible introduction of a new remedial scheme for cohabitants. It considered the merits of what it referred to as an "opt-in scheme"; that is, a scheme which would impose enforceable financial obligations on parties in the event of their separation only if they had expressly chosen to be governed by it by some formal process of registration. However, the CP provisionally rejected such an approach on the basis that it would do nothing for those who, for whatever reason, failed to opt in. It was difficult to see how it was possible to achieve the objective of the project – that is, alleviating the financial hardship of those who have not married or registered a civil partnership – by means of an opt-in system.

1.29 Instead, the paper sought to formulate a generally applicable scheme of financial relief on separation; in other words, a scheme that would apply to qualifying couples without any election on their part that it should do so. However, in order to protect individuals' autonomy, the CP provisionally proposed that cohabiting couples should be entitled to opt out of the operation of the scheme provided that certain conditions were satisfied.

1.30 The scheme devised in the CP was specifically designed for cohabitants on separation, and based on principles different from those applicable between spouses or civil partners on divorce or dissolution. The scheme conferred jurisdiction on the court to make orders for financial relief in the exercise of its discretion. Its objective was to share, more fairly than the current law is able to do, the continuing economic advantages and disadvantages arising from the parties' contributions to the relationship.

1.31 We emphasised in the CP that we did not consider that all cohabiting couples falling within our terms of reference should have access to remedies merely because their relationship comes to an end. Simply having been in a cohabiting relationship would not be sufficient to give rise to a claim. The availability of remedies under the CP's proposed scheme of financial relief was controlled in two ways:

(1) *Eligibility to apply.* The scheme set out qualifying conditions which would govern which sorts of couple were eligible. Those who fell outside the defined category would be excluded from the scheme.

(2) *The basis on which awards would be made.* Eligibility was a necessary pre-condition to making a claim, but was not in itself sufficient to justify an award. We contended that cohabiting couples should not be entitled to a share of each other's assets at the end of their relationship irrespective of the extent to which they shared their lives during the relationship. Applicants should only be able to obtain a remedy on separation if they could show that the effects of the contributions and associated economic sacrifices they had made during the relationship would otherwise be unfairly shared following separation. In many cases, neither party would be able to establish this and no claim would therefore be tenable.

THE CONSULTATION PROCESS

1.32 Before publication of the CP, the Commission conducted extensive informal consultation with a broad range of stakeholders. These are identified in Appendix E to the CP.

1.33 On publication, the CP attracted a huge amount of press and other media interest, and there has been a steady stream of articles referring to the paper since that date. The CP elicited 256 written responses. Both the Overview and the CP appear to have been downloaded from the website in much larger numbers.

1.34 During the consultation period (which closed on 30 September 2006) we held meetings with a number of interested parties. In September, the Nuffield Foundation hosted a day-long seminar on the CP which was attended by a wide range of experts in family law and policy, and related disciplines. The Institute of Advanced Legal Studies held a public meeting on the CP which was attended by nearly 100 people in early October.

1.35 We have continued to consult widely since the close of the formal consultation period and have been greatly assisted by all the comments that we have received.

1.36 We have also paid close attention to the experience of other jurisdictions which have systems of financial relief for cohabiting couples on separation. Much of our research in this area has focused on the legislation, case law and academic commentary in those jurisdictions, particularly Australia, Canada, New Zealand and Scotland. We have been unable to identify any major research projects examining the operation of those laws in any of those jurisdictions, but we have benefited from correspondence with practitioners, judges and academics. We have also drawn on recent research examining the operation of European community of property regimes.[32]

RECENT DEVELOPMENTS

1.37 There have been a number of developments relevant to the project since the publication of the CP, both in this jurisdiction and elsewhere.

Recent decisions of the House of Lords

1.38 A week before the publication of the CP,[33] the House of Lords delivered its decision in *Miller v Miller; McFarlane v McFarlane*,[34] its first consideration of ancillary relief on divorce[35] since *White v White*.[36] This decision identified three "strands" or "rationales" which underpin the exercise of the judicial power to grant relief under the Matrimonial Causes Act 1973 ("the MCA"):

[32] E Cooke, A Barlow, T Callus, *Community of Property: a regime for England and Wales?* (2006).

[33] But after the paper had been finalised for publication.

[34] [2006] UKHL 24, [2006] 2 AC 618; for comment see P Moor and V Le Grice, "Periodical Payments Orders Following Miller & McFarlane – a Series of Unfortunate Events" (2006) 36 *Family Law* 655; J Eekelaar, "Property and Financial Settlement on Divorce – Sharing and Compensating" (2006) 36 *Family Law* 754; E Cooke, "Miller/McFarlane: Law in Search of Discrimination" (2007) 19 *Child and Family Law Quarterly* 98; I Ellman, "Financial Settlements on Divorce: Two Steps Forward, Two to Go" (2007) 123 *Law Quarterly Review* 2.

[35] That is to say, financial provision and property adjustment made under the Matrimonial Causes Act 1973 ("MCA"), and equivalent provisions of the Civil Partnership Act 2004.

[36] [2001] 1 AC 596.

(1)   equality/partnership (equal sharing of "matrimonial property");

(2)   compensation for relationship-generated disadvantage; and

(3)   needs generated by or arising during the relationship.[37]

We refer later to this development when we assess the potential suitability for cohabitants of the financial relief provisions of the MCA.[38]

1.39   More recently, the House of Lords delivered its decision in *Stack v Dowden*,[39] a case concerning the division of a family home between two former cohabitants. We discuss this case in Part 2 and Appendix A.

Recent research

1.40   A number of relevant research projects in this jurisdiction have concluded, or are nearing conclusion, and we have drawn on the findings from these studies in formulating our recommendations. Two projects have examined outcomes for cohabitants following separation under the current law, with or without the assistance of lawyers and courts.[40] One study has examined the impact of information obtained by cohabitants who have visited the *Living Together Campaign* website.[41] The 2006 British Social Attitudes Survey has again examined the prevalence of the common law marriage myth and attitudes towards law reform relating to cohabitants. Another large attitudinal survey, conducted by undergraduate family law students, has examined views on remedies for cohabitants whose relationships end on the death of the other partner.[42]

---

[37]   See further *Charman v Charman* [2007] EWCA Civ 502, [2007] 2 FCR 217. For comment on the comparison between these principles and the proposals in our CP, see S Bridge, "Money, marriage and cohabitation" (2006) 36 *Family Law* 641.

[38]   Paras 4.5 to 4.10, and C.3 to C.22.

[39]   [2007] UKHL 17, [2007] 2 WLR 831. Their Lordships referred to the CP at [23], [26], [44] to [48], and [104] to [105] of their opinions.

[40]   R Tennant, J Taylor and J Lewis, *Separating from cohabitation: making arrangements for finances and parenting* (2006) Department for Constitutional Affairs Research Report 7/2006; and G Douglas, J Pearce, H Woodward, *A Failure of Trust: Resolving Property Disputes on Cohabitation Breakdown* (2007), available at http://www.law.cf.ac.uk/researchpapers/papers/1.pdf or http://www.bris.ac.uk/law/research/centres-themes/cohabit/cohabit-rep.pdf (last visited 3 July 2007); see also "Dealing with Property Issues on Cohabitation Breakdown" (2007) 37 *Family Law* 36.

[41]   A Barlow, C Burgoyne, J Smithson, *The Living Together Campaign – An investigation of its impact on legally aware cohabitants* Ministry of Justice Research Report (forthcoming, 2007). The Living Together Campaign was set up in mid-2004 by Advicenow with Government funding. It aims to highlight the differences in the law's treatment of cohabitants and spouses, and to provide practical advice to cohabitants about options open to them to protect themselves and their families: see http://www.advicenow.org.uk/livingtogether (last visited 3 July 2007).

[42]   C Williams, G Potter and G Douglas, Views of members of the public on the intestacy rules relating to cohabitation: a survey conducted by students at Sheffield and Cardiff Universities (2007, unpublished).

1.41   Data analysis from Australia has recently been published,[43] examining what impact, if any, legislation providing financial relief between cohabiting couples in the various Australian states has had on marriage rates there. On the evidence currently available, no connection has been found between the falling marriage rate and the inception of statutory remedies for cohabitants.[44]

Debate in Parliament and beyond

1.42   In October 2006, Mary Creagh MP moved an adjournment debate on Couples Living Together.[45] The Right Honourable Harriet Harman MP, who was then Minister of State with responsibility for family justice at (what was then) the Department for Constitutional Affairs spoke in that debate, indicating her support for reform.

1.43   The Social Justice Policy Group, a group advising the Conservative Party's policy review, published its final report on 10 July 2007. That paper examined a wide range of legal and policy issues relating to family, marriage and cohabitation, including the proposals made in our CP. It concluded that it would be wrong to put forward proposals ahead of the publication of our Report.[46]

Child support reform

1.44   In December 2006, the Department for Work and Pensions published its White Paper on child maintenance, following the Henshaw Report published earlier that year. The White Paper, a consultative document, made radical proposals for the overhaul of the child maintenance system. The Child Maintenance and Other Payments Bill was introduced in June 2007.[47] The Bill has no direct implications for this project.

Developments in other jurisdictions

1.45   Just before publication of the CP, the provisions of the Family Law (Scotland) Act 2006 providing a scheme of remedies for cohabitants on separation and death came into force.[48] In December 2006, two papers were published offering various recommendations for reform for cohabitants in the Republic of Ireland, one by the Irish Law Reform Commission,[49] the other by the Irish Ministry of Justice's Working Group on Domestic Partnerships.[50] It is intended that a federal Bill will at

---

[43]   We referred to this data in CP, Part 5, n 37.

[44]   K Kiernan, A Barlow and R Merlo, "Cohabitation Law Reform and its Impact on Marriage" (2006) 36 *Family Law* 1074.

[45]   Hansard HC 11 October 2006, col 129WH.

[46]   Social Justice Policy Group, *Breakthrough Britain. Volume 1: Family Breakdown* (2007), available at http://povertydebate.typepad.com/home/files/family_breakdown.pdf (last visited 10 July 2007).

[47]   All documents relating to this review and Bill are available at http://www.dwp.gov.uk/childmaintenance/ (last visited 3 July 2007).

[48]   This largely implemented recommendations of the Scottish Law Commission (Report on Family Law (1992) Scot Law Com No 135).

[49]   Rights and Duties of Cohabitants (2006) Law Reform Commission of the Republic of Ireland LRC 82-2006.

[50]   *Options Paper Presented by the Working Group on Domestic Partnership to the Tánaiste and Minister for Justice, Equality and Law Reform* (2006).

some point be introduced in the Australian Parliament, which would provide a uniform set of remedies for cohabitants in place of schemes currently applying in the various states and territories.

THE STRUCTURE OF THIS REPORT AND AN OUTLINE OF THE SCHEME

1.46   In this Report, we set out our recommendations for reform of the law as it affects the financial consequences of the breakdown of a relationship between cohabitants.

1.47   In **Part 2** we consider the strength of the case for legislative reform, and to whom any such reform should apply. We remain convinced that legislative reform is necessary. We recommend the implementation of a statutory scheme of general application conferring on certain eligible cohabitants the right to apply for financial relief on separation. Couples who wished to do so could opt out of the statutory scheme by agreement, and so be free to make their own arrangements.

1.48   In **Part 3** we consider who should be eligible to make a claim for financial relief. We first explore the types of relationship which we mean when we refer to "cohabitants" for these purposes: a couple, who are neither married to each other nor civil partners of each other, who live in a joint household. We then consider what further requirements should be imposed. We recommend that cohabitants who have a child together should be eligible, without more, to apply for financial relief. We recommend that other cohabitants should become eligible only when their cohabitation satisfies a minimum duration requirement; in other words, when they have lived as a couple in a joint household for more than a specified period. We make no recommendation as to what the precise minimum duration should be, but leave this for Parliament to decide, suggesting a range within which the selection should be made.

1.49   In **Part 4** we discuss the options for a new statutory scheme. There is a more detailed discussion of the options that we have rejected in Appendix C. We then explain the principles underpinning the statutory scheme that we are recommending, which is based on an assessment of the economic impact of cohabitation upon the parties. A claim would only be tenable if, as a result of qualifying contributions, at the end of the relationship the respondent had a retained benefit or the applicant had an economic disadvantage. The court, having regard to a number of specified factors, would then be able to make an order for financial relief reversing any retained benefit and sharing any economic disadvantage. Orders available would be wide-ranging, although periodical payments orders should not generally be available. Appendix B gives worked examples of how the scheme that we are recommending would operate in practice.

1.50   In **Part 5** we consider cohabitation contracts and opt-out agreements. We recommend that any residual doubt there may be as to the validity of cohabitation contracts should be removed by statute, whether or not our recommended scheme is enacted. We then discuss opt-out agreements, by which we mean agreements between cohabitants that our recommended scheme should not apply to them on their separation. Having power to disapply the scheme would enable cohabitants to make financial arrangements between themselves and to enforce them in the event of their separation. We make recommendations about capacity to make opt-out agreements, the formalities to be satisfied in order for such agreements to be binding, and the circumstances in which an opt-out agreement might be set aside by the court. We recommend that express declarations of trust in relation to land should not be regarded as opt-out agreements.

1.51 In **Part 6** we consider the position on death. We do not recommend that cohabitants be brought within the range of those entitled to inherit under the intestacy rules. Instead, we make various recommendations for reform of the Inheritance (Provision for Family and Dependants) Act 1975, which would be consequent upon the implementation of our recommended scheme for financial relief on separation. In particular, we recommend that where cohabitants have had a child together, the surviving cohabitant should be entitled to apply for provision under the 1975 Act without having to satisfy a minimum duration requirement. We also recommend that, in making provision for a surviving cohabitant, the court should have regard to what that person would have received had the relationship instead ended by separation.

1.52 In **Part 7** we make recommendations regarding the private international law aspects of our recommended scheme.

THE COST OF REFORM

1.53 Reform cannot be implemented without regard to cost.

1.54 The introduction of a new scheme of the sort recommended in this Report would have cost implications for Government. Although the costs of running cases can be met by court fees, initial expenditure on the creation of court forms and appropriate court rules and procedures is likely to be required. There would also be significant cost implications should Government decide to fund court action by cohabitants by means of legal aid. However, that is entirely a matter for Government – we make no recommendations about legal aid. If the Government were to exclude cases under the cohabitation scheme from the scope of legal aid, there would be no extra call on the funds of the Legal Services Commission.

1.55 It is important, however, to recognise that the operation of the current law creates very significant costs of its own. Some are more direct than others. Claims by cohabitants for a share in the family home currently take the form of an application under the Trusts of Land and Appointment of Trustees Act 1996. Such cases are eligible for legal aid, as are claims for the benefit of cohabitants' children under Schedule 1 to the Children Act 1989.

1.56 Perhaps more significant are the indirect costs caused by the inadequacies of the current law.

1.57 As the CP made clear, many cohabitants are currently unable to establish a claim to property on separation and so do not gain a share in what may be a larger or smaller pool of family assets. Common sense suggests that in many cases where this occurs the result must be to drive the economically weaker party into reliance on the State. It would be much too speculative to try to establish an overall figure for the social security costs arising from the operation of the law as it currently stands. But that figure must be a large one. The fact that, in turn, many children living with parents who have been economically disadvantaged following separation are likely to suffer comparative financial deprivation has knock-on costs of its own.

ACKNOWLEDGEMENTS

1.58 We are very grateful to a large number of individuals and organisations who have assisted us throughout the course of this project, both in the preparation of the CP[51] and since its publication. Particular thanks are due to the Nuffield Foundation, which hosted and organised a seminar in September 2006; to the Institute of Advanced Legal Studies, which hosted a public discussion evening in October 2006; to the circuit and district judges with whom we held a meeting in Cardiff earlier this year; and to the members of our legal advisory group who have assisted us throughout the project. Finally, we thank all of those who took the time to respond to our CP, or who attended meetings and conferences relating to the project over the course of the last year.[52]

---

[51] See CP, Appendix E.

[52] Members of our advisory group and individuals and organisations which responded to the CP are identified in Appendix D.

PART 2
SHOULD THERE BE REFORM?

INTRODUCTION

2.1 For many of those who have engaged in the debate about the law's treatment of cohabitants, the only question of interest is whether there should be reform at all. It is a question on which most people have an opinion. In many cases, that view is strongly held.

2.2 As we explained in Part 3 of the CP, cohabitants are far from ignored by the law. In many contexts, including financial provision on death, they already receive express statutory recognition. There is no such recognition in relation to the parties' financial and property rights on separation. Instead the law determines their ownership of particular assets by reference to the law of contract, property and trusts.

2.3 In this Part, we consider the current law as it applies to cohabitants on separation,[1] and then ask the following questions:

    (1)   Is reform necessary?

    (2)   Should there be reform:

        (a)   for cohabitants with children; and

        (b)   for other cohabitants?

    (3)   Should any reform operate:

        (a)   by requiring parties to "opt in" by a system of registration or by the self-regulation of private agreement; or

        (b)   by general application – in other words, should it apply to all "eligible" cohabitants, unless they have made an agreement disapplying the scheme, leaving them free to make their own financial arrangements on separation?

THE CURRENT LAW

2.4 Part 3 of the CP described aspects of the general law (in particular the law of property and trusts) and statute law (notably Schedule 1 to the Children Act 1989) as they apply to cohabitants. We provide an updated account of the law in Appendix A to this Report. We described in Part 4 of the CP the criticisms which have been levelled at that law: its unfairness and failure to respond to the realities of family life and the problems of family breakdown; its uncertainty; its illogicality; and its procedural complexity.

2.5 Since the close of the consultation period for our CP, there has been one major development in the current law. The House of Lords has, in the case of *Stack v*

---

[1] We consider the issues arising on death in Part 6.

Dowden,[2] considered the law of express and implied trusts of the family home for the first time since 1990.[3] *Stack v Dowden* is the first occasion on which the House of Lords has had to examine that law in the context of a dispute arising on the separation of a cohabiting couple. It is also the first time it has had to consider, in any context, the effect of a conveyance of property into joint names without an express declaration of the parties' beneficial interests.[4]

The decision in *Stack v Dowden*

2.6   The case essentially raised two issues:

    (1)   whether a standard form of words used in property transfers to more than one person[5] constituted an express declaration of trust,[6] creating a beneficial joint tenancy;[7] and

    (2)   if it did not, how the beneficial interests of joint owners were to be ascertained.

2.7   On the first issue, the House of Lords held that the form of words used in this conveyance – that the survivor "can give a valid receipt for capital money arising on a disposition of the land" – did not of itself constitute a declaration of trust.[8]

2.8   Although their Lordships all agreed on the outcome in the case before them, they were divided on the principles to be applied in determining the second issue.[9] The majority held that in a "domestic" or "consumer" context where property is conveyed to more than one person (thereby creating joint ownership at law, by way of a "joint tenancy"), there is a strong presumption that the parties are beneficial joint tenants.[10] Accordingly, if the parties separate and unless the

---

[2]   [2007] UKHL 17, [2007] 2 WLR 831.

[3]   *Lloyds Bank v Rosset* [1991] 1 AC 107.

[4]   [2007] UKHL 17, [2007] 2 WLR 831, at [40], Baroness Hale.

[5]   In particular before 1995, when the relevant words appeared on the Land Registry form used to register transfers: [2007] UKHL 17, [2007] 2 WLR 831, at [50].

[6]   Such an express declaration of trust would be conclusive of the parties' beneficial shares, in the absence of fraud or other vitiating factors, subsequent variation or proprietary estoppel: *Goodman v Gallant* [1986] Fam 106.

[7]   In which case, when the parties separated (and severed the joint tenancy), they would each be entitled to a half share of the property.

[8]   [2007] UKHL 17, [2007] 2 WLR 831, see in particular [51], Baroness Hale, and [130], Lord Neuberger.

[9]   Baroness Hale gave the leading judgment for the majority, with which Lord Hoffmann agreed; Lords Walker and Hope delivered concurring judgments. Lord Neuberger agreed with the result, but provided different reasons for his decision.

[10]   [2007] UKHL 17, [2007] 2 WLR 831, at [56] and [68] to [69]. In effect, although parties who used the valid receipt clause would not thereby be found to have made an express declaration of a beneficial joint tenancy, the existence of an implied trust on those terms will be heavily presumed. This would have the effect that the party who had contributed substantially more to the purchase price would be strongly presumed to have gifted part of that contribution to the other party: at [112] and [136], Lord Neuberger. This might be of particular concern where formerly solely-owned property is put into joint names on the insistence of a mortgage lender when the property is remortgaged, an increasingly common event.

presumption is rebutted, each will be entitled to an equal share of the proceeds of any sale (after any outstanding mortgage loan has been repaid).

2.9 Baroness Hale suggested that, while "each case will turn on its own facts",[11] it will be "very unusual"[12] for a party in a domestic case to succeed in rebutting the presumption of a beneficial joint tenancy[13] (which arises in cases of joint legal ownership) and so to obtain a larger share of the equity under a common intention constructive trust. Crucially, the mere fact that the parties had made unequal financial contributions to the acquisition of the purchase price will not rebut that presumption; the presumption of resulting trust therefore has no role to play in these cases.[14] A common intention constructive trust will only arise, and so rebut the presumption of a beneficial joint tenancy, on the basis of evidence that the parties shared an intention, "actual, inferred or imputed",[15] arising at the date of acquisition or subsequently, to hold the property differently.

2.10 However, *Stack v Dowden* was held to be one of those very unusual cases in which the presumption could be rebutted. Their Lordships were persuaded that there was evidence that the parties intended to hold the beneficial interest in unequal shares, which corresponded closely to their respective financial contributions to the acquisition of the property.

2.11 The majority identified several factors, not an exhaustive list, which the court might be invited to consider in determining the parties' true intentions:[16]

(1) the parties' financial contributions to the acquisition of the property;

(2) any advice or discussions at the time of the transfer which cast light upon their intentions then;

(3) the reasons why the home was acquired in their joint names;

(4) (where applicable) the reasons why the survivor was authorised to give a valid receipt for the capital monies;

(5) the purpose for which the home was acquired;

(6) the nature of the parties' relationship;

(7) whether the parties had children for whom they both had responsibility to provide a home;

(8) how the purchase was financed, both initially and subsequently;

(9) how the parties arranged their finances, whether separately or together or a bit of both;

[11] [2007] UKHL 17, [2007] 2 WLR 831, at [69].

[12] [2007] UKHL 17, [2007] 2 WLR 831, at [68] and [69].

[13] Or the existence of a tenancy in common in equal shares.

[14] [2007] UKHL 17, [2007] 2 WLR 831, at [68]; though compare Lord Hope, at [11].

[15] [2007] UKHL 17, [2007] 2 WLR 831, at [60]. See A.30 and following.

[16] Taken from [2007] UKHL 17, [2007] 2 WLR 831, at [69] and [70], Baroness Hale.

(10)   how the parties discharged the outgoings on the property and their other household expenses;[17]

(11)   the parties' individual characters and personalities;

(12)   whether the parties were cohabiting or married;[18]

(13)   indirect contributions, such as financing or constructing an extension or making improvements to the property which added significantly to its value; and

(14)   any other factors indicating that the parties' intentions may have changed over time.

THE CONTINUING CASE FOR STATUTORY INTERVENTION

2.12   When considering the case for reform in the CP, we asked "Can we not leave it to the judges?".[19] We observed that, whatever else might be thought about the merits of judicial development of the law in this area,[20] "unless and until the right case happens to come along, and reaches the House of Lords, no real progress can be made".[21] Despite *Stack v Dowden*, we consider that, should reform be deemed desirable as a matter of social policy,[22] the need for statutory intervention remains.

2.13   The CP highlighted various ways in which the current law may be inadequate in dealing with the financial consequences of relationship breakdown between cohabitants.[23] The findings of recent empirical research reinforce the view that the current law can produce unfair outcomes for cohabitants, in particular for the primary carer of children who may experience significant economic disadvantage following separation.[24] Moreover, several key points remain undecided or unclear after *Stack v Dowden*. Their Lordships were not required to address the issue of how trusts arise in the context of sole ownership, in particular whether making

---

[17]   Baroness Hale suggests, at [69], that where parties are joint owners, it will be easier to infer "that they intended each should contribute as much to the household as they reasonably could and that they would share the eventual benefit or burden equally"; by contrast, a different approach might be warranted in sole owner cases.

[18]   See [40] and [69], where Baroness Hale suggests that "mercenary considerations may be more to the fore" in the cohabitation context than in marriage, though "it should not be assumed that they always take pride of place over natural love and affection".

[19]   CP, para 5.98.

[20]   See concerns described at CP, paras 5.100 to 5.101; see also *Stack v Dowden* [2007] UKHL 17, [2007] 2 WLR 831, at [102] to [105], Lord Neuberger.

[21]   CP, para 5.100.

[22]   Considered at para 2.27 and following.

[23]   See generally CP, Part 4.

indirect financial contributions to the acquisition of property suffices to establish an interest.[25] The party in such a case who principally made non-financial contributions, such as raising the couple's children, will continue to struggle to obtain any share in the family home on separation, unless there is evidence[26] of an express common intention to share.[27] And it remains unclear how a party who had chiefly made domestic contributions would fare in a joint ownership case: what would be the result of the application of the factors identified in *Stack v Dowden*?[28]

2.14 Like all cases in this field, *Stack v Dowden* dealt with a particular set of facts, applying and developing general principles of property and trust law. The speeches contain some broad statements of principle that endeavour to shape the general law in a way that is thought apt for the domestic context. But, as Baroness Hale said, "the precise question" which arose in the case was "the effect of a conveyance into joint names without express declaration of the beneficial interests".[29] The case is far from offering, and does not purport to offer, a comprehensive solution to the hardships that can arise for cohabitants on separation.

2.15 This is not to criticise the House of Lords. It is an inevitable consequence of the limits on what the general law can do. The law of property and trusts can only be used, in this context, in order to establish ownership of individual assets. The law of common intention constructive trusts, to which resort is had in the absence of an express declaration of trust, is based on the parties' intentions regarding the ownership of the asset in dispute. While those intentions may change over time, the constructive trust cannot accommodate "contingent" intentions. It cannot simultaneously provide that the parties hold the property in particular shares while they stay together but will hold in different shares should they separate.[30] Moreover, since the parties' shares are to be determined by reference to their

---

[24] R Tennant, J Taylor and J Lewis, *Separating from cohabitation: making arrangements for finances and parenting* (2006), Department for Constitutional Affairs Research Report 7/2006; G Douglas, J Pearce, H Woodward, *A Failure of Trust: Resolving Property Disputes on Cohabitation Breakdown* (2007), paras 10.2 to 10.7, available at http://www.law.cf.ac.uk/researchpapers/papers/1.pdf or http://www.bris.ac.uk/law/research/centres-themes/cohabit/cohabit-rep.pdf (last visited 3 July 2007); see also "Dealing with Property Issues on Cohabitation Breakdown" (2007) 37 *Family Law* 36.

[25] For example, one party pays the utility bills enabling the other to pay the mortgage instalments. See CP, paras 3.28 to 3.30 and 4.10 to 4.11 for discussion. For comment on this issue, see [2007] UKHL 17, [2007] 2 WLR 831, at [63], Baroness Hale, at [26], Lord Walker; contrast [141], Lord Neuberger.

[26] Obtaining reliable oral evidence on such matters can be very difficult, and even where documents are drawn up, they may be left unsigned: G Douglas, J Pearce, H Woodward, *A Failure of Trust: Resolving Property Disputes on Cohabitation Breakdown* (2007), see n 24 for URL.

[27] The classic case of *Burns v Burns* [1984] Ch 317.

[28] See para 2.11.

[29] [2007] UKHL 17, [2007] 2 WLR 831, at [48].

[30] [2007] UKHL 17, [2007] 2 WLR 831, at [62], Baroness Hale. Parties who wished to provide in advance that they would divide their assets differently on separation would need to enter into a contract or express trust to that effect; but see CP, para 3.15 to 3.19 on the uncertain legal status of cohabitation contracts.

intentions,[31] the court cannot substitute its own view of what is the fair outcome on separation.

2.16 The general law, therefore, is not equipped to provide a comprehensive solution to problems arising on separation, responding to the economic consequences of the parties' contributions to their relationship. Moreover, since it is limited to addressing the beneficial ownership of individual assets, the general law of property and trusts offers very little remedial flexibility. It provides no scope for orders that take effect, for example, over parties' pension funds. It offers no assistance where parties do not own the home that they have shared[32] and do not have capital assets. A coherent set of statutory remedies providing financial relief between cohabitants would provide a way of doing better justice between the parties on separation, while respecting the interests of affected third parties.[33]

Express trusts and conveyancing

2.17 Before addressing the central question of whether there should be statutory reform, it is necessary to comment further on the issue of express declarations of trust and conveyancing practice raised by *Stack v Dowden*.

2.18 The facts of Stack *v Dowden* required the House of Lords to consider the significance of wording on HM Land Registry ("Land Registry") property transfer forms used before 1995 to indicate whether Land Registry needed to enter a restriction on the land register.[34] When property is transferred to more than one person, the current Land Registry document – Form TR1 – appears to require the transferees to indicate whether they shall hold the property as beneficial joint tenants, tenants in common in equal shares, or on some other basis specified by them (for example, tenants in common in shares of 60:40).[35] Where this section is completed and the form signed by the transferees, it constitutes an express declaration of trust that conclusively determines the extent of the parties' interests in the property.

2.19 However, notwithstanding this apparent requirement, in some cases no express declaration of trust is executed and the law of implied trusts must therefore be invoked by any person claiming beneficial entitlement.[36] In *Stack v Dowden*, Baroness Hale suggested that an option might be added to TR1 enabling parties expressly to decline to specify their shares and so to rely on the law of implied trusts.[37]

---

[31] Though see Appendix A, n 62.

[32] For rented property, see existing tenancy transfers: Family Law Act 1996, sch 7.

[33] Just as third parties' interests are protected in the course of proceedings for financial relief on divorce: para 4.146.

[34] On the basis that a survivor would not be able to give a valid receipt, for the purposes of overreaching, without appointing a second trustee: Law of Property Act 1925, s 2(1)(ii).

[35] Form FR1, which applies to first registration, is to the same effect.

[36] *Stack v Dowden* [2007] UKHL 17, [2007] 2 WLR 831, at [52], Baroness Hale. We understand that the practice of Land Registry in such cases is to enter a restriction on the land register.

[37] [2007] UKHL 17, [2007] 2 WLR 831, at [52].

2.20   Moreover, recent research indicates that, even where parties do declare their beneficial interests on the relevant form, they may not fully appreciate the effect of the arrangement that they have thereby made.[38] Couples who buy a home together may be well-informed about the significance of the right of survivorship for beneficial joint tenants,[39] but it seems that many may be ill-informed about, or simply fail to take on board, the effect of severance on beneficial joint tenancies. Couples who opt for a beneficial joint tenancy may not appreciate that the party who made the larger contribution will not be able to recover that greater investment in the event of separation, even if separation occurs only shortly after the transfer was made.[40] The researchers report that this lack of interest in, or lack of appreciation of, the legal position reflects the fact that when buying a house together couples find it difficult to contemplate the possibility that they might separate. Couples may also consider it unromantic or embarrassing to discuss such matters, particularly in so far as they wish to protect their own financial position against the other party.

2.21   The problem may be compounded by the fact that joint purchases are inevitably treated as non-contentious matters and the parties often do not have separate legal advice. Many parties may be reluctant to pay for the detailed advice that may be necessary, not least because conflict of interest may prevent the conveyancer from advising each party adequately and so require the engagement of another adviser. The recent research[41] suggests that advice provided to parties at the time of purchase may often not be sufficient to ensure that parties' decisions about how they will hold the property are properly informed.[42]

2.22   It may also be said that the law provides rather limited options for forms of property holding. The severance of a beneficial joint tenancy inevitably gives rise to ownership in equal shares. A cohabitant who paid all or most of the purchase price of a house, and was content for it to be held with his or her partner on a beneficial joint tenancy in contemplation of a long cohabitation, may be aggrieved to find that if the joint tenancy is severed on separation he or she will have only a 50% share. Some may contend that it should be possible to create joint ownership in unequal shares but with a right of survivorship, and that this option

---

[38]   G Douglas, J Pearce and H Woodward, *A Failure of Trust: Resolving Property Disputes on Cohabitation Breakdown* (2007), see n 24 for URL, paras 5.9 to 5.10; also reported in "Dealing with Property Issues on Cohabitation Breakdown" (2007) 37 *Family Law* 36, referred to in *Stack v Dowden* [2007] UKHL 17, [2007] 2 WLR 831, at [67], Baroness Hale.

[39]   This doctrine means that, on the death of any joint tenant, the survivor(s) become beneficial owners of the whole: no part of the property devolves with the deceased's estate. Contrast the position of tenants in common who own distinct shares that will devolve with their estate on death.

[40]   G Douglas, J Pearce and H Woodward, *A Failure of Trust: Resolving Property Disputes on Cohabitation Breakdown* (2007), see n 24 for URL, para 5.10.

[41]   G Douglas, J Pearce and H Woodward, *A Failure of Trust: Resolving Property Disputes on Cohabitation Breakdown* (2007), see n 24 for URL, ch 5. This finding is echoed in R Tennant, J Taylor and J Lewis, *Separating from cohabitation: making arrangements for finances and parenting* (2006) p 79.

[42]   This is particularly the case where a partner is brought onto the legal title of a previously solely-owned property when that property is remortgaged.

may prove attractive to a significant number of couples.[43] But that is not an issue that falls within the scope of this project, not least because it has significance for all transferees of land, not just cohabiting couples. We therefore do not feel it appropriate to consider the matter in depth or to make any specific recommendations on it now.

2.23 However, we do think it appropriate for us to observe that this recent research clearly raises a number of important issues, both for legal practice and future reform. The researchers have suggested that some of the unfair outcomes identified in the course of their recent project might be prevented by appropriate reforms to conveyancing law and practice.[44] Concerns have been expressed about Form TR1, which is not easily understood by the lay person. It includes no explanation of the legal terms used,[45] and many practitioners we have spoken to, including members of the Law Society's Family Law and Land Law and Conveyancing Committees, say that they find the forms unhelpful. The Land Registry forms on which the declarations of trust are made cannot be a substitute for legal advice. However, it has been suggested that, suitably amended, the form could be a useful means of providing co-purchasers with clear information about the different models of beneficial ownership available to them and the implications of each, or about the importance of co-purchasers obtaining separate advice.

2.24 Land Registry is planning to conduct its own consultation exercise later this year as part of its review of the Land Registration Rules 2003, including Form TR1. We would encourage those who wish to propose changes to that form, or other measures that Land Registry itself might take to increase public understanding in this area, to respond to that consultation exercise with suggestions of specific wording that could be used for this purpose.[46]

2.25 Pending the introduction of a scheme of financial relief between cohabitants on relationship breakdown, decisions made at the time of purchase will often continue to determine outcomes on separation, which may be many years later. Indeed, even following any such reform, those decisions would remain determinative for parties who were ineligible to apply for financial relief under any new scheme, and for all couples in their dealings with third parties. While it is not the purpose of this project to address conveyancing issues, we encourage Land Registry and relevant professional bodies to investigate what more might be done to address the problems outlined here. The law cannot oblige those purchasing property to make careful and sensible decisions. But it may be that more could be done to maximise parties' opportunities to do so and to encourage a culture in

---

[43] Indeed, this possibility has been suggested by G Douglas, J Pearce and H Woodward, *A Failure of Trust: Resolving Property Disputes on Cohabitation Breakdown* (2007), see n 24 for URL, para 10.32.

[44] G Douglas, J Pearce and H Woodward, *A Failure of Trust: Resolving Property Disputes on Cohabitation Breakdown* (2007), see n 24 for URL, paras 10.28 to 10.31.

[45] A separate public guide is published by Land Registry, available at http://www.landregistry.gov.uk/assets/library/documents/public_guide_018.pdf (last visited 3 July 2007).

[46] It is important to bear in mind that the form exists primarily for Land Registry purposes, and that it is a universal form, used not only for cohabiting purchasers, but across the board.

which couples feel able to discuss the financial implications of their relationships directly.

SHOULD THERE BE NEW STATUTORY REMEDIES?

2.26 We turn now to the central question with which this project is concerned. Should new statutory remedies providing financial relief between cohabitants be introduced at all?

2.27 Our project has prompted a flood of comment in the media on this basic question. In many instances, the issue has been discussed in terms of whether cohabitants should have access to the same legal rights as spouses, an option that we specifically rejected in the CP. Newspaper headlines about the possibility of reform indicate the range of opinion. On the one hand: "Why marriage matters",[47] "If you want financial rights – get married",[48] and "'Divorce' payouts for partners could spell end of marriage".[49] On the other hand: "Law gets fairer for couples",[50] "Time the law caught up with society over those who 'live in sin'",[51] and "Easing the pain of separation".[52] Some commentators objected that our provisional proposals did not go far enough.[53]

2.28 Reaction amongst our consultees was, predictably, no less varied.

2.29 In order to gain as much understanding of consultees' opinions as possible, the CP did not ask the simple question "Should there be reform?". It instead asked consultees to comment on its provisional view that in cases where cohabitants have children there should be new statutory remedies and invited consultees' views on whether reform is also warranted in any cases involving cohabitants without children.[54] The responses to those particular questions are discussed below.[55]

2.30 We nevertheless received a significant number of emails, many relatively brief, from individuals who commented on the basic question of whether or not there should be any reform. Most of those emails expressed, one way or another, antagonism towards reform or towards cohabitants. Some responses reached us even before our CP had been published and so, although instructive in very general terms, did not address our provisional views on cohabitation. Many others did not directly respond to any of our consultation questions.

2.31 Opposition to reform appeared to be based on various grounds and on various assumptions about what reform might entail. Many stated that they did not

[47] Anne Atkins, Sunday Express, 4 June 2006.

[48] Jenny McCartney, Sunday Times, 4 June 2006.

[49] Tom Whitehead, Daily Express, 1 June 2006.

[50] The Sun, 27 June 2005.

[51] Patrick Collinson, The Guardian, 2 July 2005.

[52] Headline accompanying letter from David Allison (Cohabitation committee chair, Resolution), The Times, 15 June 2007.

[53] For example, "The way we live now", editorial comment, The Guardian, 1 June 2006.

[54] CP, paras 5.113 and 5.114.

[55] See para 2.64 and following, and para 2.75 and following.

support the extension to cohabitants of the law applicable to spouses on divorce. Others were concerned that a cohabiting partner ought not to be able automatically to claim a stake in their property. Since the CP rejected both of these options, our provisional proposals could be said to accommodate these particular concerns.[56]

2.32 Although it was often difficult to establish the nuanced opinions of the senders of such emails, we have in the following discussions of potential reform for couples with and without children taken such responses as opposing the introduction of any sort of reform for any sort of cohabitant.

2.33 We also received a large number of detailed responses from other individuals and various organisations. Many of the organisations represent the views of thousands of people, including those who work professionally with families. These responses also yielded a wide range of opinion, both on the specific detail of our proposals and on the larger questions of general policy. The majority of such responses were supportive of reform of some sort.

2.34 In the following sections, we review the arguments put to us by advocates and opponents of reform. Many of those who opposed reform did so for reasons relating to the overall shape of family policy, and its impact on the institution of marriage, the prevalence of cohabitation, the autonomy of cohabitants, and personal relationships generally. They also highlighted the importance of public information to ensure that people properly understand their position under the current law. Advocates of reform, by contrast, pointed to what they regard as the unfairness, uncertainty and hardship generated by the current law.

2.35 It is difficult to distil an understanding of public opinion on the issue of reform purely on the basis of responses to our consultation. While those who supported and opposed reform clearly felt strongly about the issue, the responses do not form a nationally-representative sample of public opinion. For that, we have to look to the British Social Attitudes survey, most recently carried out in summer 2006, which is conducted on a randomly selected and statistically significant sample and is therefore the best available source of data on the views of the population.[57] Like earlier surveys, the 2006 British Social Attitudes survey reveals a majority in favour of providing financial remedies between cohabitants. The presence of children in a relationship and a long duration both greatly increase the levels of support for making financial relief available on separation. Indeed, majorities of respondents to the survey supported reform that treated spouses and cohabitants in the same way in many situations.[58] As we explain in Part 4, we are not recommending that cohabitants be subject to the current law applicable between spouses and civil partners on dissolution. But this survey evidence forms an important part of the context in which we have to evaluate the responses that we received.

---

[56] CP, paras 6.15 to 6.23 and 6.239; 6.34 to 6.45 and 6.111 to 6.114.

[57] This year's survey interviewed nearly 4000 individuals; questions relating to cohabitation law reform were put to a sub-set of around 3000 people.

[58] A Park et al, *British Social Attitudes. The 24th Report* (forthcoming, January 2008).

Family policy: supporting marriage and family stability

2.36 The last year has seen considerable debate about the legal and fiscal support provided for families, and the ways in which welfare benefit and tax policy might be used to encourage or discourage particular family forms. Many participants in that debate, drawing on research findings that marriage is often associated with the best outcomes for children, are concerned about falling marriage rates and increasing cohabitation and parenthood outside marriage. They fear that giving cohabitants additional legal recognition may encourage these trends. Others argue that all families with children should be supported, regardless of the legal form that they take.

2.37 Reflecting this debate, our consultees expressed a wide range of views about marriage and cohabitation. A few took issue with the emphasis we placed in the CP on supporting marriage. But others were concerned that any further legal recognition of cohabitants would undermine the institution of marriage. For example, the consultation response from Marriage Resource[59] simply read:

> We recognise that the current law "is uncertain and capable of producing unfair outcomes", but we feel that anything that is done will weaken the institution of marriage in the nation when it is already under many pressures. We appreciate the work that has been done, but our view is that new statutory remedies should not be provided.

2.38 The Evangelical Alliance[60] similarly observed that they were:

> not persuaded that ... reform is necessary. Naturally, there are individuals who suffer from the current absence of specific legislation to cover the situation when an uncommitted relationship breaks up. The church recognises and sympathises with the very human and tragic consequences of such life events. Nevertheless, we doubt that new legislation is the answer. The fact remains that the UK already has an established legal arrangement that couples can opt into if they want to create mutual rights and obligations. This is called marriage. We concur with those who express fears that imposing rights and duties on cohabiting couples – which would amount to a "cut price" or "reduced" version of marriage – will undermine the crucial institution of marriage itself and will result in fewer couples actually marrying. This in turn will continue to have serious consequences for society.

2.39 As we said in the CP,[61] we fully support initiatives designed to encourage stable family relationships. We also acknowledge and respect the fact that many wish to promote marriage, whether for religious or secular reasons. Our present concern, however, is with those relationships that are not, for whatever reason, formalised by marriage or civil partnership and that sadly founder.

2.40 The potential effects on social behaviour of legal change of the sort being contemplated in this project are difficult to predict.

---

[59] A Christian charitable organisation working in the field of marriage support.

[60] An organisation founded in 1846 which acts as an umbrella body for Britain's Evangelical Christians, of whatever denomination.

2.41 Take, for example, last year's highly-publicised House of Lords' decision on the law governing ancillary relief on divorce.[62] Reaction to that decision highlighted how the current law, by providing financial relief between spouses but not between cohabitants, may provide the economically stronger party with compelling reasons to shun marriage in preference to cohabitation.[63] Some consultees suggested that introducing new remedies between cohabitants would, in turn, reduce the numbers of cohabiting couples and increase single-person households.[64]

2.42 The law is clearly not an irrelevant factor, and the incentive structure it creates may affect individuals' decisions about their personal relationships, at least where other considerations are finely balanced. However, we think that it is important not to over-estimate the influence that the law has on people's behaviour in relationships. As we discussed in the CP, research suggests that even where individuals are provided with accurate information about their legal position,[65] the law may have relatively little effect on what people do: in particular, in deciding whether to start or end a relationship, and whether to cohabit or to marry or register a civil partnership.[66] Indeed, recent research finds that some cohabitants think that it would be wrong to take on what they view as the serious commitment of marriage for legal or financial reasons.[67] This view is shared by Relate, the UK's largest provider of relationship counselling, who made the following observation in their consultation response:

> We support a change in legislation simply because it is necessary in a world where cohabitation is on the increase. We do not believe that

---

[61] See, in particular, paras 5.30 to 5.40.

[62] *Miller v Miller; McFarlane v McFarlane* [2006] UKHL 24, [2006] 2 AC 618.

[63] The Family Law Bar Association response frankly observed that when legal advice on this issue is sought, such a party is advised strongly not to marry, not least given that English law does not enforce pre-nuptial agreements. It noted that many consider that a change in the law to render such agreements enforceable would bolster the institution of marriage.

[64] Like the rise in cohabitation and decline in marriage, "solo living", attributed to various factors, is already a rising social trend: see "Solo living across the adult lifecourse", Centre for Research on Families and Relationships, Research Briefing 20 (2005).

[65] See below, from para 2.46 and following.

[66] See for example, R Tennant, J Taylor and J Lewis, *Separating from cohabitation: making arrangements for finances and parenting* (2006) Department for Constitutional Affairs Research Report 7/2006, p 139; M Hibbs, C Barton and J Beswick, "Why marry? – Perceptions of the Affianced" (2001) 31 *Family Law* 197; J Eekelaar and M Maclean, "Marriage and the Moral Bases of Personal Relationship" (2004) 31 *Journal of Law and Society* 510; A Carling, S Duncan and R Edwards (eds), *Analysing Families: morality and rationality in policy and practice* (2002); C Smart and P Stevens, *Cohabitation Breakdown* (2000) p 50; J Lewis, "Marriage, Cohabitation and the Law: Individualism and Obligation" and J Lewis, J Datta and S Sarre, "Individualism and Commitment in Marriage and Cohabitation" (1999) Lord Chancellor's Department Research Series Nos 1/99 and 8/99.

[67] See A Barlow, C Burgoyne, J Smithson, *The Living Together Campaign – An investigation of its impact on legally aware cohabitants* Ministry of Justice Research Report (forthcoming, 2007), ch 4 and 5. British Social Attitudes survey 2000 found that just 9% of the public agreed that "There's no point getting married - it's just a piece of paper" indicating the high social value which continues to be attached to marriage: A Barlow, S Duncan, G James and A Park, "Just a piece of paper? Marriage and cohabitation", in A Park, J Curtice, K Thompson, L Jarvis and C Bromley (eds), *British Social Attitudes: Public policy, social ties. The 18th Report* (2001).

it would provide a disincentive to marriage, as our experience is that people rarely get married for financial reasons. The argument that they do is even less plausible when we consider the still common misconception that there is such a thing as a 'common law marriage'. Nor do we believe a change in the law would encourage cohabiting people to separate – another decision rarely propelled by money.

2.43 Recently published analysis of Australian data (where there have been statutory remedies between cohabitants in New South Wales since the mid-1980s) indicates that there is no statistical evidence of a relationship between the introduction of those laws and the continuing decline in the marriage rate.[68] Figure 5 illustrates the marriage rate in four states since 1971, the vertical line indicating the point when the State Parliament introduced a new regime of financial relief between cohabiting couples. The researchers analysed the data in order to see whether the intensity of decline in the marriage rates after the State legislation was greater than would be anticipated from the prior trend. On the basis of the best available data,[69] there was no statistical evidence of a relationship between the falling marriage rates and the introduction of remedies for cohabitants.

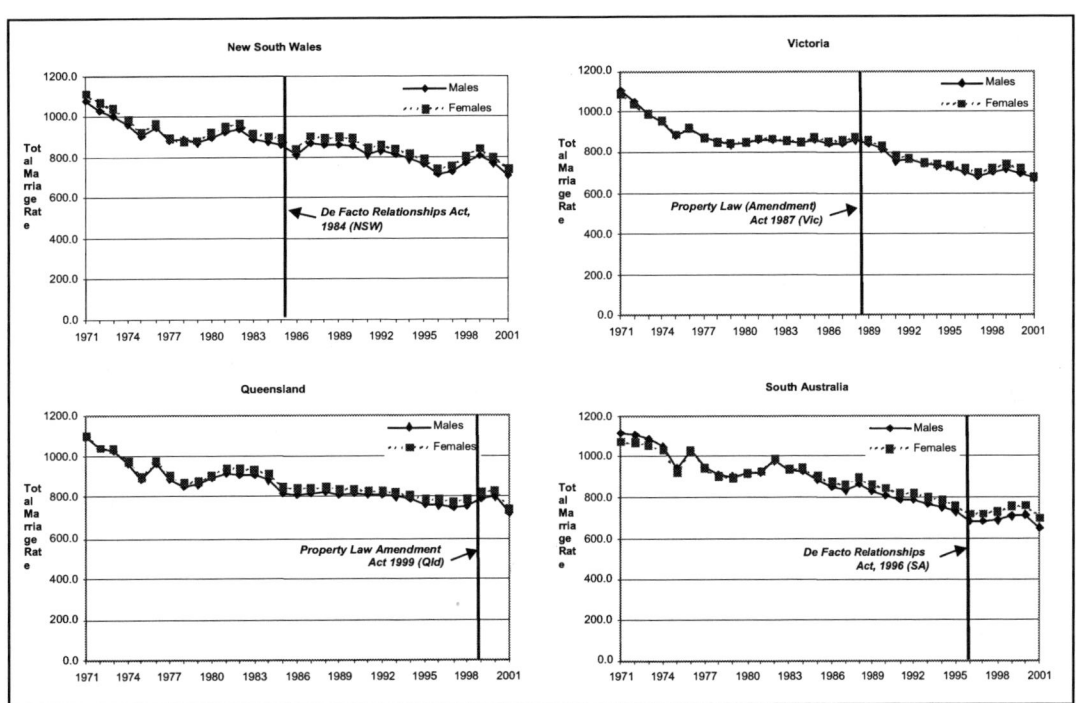

Figure 5: Marriage Rates Before and After Cohabitation Law Reform[70]

2.44 The promotion and protection of strong marriages may be priorities for legal and social policy. But we do not consider that pursuit of such a policy would be incompatible with the introduction of focused remedies providing financial relief

---

[68] K Kiernan, A Barlow and R Merlo, "Cohabitation Law Reform and its Impact on Marriage" (2006) 36 *Family Law* 1074.

[69] The researchers describe the limitations of the available data at p 1074 of their article. Inevitably the analysis is also restricted by the fact that the earliest legislation was in 1984.

between cohabiting couples on relationship breakdown. Nor, therefore, do we consider that simply introducing remedies between cohabitants would of itself undermine marriage. As we said in the CP, both the institution of marriage and individual marriages can be supported whilst also recognising and responding to the factual reality of cohabitation and the hardship that can arise when such relationships end. It seems to us that marriage does not need to be supported by perpetuating the hardship experienced by others when alternative forms of personal relationship end.[71]

2.45 Cohabiting relationships are currently more prone to breakdown than marriages.[72] But we do not accept that new remedies would inevitably aggravate that trend; they may even help to stem it.[73] One factor contributing to the present fragility of cohabiting relationships may be precisely the current law's failure to ensure a fair distribution between the parties of the economic consequences of separation. Cohabitation may therefore be viewed by some individuals as a "responsibility-free" option, from which they can walk away without any financial consequences. The introduction of a scheme of financial relief may prompt couples to consider more carefully whether and on what basis they should cohabit. But it may also help to reinforce the commitment which cohabitants make to each other, not least by protecting the position of the party who was or would be more economically vulnerable should the parties separate. Indeed, the introduction of remedies between cohabitants may even lead some couples to formalise their relationship. If financial responsibility attached not only to marriage and civil partnership but also to cohabitation, the economically stronger party's current incentive to refuse to marry or register a civil partnership may to some extent be reduced.

Public education and relationship support

2.46 Many of our consultees, both those in favour of reform and those against, felt that considerably greater efforts can and should be made to educate the public about the legal implications of marriage, civil partnership and cohabitation. Several consultees, particularly (but by no means exclusively) those opposed to reform, also wanted far greater emphasis to be given to relationship support and non-legal education, particularly in relation to marriage. Opponents of reform

---

[70] First published in K Kiernan, A Barlow and R Merlo, "Cohabitation Law Reform and its Impact on Marriage" (2006) 36 *Family Law* 1074. Reproduced here with kind permission of Professor Kathleen Kiernan, and *Family Law*.

[71] CP, para 5.34.

[72] See data from the Millennium Cohort Study reported in a plenary paper by K Kiernan, "Partnership and Parenthood in the UK" at the Family and Parenting Institute's Parent Child 2006 Conference, London, November 2006: 95% of mothers who were married to the father at birth were still with the father three years after the birth; 83% of mothers who had been cohabiting with the father at the birth were still with the father, 32% having married him; see also analysis in H Benson, *The conflation of marriage and cohabitation in government statistics* (2006), published as Appendix 3 to Social Justice Policy Group, *Breakdown Britain: interim report on the state of the nation - Fractured Families* (2006), available at http://povertydebate.typepad.com/ (last visited 3 July 2007); and sources cited in CP, para 2.36, n 67.

[73] As we suggested at CP, para 5.39, some cohabitants who had been seeking to avoid the financial consequences of marriage might be inclined to marry after all if cohabitation also carried some financial consequences.

emphasised education as a way of enabling individuals to make responsible, informed choices about their relationships. For example, Christian Action Research and Education ("CARE") said:

> That the current law is unfair, uncertain and illogical may be justification for seeking some clarity but it does not necessarily justify the wholesale review of law as it applies to cohabiting couples. Couples who cohabit undertake a "risk" in choosing not to marry in order to "gain" from the "freedom" of cohabitation, to avoid a possible divorce or for ideological reasons. This apparent desire for flexibility means that cohabitants already "opt in" to a situation that could place them at risk in the future. This might be walked into unknowingly or deliberately but whilst living in a free society it is still the responsibility of the couple to understand what situation they are in. As a result of this one cannot make the law "fair" or even "certain" in dealing with the results of separating cohabitants, in fact, it may be that it should remain "unfair" in order to encourage couples to marry or formalise their relationship through a declaration of trust or civil partnership.

2.47 By contrast, some supporters of legal reform were concerned that it was dangerous to give too much weight to the concepts of autonomy and informed choice. As we discuss below, the reality for many individuals, some felt, would always be rather different.[74]

2.48 We do not view reform of the law relating to cohabitants as an alternative to or substitute for the promotion of marriage, self-regulation, public information and education, relationship support and other initiatives aimed at reducing family breakdown. A coherent family policy could involve all these strategies.

2.49 We agree that public information and education are crucial, whether or not the law is reformed. Surveys continue to find widespread belief in the "common law marriage myth" that the law treats cohabiting couples, perhaps after they have been living together for a certain period of time, as if they were married.[75] The need for improvements in the delivery of information and advice to cohabitants has been highlighted in recent research studies.[76]

2.50 It is important, however, to evaluate the impact that the provision of information has. A recent research study has examined the effects of the existing internet-based public information campaign about cohabitation sponsored by what was the Department for Constitutional Affairs.[77] We are aware that some believe that

---

[74] See para 2.55.

[75] A Park et al, *British Social Attitudes. The 24th Report* (forthcoming, January 2008).

[76] G Douglas, J Pearce and H Woodward, *A Failure of Trust: Resolving Property Disputes on Cohabitation Breakdown* (2007), see n 24 for URL, para 5.42; and R Tennant, J Taylor and J Lewis, *Separating from cohabitation: making arrangements for finances and parenting* (2006), Department for Constitutional Affairs Research Report 7/2006, where a number of suggestions are made at 8.4. Note also recent interesting findings about the prevalence of unqualified references to "common law marriage" in the media: R Probert, "Why Couples still Believe in Common-law Marriage" (2007) 37 *Family Law* 403.

[77] A Barlow, C Burgoyne and J Smithson, *The Living Together Campaign: an investigation of its impact on legally aware cohabitants*, Ministry of Justice Research Report (forthcoming, 2007).

this campaign was not sufficiently well-funded to achieve the type of coverage necessary to make a real impact on public misconceptions about cohabitation. However, the research study focused on those who had obtained the information and examined the effect that the information had on their behaviour.

2.51 The researchers found that many of those who had accessed the website found the information there helpful and that a significant number intended to take action as a result of the information obtained. Participants in the survey identified various things that they now intended to do, amongst the most common of which were: to discuss the matter with their partner (36%); to make a will (29%); to seek further legal advice (28%); and to make a "living together agreement" or a cohabitation contract (19%).[78] However, very few had actually taken any action. Various reasons were offered for this inactivity.[79] Over a third "hadn't yet got around to it", but almost as many had encountered an obstacle which was preventing them acting on the information: lack of agreement from their partner (where needed); concern that legal advice was required but could not be afforded; and concern that taking any further steps might cause problems with their partner.[80] A significant minority felt that they did not need to take any action; it appears that some of them were banking on the hope that the need for legal protection would not arise or found thinking about the legal aspects of their relationship "negative".[81]

2.52 These findings suggest that too much weight can be placed on the potential of information to solve the problems encountered by cohabitants. The researchers conclude that taking legal action:

> is often inhibited by practical barriers … and is often a long piecemeal process rather than a single event[,] leaving cohabitants legally vulnerable [often] for … long periods of time.[82]

2.53 Some of our consultees might respond to the suggestion that education often does not lead to action by arguing that, once armed with the relevant information, cohabitants have only themselves to blame if they later find themselves in difficulty. They might contend that the role of the State should begin and end with

---

[78] Only 3% indicated that they now intended to marry as a result: A Barlow, C Burgoyne and J Smithson, *The Living Together Campaign: an investigation of its impact on legally aware cohabitants* Ministry of Justice Research Report (forthcoming, 2007) p 6. The main survey had 102 respondents.

[79] A Barlow, C Burgoyne and J Smithson, *The Living Together Campaign: an investigation of its impact on legally aware cohabitants* Ministry of Justice Research Report (forthcoming, 2007) p 6.

[80] These reflect factors that we had suggested might inhibit legal action: CP, paras 5.16 to 5.29. And see findings of R Tennant, J Taylor and J Lewis, *Separating from cohabitation: making arrangements for finances and parenting* (2006) Department for Constitutional Affairs Research Report 7/2006, p 56 and following.

[81] A Barlow, C Burgoyne and J Smithson, *The Living Together Campaign: an investigation of its impact on legally aware cohabitants* Ministry of Justice Research Report (forthcoming, 2007) pp 6, 7 and 52.

[82] A Barlow, C Burgoyne and J Smithson, *The Living Together Campaign: an investigation of its impact on legally aware cohabitants* Ministry of Justice Research Report (forthcoming, 2007) p 11.

the provision of information; thereafter it is for individuals to take responsibility for themselves within the existing legal framework.

2.54 This is a justifiable standpoint. However, many other consultees would take issue with it. Many would consider the harshness of the consequences in some cases too stiff a penalty for disadvantaged individuals' failure to take legal steps that were theoretically open to them.[83] In reality, many cohabitants' options are narrower than the theory would suggest. As a result, even if they were made aware of the dangers of their current position, they would not be practically able to do anything to improve it.[84]

2.55 Take the position of cohabitants who have children and have been living together for a long time. The mother stays at home to look after the children and has no real prospects of re-entering the job market at a level that would enable her to afford the child-care that her absence from home would require. Her partner is able to provide for the family, but there is not a lot of extra money to go around. In order to obtain any long-term economic security in case of the relationship ending, she would first have to persuade him that he should take steps to protect her position. It may well be that he is quite happy with the status quo, which favours him.

2.56 Even if she were able to overcome this initial hurdle and persuade her partner that something should be done, they would then have to decide what steps were appropriate. It might be thought that the obvious answer is that they should marry. But research suggests that many couples are discouraged from taking this step because of the financial outlay that a wedding is perceived to entail. They are not willing to get married unless they can do it "properly", and many cohabitants think it wrong to marry purely for legal or financial reasons.[85] The alternative would be for them to declare an express trust over their home or enter into a contract for her benefit. However, such arrangements may be complex and require legal advice. The couple may simply conclude that the issue is not sufficiently pressing to take any further, and that they have other spending priorities.[86] As noted above, research suggests that while individuals may be

---

[83] CP, para 5.28.

[84] See, for example, the respondents to the Living Together Campaign Survey who needed their partner's agreement: para 2.51; similar observations were also made by a number of consultees, including Resolution, the Law Society, the Association of Women Solicitors, and the Mission and Public Affairs Council of the Church of England.

[85] See sources cited in CP, Part 5, n 62.

[86] See for example findings of A Barlow, S Duncan, G James and A Park, *Cohabitation, Marriage and the Law* (2005) pp 71 to 72; and A Barlow, C Burgoyne, J Smithson, *The Living Together Campaign – An investigation of its impact on legally aware cohabitants* Ministry of Justice Research Report (forthcoming, 2007) p 6.

aware of the potentially vulnerable nature of their position in law, optimism bias persuades many that, in their case, the need for protection will not arise.[87]

2.57 Assume, though, that the woman was unhappy with such a conclusion. She cannot take the required steps without the acquiescence of her partner. The only options are for her to leave the relationship or to stay in it without protection and so to be vulnerable should he later end the relationship. But separation does not solve the problem; it merely causes it to crystallise. And it is in no one's interests for the family to break up, particularly not those of the children.

2.58 As we indicated above, this is not to say that we do not place considerable weight on the importance of steps being taken to improve public understanding of the law: we do. But we consider that information provision cannot be regarded as a satisfactory cure, by itself, for the hardship experienced by many cohabitants and, by extension, their children, on separation.

Uncertainty, unfairness and hardship under the current law

2.59 Consultees who supported reform naturally tended to highlight the problems currently faced by cohabiting couples under the current law.[88]

2.60 Many organisations supported reform. We have already quoted the views of Relate.[89] Resolution, the association for solicitors specialising in family law, also called for reform:

> Injustice is caused by the confusing and complex rules of property and trust law and the requirement to look back at what has been said and done by a couple during their relationship rather than at what is fair at the time of separation. The prospects of success are hard to predict and clients cannot afford to risk litigation which may be costly and ultimately unsuccessful. The law should be clear and reasonably predictable. The current law increases the distress of relationship breakdown and does not produce fair outcomes.

2.61 The Association of District Judges, whose members deal with the problems generated by the current law on a daily basis in county courts across England and Wales, said that:

---

[87] A Barlow, C Burgoyne, J Smithson, *The Living Together Campaign – An investigation of its impact on legally aware cohabitants* Ministry of Justice Research Report (forthcoming, 2007) p 6. Relatively low rates of will-making amongst all categories of the population, not just cohabitants, further illustrate this problem In relation to cohabitants, see A Barlow, S Duncan, G James and A Park, "Just a piece of paper? Marriage and cohabitation", in A Park, J Curtice, K Thompson, L Jarvis and C Bromley (eds), *British Social Attitudes: Public policy, social ties. The 18th Report* (2001) p 45: only 10% of past and present cohabitants had made or changed a will in light of their cohabitation.

[88] See also the research findings of R Tennant, J Taylor and J Lewis, *Separating from cohabitation: making arrangements for finances and parenting* (2006) Department for Constitutional Affairs Research Report 7/2006 and G Douglas, J Pearce, H Woodward, *A Failure of Trust: Resolving Property Disputes on Cohabitation Breakdown* (2007), see URL at n 24; see also "Dealing with Property Issues on Cohabitation Breakdown" (2007) 37 *Family Law* 36.

[89] Para 2.30.

A new scheme would provide remedies that are long overdue. Inequities caused by the uncertainty that currently arise could be significantly reduced and eliminated, giving applicants a "right" in their own action. Presently applicants, for the benefit of the family, have to adopt and adapt a series of legal devices in an attempt to obtain a fair financial settlement, which currently is not always possible. … Such unfairness can and does occur with regularity on the separation of partners where little or no thought has been given to the impact of the financial responsibilities that can arise. The consequences can be catastrophic for the vulnerable partner, the children, and the family.

2.62 We also received a detailed response from the Mission and Public Affairs Council of the Church of England.[90] The Council emphasised that marriage warrants a special position within the social and legislative framework of society. Nevertheless, it acknowledged that:

> … there is also strong Biblical precedent not only for upholding standards but also for introducing laws to address situations that fall short of biblical ideals.

Consequently:

> … as was affirmed in a General Synod of February 2004[91] the Church of England recognises that there are some issues of hardship and vulnerability for people whose relationships are not based on marriage and that these need to be addressed by the creation of new legal rights.

2.63 They therefore expressed their position in the following terms:

> The test we would commend in assessing possible solutions is whether they will genuinely correct injustices without at the same time downgrading or creating disincentives to marriage. It is in our view perfectly justified in terms of public policy for marriage to continue to confer particular benefits and privileges not available to those who choose not to commit to an enduring legal relationship, so long as adequate steps are taken to prevent manifest injustice.

The case of cohabitants with children

2.64 In the CP, we provisionally proposed that the unfairness created by the current law in cases involving cohabitants who had children together is such that statutory reform is merited.[92] In particular, we pointed to evidence that couples living together with children[93] tend to adapt their individual roles with the result

---

[90] The Council is the body responsible for overseeing research and comment on social and political issues on behalf of the Church.

[91] Which concerned cohabiting couples and other sorts of home-sharers.

[92] CP, para 5.113.

[93] We discuss in Part 3 how cohabitants who have children together (as joint legal parents) may or may not differ, for the purposes of eligibility to apply for relief, from other cohabitants with children, eg step-children.

that the family lives together as a financially interdependent unit, creating economic vulnerability for one party in the event of separation. We also emphasised the potential for any hardship experienced by a cohabitant on separation to be passed on to any children living with that cohabitant.[94]

2.65 Data from the 2006 British Social Attitudes survey shows that a majority of respondents thought that cohabitants with children should have access to financial remedies on relationship breakdown.[95] Further, there was considerable support[96] from those of our consultees who addressed the question in the CP for reform in these cases. Even some of those who appeared to oppose any reform in principle qualified their position to some degree where children were involved.

2.66 The current law in these cases is different from that applicable to cohabitants without children, to the extent that Schedule 1 to the Children Act 1989 empowers the court to make various orders for financial provision for the benefit of children.[97] We explained in the CP why Schedule 1 does not provide adequately for cohabitants and their children.[98] That assessment was supported by several consultees with experience of the area. One Parent Families, a charity that provides advice to and represents the interests of lone parents, said:

> We are only too well aware of the limitations of Schedule 1 to the Children Act 1989 … . Even if the relationship breakdown occurs whilst children are comparatively young, mothers may be reluctant to seek orders under the Act knowing that they could be homeless upon cessation of their children's dependency. We invariably point out that they would be better off being homeless whilst their children were dependent, [since] they would at least be entitled to priority for social housing. Orders under Schedule 1 can also generate inter-generational conflicts of interest, with parents putting pressure on children either to extend or restrict their education depending on their financial interest.

2.67 These observations highlight some of the practical problems experienced in using Schedule 1. Schedule 1 provides no mechanism for sharing the capital in the property between the primary carer and the other party, so if the primary carer is unable to establish any beneficial interest in the property, he or she will be left empty handed. Pursuing a claim under Schedule 1 may provide the primary carer and children with accommodation during the children's minority or while they are still in education, but only at the risk of leaving the primary carer homeless when the order ceases to have effect. Since the children will by then no longer be dependent, the primary carer will cease to have a "priority need" for social housing, and, having had his or her employment disrupted over the past years by

---

[94] CP, para 5.70.

[95] A Park et al, *British Social Attitudes. The 24th Report* (forthcoming, January 2008).

[96] A majority of those who commented on the provisional proposal (or expressed a general view on the case for reform) agreed that statutory reform is merited in cases involving cohabitants who have children together.

[97] Child support is also payable where the children are still dependent. The law and administration of child support, which fall outside our terms of reference, are currently under reform: see the Child Maintenance and Other Payments Bill 2007.

[98] CP, para 4.34 to 4.46

discharging child-care obligations, may be unable to afford satisfactory housing alone.

2.68 In any event, as we explained in the CP, the reality in the vast majority of cases, where resources are limited, is that the relative lack of remedial flexibility offered by Schedule 1 makes its use unfeasible.[99] Many of the solicitors with whom we have consulted have suggested that Schedule 1 at best provides a bargaining tool in negotiations over securing a beneficial share in the family home under the general law of property and trusts. They did not consider it a realistic or satisfactory remedy in its own right in the vast majority of cases.[100]

2.69 We are aware that some who sympathise with the view that the law applicable to cohabitants with children is in need of reform may feel that the focus of reform should be the children rather than the parents. This might suggest that the most appropriate means of reform would be to amend (and perhaps extend) the provisions of Schedule 1 which operates solely for the benefit of children.

2.70 While the interests of children are fundamental to our recommendation that there should be reform for cohabitants with children, we do not share the view that reform should assist children alone. We agree with the many consultees who thought it unacceptable that a parent who has taken joint decisions during the course of a cohabiting relationship for the benefit of the family (and in particular the children) should not be able to require his or her ex-partner to share any disadvantages that flow from those decisions.

2.71 However, irrespective of the claims of the adult parties, we have concluded that it would not be possible to address the problems affecting the children of separated cohabitants adequately by means of changes to the Children Act. As preceding paragraphs explain,[101] the practical difficulties that currently prevent many children benefiting under the Children Act flow precisely from the focus of that Act on the children to the express exclusion of their parents. It is to a very great extent the failure of the law to ensure fairness between the adult parties that creates situations in which the Children Act cannot properly operate. It is obviously not the place of a Children Act to benefit adult parties.

2.72 Rather, we believe that the best way to ensure the welfare of the children of separated cohabitants is to introduce remedies that are more capable of bringing about a fair balancing of the adult parties' positions than the current law. This in turn would allow Schedule 1 to operate for the benefit of the children without the need for any amendment to the Children Act. It would also, irrespective of Schedule 1, provide the parent with care with his or her own means to prevent

[99] CP, paras 4.34 to 4.46. We disagree with the view expressed by the Social Justice Policy Group (an independent group reporting to the Conservative Party) that the "potential inequities" arising from the differences in legal regime for marital and cohabiting cases "are largely dealt with by sensible and appropriate interpretation of the legislation by judges": *The State of the Nation Report: Fractured Families* (2006) p 96. The cases referred to by the Group involve parties with substantial asset pools and so are not representative.

[100] See also findings of R Tennant, J Taylor and J Lewis, *Separating from cohabitation: making arrangements for finances and parenting* (2006) Department for Constitutional Affairs Research Report 7/2006, who highlight the problems for those with "middle financial circumstances": p 121.

[101] See also CP, para 4.34 to 4.46.

the children suffering hardship. Any attempt to reform the law which did not address the position of the adult parties would be incapable of supporting the children in this way.

2.73 The Mission and Public Affairs Council of the Church of England[102] was particularly concerned about cases involving cohabitants with children and agreed that reform should address the position of the adults as well as the children:

> Whilst we support marriage as being the best context for the nurturing of children because we believe it has greater potential for creating a stable, committed and healthy environment for children, we also recognise the importance of more recent legislation that [ensures] the rights and welfare of children regardless of the relationship of the parents. In becoming parents, people put themselves within the legitimate interest of both state and law. Provision for the main carer will affect the outcomes for the children arising from any relationship breakdown. This means we are sympathetic to reform that addresses the effect of relationship breakdown on children and those who make sacrifices to care for them. … We are persuaded … that it is appropriate for the state to invest in the protection of parenting and to provide a safety net for adults as well as remedies for children. We agree that, because of the potentially lifelong impact of parenting [on earning capacity, pensions etc], remedies should apply even when children of the family have grown up.

2.74 We agree with those consultees who argued that reform is warranted for cohabitants with children. The current law fails to provide a coherent response to relationship breakdown in these cases and does not take fair account of the economic consequences of the parties' contributions to the relationship. This disadvantages both cohabitants who have reduced or ceased paid employment in order to raise a family, and children who are still dependent when the parties separate. As we have already argued,[103] we do not consider that reform of the current law would necessarily be incompatible with the support of marriage and stable family relationships. Nor do we think that public information campaigns, while vitally important, provide an adequate response to the reality of the economic hardship faced by many cohabitants and, indirectly, their children under the current law.

The case of cohabitants without children

2.75 The CP did not reach any provisional conclusion about whether reform should extend to cohabitants without children; instead we invited the views of consultees.[104]

2.76 Consultees were more divided on this issue and a number were undecided. The majority considered that reform is not warranted in such cases. However, most of

---

[102] The Council is the body responsible for overseeing research and comment on social and political issues on behalf of the Church.

[103] Para 2.33 to 2.56.

[104] CP, para 5.114.

the legal practitioners, academics and organisations who addressed this question supported reform for cohabitants without children. The majority of respondents to the British Social Attitudes survey also favoured extending financial relief to cohabitants without children, depending on the duration and other circumstances of the relationship, such as contributions that each party made towards the other's wealth and financial sacrifices made for the benefit of the other party.[105]

2.77 There is evidence that cohabitants without children have the same potential to encounter unfairness on separation as cohabitants with children. We note in particular the observations of researchers who have recently been examining outcomes for cohabitants who separate under the current law. Their findings show that injustices currently arise between cohabitants without children who (just like those with children) are subject to the deficiencies of the general law of property and trusts.[106] As we explained earlier, the problems generated by that law are not confined to the effects of caring for children during the relationship.[107] Some consultees specifically observed that the problem of role-allocation within relationships, including care-giving for adult dependants, also occurs between cohabitants without children, creating an economic imbalance between the parties.

2.78 It therefore appears that the problems caused by unfair outcomes on separation are not confined to cases involving children. However, as we discussed in the CP, the simple fact that unfairness may arise may not, of itself, necessarily justify providing new remedies.[108] It might be argued that the relationship between cohabitants who have neither made the commitment entailed in marriage or civil partnership nor become parents together does not exhibit a type or level of commitment or any other key characteristic that justifies giving them access to financial relief.[109] A number of consultees took that approach and opposed reform for cohabitants without children. Those who took this view felt that the general arguments against reform examined above[110] told more strongly against reform in these cases than between cohabitants with children.

2.79 Supporters of reform offered a different assessment. For example, a majority of the Mothers' Union[111] members who contributed to their consultation response favoured reform for cohabitants without children, provided the relationship had lasted beyond a minimum duration. One member observed that it is difficult to differentiate between couples simply by reference to whether they have or do not have children, as there may be all sorts of reasons why a couple do not have

---

[105] A Park et al, *British Social Attitudes. The 24th Report* (forthcoming, January 2008).

[106] G Douglas, J Pearce, H Woodward, *A Failure of Trust: Resolving Property Disputes on Cohabitation Breakdown* (2007) paras 10.4 to 10.7, available at http://www.law.cf.ac.uk/researchpapers/papers/1.pdf or http://www.bris.ac.uk/law/research/centres-themes/cohabit/cohabit-rep.pdf (last visited 3 July 2007).

[107] See para 2.12 and following.

[108] Para 2.26 and following.

[109] CP, paras 5.74 to 5.86.

[110] From para 2.36.

[111] A Christian women's organisation, committed to marriage and the family.

children. The lack of children does not of itself necessarily connote a lack of commitment or interdependence.

2.80 Professor Anne Barlow, a leading researcher of marriage and cohabitation, offered the following observations on this issue:

> Cohabitants are a diverse group in terms of their expectations, commitment and styles of relationship ... and this is possibly more so where there are no children. However, a shared household plus an intimate relationship can and often does generate financial dependence or interdependence which causes hardship on relationship breakdown or death of a partner even without children. The longer the relationship, the more likely this is. It is also seen by many as a valid or even superior alternative to marriage in terms of providing emotional commitment and social stability and is certainly a socially accepted partnering style. It performs a variety of roles. It often coincides with or replaces engagement in 'trial marriage' cohabitations and has replaced marriage both in the youngest age range and among some of those who have experienced a failed marriage of their own or of their parents. These relationships are not necessarily uncommitted or short term, with research showing the average length of cohabitations increasing over time and not necessarily very short term .... . It would therefore seem appropriate to include these couples and couples where there is a child of only one partner ... within any proposed reforms but possibly on a different basis to those with children of the relationship.

2.81 To our knowledge, no jurisdiction which has legislated in this field has confined remedies to cohabitants with children. We have weighed all of the arguments for and against reform made to us by our consultees, and taken into account the recent research findings about outcomes for cohabitants under the current law, and the British Social Attitudes survey data about public opinion discussed above. We are persuaded that, subject to the imposition of a minimum duration requirement,[112] cohabitants without children should be covered by a new statutory scheme.

AN OPT-IN SCHEME OR A SCHEME OF GENERAL APPLICATION?

2.82 The next important question is the basis on which a new scheme should operate. There are two basic options:

(1) a scheme whereby remedies are only available between couples who have earlier "opted in" by formal registration of their relationship or who self-regulate; or

(2) a scheme which is available between all couples whose relationship satisfies general eligibility criteria, unless they have reached an agreement disapplying the statutory scheme, in which case the parties' own financial arrangements (if any) would apply ("a scheme of general application").

In the CP, we provisionally favoured the second model.[113]

2.83 Most consultees agreed with our provisional view, subscribing to the arguments that we had made in the CP. Rebecca Probert, a leading academic commentator, argued the case against opt-in regimes in the following terms:

> First, since the Civil Partnership Act, the vast majority of couples have the possibility of opting in to either marriage or civil partnership. Secondly, the experience of the Netherlands would suggest that the demand for an alternative to marriage is relatively low. … [Thirdly] it is possible that an opt-in regime might be seen as controversial – being perceived as a direct competitor to marriage – and so jeopardize the much-needed reform of the law relating to cohabitants.

2.84 Indeed, those who wish to do so can effectively opt into legal protection, with the agreement of their partner, by the use of contracts[114] and express declarations of trust.

2.85 Most importantly, as Probert points out:

> … while some cohabiting couples might welcome an alternative status, it is the position of those who do not realize that they need to opt in that poses the far more pressing problem.

2.86 We agree that our priority should be to address the position of those who are vulnerable under the current law, and who either do not know that they must opt in to obtain protection or who are unable, for whatever reason, to do so. If we want to remove more couples from the scope of property and trust law and the unsatisfactory outcomes that it often produces on separation, and thereby provide better basic justice between cohabitants, then an opt-in approach is not the answer.

2.87 We appreciate that, at least in theory, the choice between opt-in and opt-out should make no difference to outcomes. Equipped with the same information, parties ought to reach the same destination (within the scheme or outside it), whether positive action is required in order to come within, or to remain outside, the scope of the scheme. If so, an opt-out scheme would do no better at protecting the vulnerable than an opt-in: the individual who would fail to persuade his or her partner to opt in would equally come under pressure to opt out. However, we consider that such arguments underestimate the practical significance of the default position, combined with the likelihood that many couples who do not actively intend to fall outside the scheme would either not address their minds to the issue or postpone taking action for the sorts of reasons discussed earlier. Only an opt-out scheme would ensure protection in the

---

[112] See Part 3, where we also address the scope of "cohabitants with children" for the purpose of criteria governing eligibility to apply for relief.

[113] CP, paras 5.42 to 5.63 and 5.111 to 5.112.

[114] The legality of cohabitation contracts has not been conclusively determined (see CP, para 3.15 to 3.19). We recommend in Part 5 that a straightforward provision be enacted to confirm, for the avoidance of any doubt, that they should not be regarded as unlawful on grounds of public policy: see para 5.8.

absence of positive action by the parties; and because of the tendency of people not to get around to things, an opt-in scheme, just like the current law, would leave many unprotected. Moreover, conferring eligibility to apply for financial relief by default may improve the bargaining position of the more vulnerable party where the other party would prefer that the relationship continue on that basis than not continue at all.

2.88 As we discussed earlier, research suggests that providing people with information about the law and what they should do to protect their legal position does not guarantee that they will take those steps, or even be able to do so.[115] Indeed, while there was considerable support among respondents to the Living Together Campaign survey for opt-in regimes, the fact that so few of those individuals had taken action based on the information that they had obtained suggests that few would in practice register their relationship or be able to do so.[116]

2.89 Many of the minority of consultees who argued for an opt-in approach[117] were motivated by issues other than financial relief on separation. Instead, some were long-term cohabitants who wished to have a way of registering their relationship in order to obtain tax and pension benefits akin to those attaching to marriage and civil partnership. Since these issues fall outside our terms of reference, any opt-in scheme that we might recommend could not, in any event, offer those benefits.

2.90 Others who preferred the opt-in approach were concerned to protect the autonomy of cohabitants: individuals who have chosen not to become spouses or civil partners ought not, it was argued, have financial remedies imposed upon them. Indeed, they should be encouraged positively to address the consequences of their relationship. John Passmore, a barrister, who limited his remarks to childless relationships, argued that any relationship:

> functions at the highest level which is desired by *both* parties. If one party wants more, he or she has to make do with what the other is prepared to give, or find another acquaintance, friend or sexual partner who is prepared to give more. What the law should do is provide legal statuses for relationships, which people can opt for, and the available options should be made well known. What the law should not do is exert any pressure on people to have one sort of relationship rather than another … . An "opt out" system would exert pressure of this sort.

2.91 Attractive though this argument may seem, we believe that it does not account for a crucial factor. This is that an opt-in scheme is likely to leave too many economically vulnerable people facing unjustified hardship on separation. The factors that led to their economic vulnerability are all too likely to be the same factors that led them to agree with an economically stronger partner not to opt in, meant that they failed to convince their partner to opt in, or led them to be

---

[115] From para 2.42 to 2.58.

[116] A Barlow, C Burgoyne, J Smithson, *The Living Together Campaign – An investigation of its impact on legally aware cohabitants* Ministry of Justice Research Report (forthcoming, 2007).

[117] Either instead of, or alongside, a scheme of general application.

understandably ignorant of the law, in the first place. A scheme of general application would better address that problem.[118]

2.92 However, we do place considerable weight on the concerns of those who preferred some form of opt-in solution: facilitating and protecting party autonomy. We consider that it is important to recommend a scheme which provides some encouragement for parties to discuss the financial implications of their relationship. Failure to communicate about such matters may leave parties unaware that they have divergent views about their relationship and so store up trouble for the future.

2.93 We do not, therefore, agree with those who argued in favour of a scheme that would apply compulsorily to all eligible couples, making no allowance for alternative arrangements. Instead, we agree with the majority who favoured a scheme of general application, but which would permit couples who wished to do so to agree to disapply the scheme. They would then be able, if they wished to do so, to make their own financial arrangements determining how their resources would be divided in the event of separation.[119] We consider that this model strikes the appropriate balance between, on the one hand, the need to provide a fairer means of resolving the property and financial disputes that can arise between cohabitants on separation than that provided by the current law, and, on the other hand, the importance of preserving individuals' freedom to conduct their private relationships on their own terms.

2.94 **We recommend that legislation should create a scheme of general application, whereby cohabiting couples would be entitled to apply for financial relief on separation:**

   (1) **provided they satisfy statutory eligibility criteria;**

   (2) **but not where they had reached an agreement disapplying the statutory scheme ("an opt-out agreement"), in which case the parties' own financial arrangements (if any) would apply.**

2.95 We discuss the issue of eligibility criteria in Part 3. We discuss in Part 5 how couples should retain the freedom to make agreements to "opt out" of our recommended scheme.

OTHER ISSUES RAISED BY CONSULTEES

2.96 Many consultees took the opportunity to draw our attention to related issues of concern. These all fall outside our terms of reference; indeed, some are criticisms directed at the scope of those terms of reference. We briefly report these observations for the benefit of those who may in future be called upon to examine these issues.

---

[118] This is the model currently used for legal recognition of cohabitants, for example to determine eligibility to apply for financial provision from the estate of the deceased partner under the Inheritance (Provision for Family and Dependants) Act 1975: see Part 6.

[119] Indeed, they might provide simply that the property should be divided in accordance with the parties' express beneficial entitlement to the assets that they own.

2.97 The Odysseus Trust (an organisation which supports the activities of Lord Lester of Herne Hill QC in his work as a member of the House of Lords) called for a wholesale review and rationalisation of all aspects of the law regarding cohabitants. Some of the issues raised by the Trust's response have been addressed by previous Law Commission projects, or have been the subject of recent legislation.[120]

2.98 As we have already indicated, several consultees, notably those who wanted a new opt-in status to be created for cohabitants, were concerned about what they view as the discriminatory treatment of long-term cohabitants as compared with spouses and civil partners, particularly in relation to tax and pension rights.[121] Conversely, CARE,[122] which has done a considerable amount of work in recent years on the treatment of families by the tax and benefits system, suggested that if cohabitants were to have access to financial relief on separation, they ought also to attract some of the tax disadvantages to which spouses and civil partners are subject.[123]

2.99 The range of relationships covered by our terms of reference also attracted comment. Several consultees expressed disappointment that the project was not dealing with various other types of home-sharing, care-giving and economically interdependent relationships, including parents and couples who have never shared a household, where financial hardship can also arise.

2.100 We have accepted in the past that the position of other home-sharers may warrant review.[124] But as our experience in the Sharing Homes[125] project demonstrated, one size does not fit all, and it was therefore necessary to confine the present project to the position of cohabitants as a specific type of home-sharers. Moreover, the fact that proponents of legal reform for parties such as blood relatives who live together often focus on issues such as tax[126] suggests that a wider review, of a sort that would not necessarily be suited to the Law Commission, may be appropriate.

2.101 Another category of relationship highlighted by some consultees was religious marriages that are not recognised by the law of England and Wales.[127] This issue arises where the marriage ceremony has not complied with the formalities

---

[120] See Mental Incapacity (1995) Law Com No 231 and the Mental Capacity Act 2005, s 4(7)(b); and Claims for Wrongful Death (1999) Law Com No 263, see now Department for Constitutional Affairs, *The Law on Damages* CP 9/07 (2007).

[121] See also the recent findings of A Barlow, C Burgoyne, J Smithson, *The Living Together Campaign – An investigation of its impact on legally aware cohabitants* Ministry of Justice Research Report (forthcoming, 2007).

[122] Christian Action Research and Education.

[123] For example, rules regarding the taxation of transactions between "connected persons".

[124] Sharing Homes (2002) Law Com 278, Part 6, paras 7 to 9.

[125] See para 1.14 and following.

[126] *Burden and Burden v UK* (2007) 44 EHRR 51.

[127] It is difficult to obtain reliable data on how many such cases there are.

prescribed by the law of England and Wales[128] and the parties have not contracted a civil marriage at any point.[129] The position of these individuals is in many ways very different from that of cohabitants, as that term is generally understood. They have made the commitment of marriage, albeit not in a form that is recognised by the civil law. We are unable to address the specific concern of this group of people – that their marriages should be recognised in law – in the context of this project. But we have been mindful in developing our recommendations that parties to such religious marriages who live together are treated by the law as cohabitants, and so fall within the scope of our current work.

CONCLUSIONS

2.102 The CP concluded its discussion of the case for reform by noting that, ultimately, it is for Government and Parliament to decide as a matter of social policy whether the introduction of financial relief for cohabitants on separation would be appropriate and, if so, for which categories of cohabitants. That of course remains the case.

2.103 We are, however, firmly of the view that reform is required. Consultation has confirmed our provisional view that reform should address the position of cohabitants who have children together. We have also concluded that reform should extend to couples who have not had children, but only where they have satisfied a minimum duration requirement. Reform should comprise a new statutory scheme of financial relief for cohabitants. This should not be a system into which couples could opt in. It should be a scheme of general application under which all couples satisfying statutory eligibility criteria would be entitled to apply for financial relief on separation, save where they had agreed to disapply the statutory scheme, in which case they would be free to make and enforce their own arrangements.

2.104 The following Parts consider the operation of the scheme that we are recommending in more detail.

[128] The law requires, in particular, that appropriate notice be given (for civil marriages) at the local register office, that the ceremony be conducted in the register office or in approved or registered premises (non-Anglican churches, mosques and temples can be registered for this purpose, but many are not) at a particular time, and that the marriage is registered. Different rules apply to Church of England/Church in Wales, Jewish and Quaker marriages. Reform recommendations which would have made it easier for members of other faiths to contract valid marriages within their religious traditions have not been enacted: General Register Office, *Civil Registration: Delivering Vital Change* (2003), available at http://www.gro.gov.uk/Images/en_tableofcontents_v1_tcm69-3576.pdf (last visited 3 July 2007).

[129] See CP, paras 9.162 to 9.165.

PART 3
ELIGIBILITY FOR REMEDIES ON SEPARATION

INTRODUCTION

3.1 In Part 2, we recommended the introduction of a new statutory scheme of general application, so that couples who satisfy certain eligibility criteria would be able to apply for financial relief unless they had made a valid opt-out agreement.[1] We now address those eligibility criteria in more detail. We deal with eligibility to apply for provision on death under the Inheritance (Provision for Family and Dependants) Act 1975 in Part 6.

3.2 Eligibility rules for the new scheme must be clear, principled and easy to apply. The more uncertain and complex they are, the more time and costs will be spent in resolving disputes, and the greater the potential for nuisance claims and for unnecessary intrusion into the minutiae of the parties' lives together.

3.3 We are aware that eligibility criteria are likely to be the aspect of any new scheme that is most readily understood and remembered by the general public. Public information campaigns, which should be conducted not only immediately before the implementation of any new law but also as a longer-term initiative,[2] should communicate clearly the point at which a couple would become eligible under the scheme.

WHO ARE "COHABITANTS"?

3.4 In the CP, we first sought consultees' views on the basic definition that should be used to identify "cohabitants". In many parts of the current law, cohabitation is defined by analogy with marriage or civil partnership: two people who are neither married to each other nor civil partners but who are living together as husband and wife or as if they were civil partners. We asked consultees whether they wanted to use that formulation or some other.[3]

3.5 Although a significant minority of consultees supported the marriage analogy, largely on the basis that it was well-established and workable, just over half of those who answered the question indicated that they would prefer some alternative.[4] Some considered that the marriage analogy could not appropriately be applied to couples who had not married and who may specifically have rejected marriage, and that such couples should not (or would not want to) be described as if they had. Some believed that the marriage analogy might be contributing to the common law marriage myth. It has also been suggested that the meaning of the equivalent "civil partnership analogy", used to describe relationships between same-sex cohabitants, is less than clear.

---

[1] See Part 5. We explain in Part 6 why we are not recommending a similar right to opt out of the Inheritance (Provision for Family and Dependants) Act 1975.

[2] See para 2.46 to 2.58.

[3] CP, para 9.32.

[4] A small number of consultees made other observations without expressing a preference on the choice of definition.

3.6 One consultee expressed particular concerns about the marriage analogy in so far as it implies that the couple are "not married to each other": parties to religious marriages not recognised as a marriage by the law of England and Wales may take exception to being described in those terms.[5] Whatever definition were ultimately adopted, it would clearly be necessary to distinguish between those whom the law of England and Wales recognises as spouses,[6] who must fall outside the scheme, and those whose relationship is not recognised as a marriage, and who may therefore fall within the scheme. It should be possible to draw this line in a way that neither confuses people, nor causes offence to those who have entered into religious marriages.

3.7 But while most opposed use of the marriage analogy, there was no clear view about what alternative concept should be used. Some liked the concept of living together as a couple;[7] others were attracted by the concept applied by adoption law of living as partners in an enduring family relationship.[8]

3.8 We do not ourselves think that the latter formulation would be sufficiently clear for the purposes of our recommended scheme. The adoption legislation was intended to widen the class of people who could put themselves forward as prospective adopters. Persons applying to adopt as a couple will consider that they have the relevant type of relationship.[9] By contrast, the potential for dispute between the parties regarding eligibility to apply for financial relief on separation is rather greater. We therefore think that more certain, clear-cut eligibility requirements are desirable in this context.

3.9 On balance, we take the view that the problems associated with the marriage analogy outweigh its advantages. We are particularly concerned that the language used by the law[10] should not contribute to public misunderstanding regarding the status of different types of relationship. Notwithstanding the arguments for consistency with existing legislation, we therefore favour the adoption of language which would be readily understood by the public, avoid

---

[5] As we discussed in the CP, para 9.162 to 9.165 and here at para 2.101, couples who marry in accordance with religious traditions in this jurisdiction or abroad in circumstances that do not create a marriage under, or recognised by, the law of England and Wales (even as a void marriage), do not qualify as "spouses" for the purposes of matrimonial law. Where parties to such marriages in fact live in a joint household, they fall within the concept of cohabitant where that is used for the purposes of the law of England and Wales, and so would fall within the scope of our recommended scheme. While they expressed some reservations about aspects of the proposed scheme, this indirect protection of parties to religious marriages was welcomed by the Association of Muslim Lawyers and by one individual consultee.

[6] Or civil partners: see Civil Partnership Act 2004, sch 20.

[7] This concept has been adopted by some other jurisdictions that have legislated in this area, including New South Wales, Tasmania, Australian Capital Territory, New Zealand and Sweden.

[8] Adoption and Children Act 2002, s 144(4). This language has been replicated in the Human Tissue and Embryos (Draft) Bill 2007, cl 60(2)(c), for the purposes of eligibility to apply for parental orders following a surrogacy arrangement. A number of other formulations were suggested by some of our consultees.

[9] And so the only person likely to challenge that assessment is the adoption agency.

[10] And in official materials such as court and welfare benefits guidance notes and forms: see CP, para 9.31.

potential confusion with the status of marriage and civil partnership, and clearly identify the type of relationship which falls within the scope of the scheme.

3.10 We consider that the marriage analogy and adoption law formulations should not be used. However, as we are not drafting a Bill, it is not appropriate for us to recommend a definition, in the sense of the specific form of words that should appear in legislation enacting our scheme. Instead, we focus on describing the type of relationship with which we are concerned in this project.

3.11 In our view, the essential type of relationship that should be covered by any new scheme is that of a couple who share a household. We discuss below the sort of factors that the courts may wish to take into account in determining whether the parties had such a relationship.[11] Most consultees who addressed this issue agreed with our provisional proposal that in order to fall within our scheme, the parties must at least share a joint household. This requirement seems to us to be an integral aspect of "cohabitation", distinguishing it from other intimate relationships where the parties do not live together. It is a concept already known to the law and is relatively easy to apply. There inevitably remain grey areas around its edges.[12] But the core requirement seems sound, and the questions it raises are familiar to the courts in other contexts.[13]

3.12 We do not anticipate that a definition based on these concepts should entail any substantive difference in application from the marriage analogy, subject possibly in relation to one issue.[14] However, since the marriage analogy continues to be used extensively elsewhere in the statute book,[15] whatever specific form of words is adopted, we would encourage Government to consider whether it may be appropriate to employ the concept of a couple sharing a household in those contexts too. As well as alleviating the problems of public misunderstanding that may arise from the use of the marriage or civil partnership analogy, this strategy would preclude scope for sterile argument about whether any difference was intended where different terms are used.

3.13 **We recommend that persons should be cohabitants for the purposes of being eligible to apply for financial relief on separation where:**

(1) **they are living as a couple in a joint household; and**

(2) **they are neither married to each other nor civil partners.**

---

[11] Para 3.14 and following

[12] When does a "living apart together" relationship actually become cohabitation; when does one party living elsewhere during the working week disrupt the joint household? See *Kotke v Saffarini* [2005] EWCA Civ 221, [2005] 2 FLR 517, discussed at CP, para 9.36.

[13] The concept of "household" is used in existing legislation concerning cohabitation (such as the Inheritance (Provision for Family and Dependants) Act 1975 and Fatal Accidents Act 1976), and in the context of divorce for determining what constitutes "living apart" for the purposes of identifying whether the parties have separated: MCA, ss 1(2)(d) to (e) and 2(6).

[14] Regarding some relationships between parties who are related by family: see para 3.64 and following.

[15] We recommend that the definition in the Inheritance (Provision for Family and Dependants) Ac 1975 be amended: see Part 6.

For these purposes, references to marriage and civil partnership should be taken to denote relationships recognised as such for the purposes of the law of England and Wales.

A statutory checklist?

3.14 We provisionally proposed that, in order to assist the court in identifying relationships falling within the definition of "cohabitants", new legislation should contain a non-exhaustive checklist of factors to which the court should have regard. We invited consultees' views on what factors might be listed.[16]

3.15 Most consultees who addressed this issue supported this approach. They felt that a checklist would enable the courts to take a flexible approach to identifying couples, and would give room to the courts to be sensitive to cultural differences. Almost all of the small number of consultees who addressed the related issue of how to determine the point of separation[17] felt that this could readily be identified in individual cases by reference to the checklist of factors used to determine whether the parties had been cohabiting. Others remarked, however, that checklists may be less useful in ascertaining eligibility to apply than in exercising a discretion to award relief once eligibility has been established.

3.16 We think that checklists have merit. They fulfil a different function here from that which they have in guiding the exercise of a discretion. Here, the issue would be a simple one of fact: were the parties living as a couple in a joint household? Or, to determine the point of separation: when did they cease to do so? A checklist would serve as a useful reminder to the parties and the court of those matters that are relevant to the determination of those issues. But it would operate merely as an aid in making the relevant finding of fact, and would not form part of the definition.[18] Moreover, as the courts acknowledge,[19] there are many sorts of "couple" relationships: they do not fit an exact pattern. A checklist can reflect and draw attention to that. Any checklist must, therefore, be understood to be non-exhaustive; and satisfaction of all or any items on the list would be neither necessary nor sufficient to establish the existence of a cohabiting relationship.

3.17 We have decided that it would be preferable not to recommend a statutory checklist. The courts currently identify cohabitants in various contexts (usually by reference to the marriage or civil partnership analogy) without the assistance of a statutory checklist. Some consultees warned that statutory checklists can encourage a "box-ticking mentality" and lead to an undesirable degree of rigidity or confusion about the status and importance of items on the list. Particularly since the concept of living as a couple in a joint household can readily be understood as a matter of plain English, we do not think that a statutory checklist is necessary.

---

[16] CP, paras 9.55 to 9.56.

[17] CP, para 9.114(5) and para 9.124. Separation would be of principal importance in establishing the time limits for bringing a claim.

[18] The courts are already alive to this in the use of the checklists adopted by case law: *Re J (Income Support: cohabitation)* [1995] 1 FLR 660.

[19] *Re Watson (deceased)* [1999] 1 FLR 878.

3.18 Nevertheless, it may be helpful if we outline here some of the central factors that we think a court would wish to have in mind when deciding whether the parties' relationship was that of a couple.

3.19 It is clear from consultees' suggestions that there is an enormous range of factors that could be examined, which is itself a reason not to attempt to single out any particular group of factors to appear in statutory form. However, the "six signposts" currently used by social security law,[20] and adopted by the judges to identify cohabiting couples under the "marriage analogy" definition, may provide a convenient starting point. Between them, they cover in general terms many of the more specific factors which some consultees suggested. Indeed, many consultees simply advocated adoption of this list:

(1) existence of a joint household;[21]

(2) stability of the relationship;

(3) financial arrangements;

(4) responsibility for children;[22]

(5) sexual relationship;

(6) public recognition of the relationship.

Some of these factors merit separate comment.

3.20 It may at first sight seem counter-intuitive for the stability of the relationship[23] to be relevant in a context where that relationship has just ended. Some consultees expressed concern that such a requirement might prejudice applicants who had been victims of domestic violence, and whose relationship may appear to be highly unstable. However, we consider that, applied with sensitivity in those cases, stability is an important factor, to some extent implicit in the express requirement that the parties had a joint household. As we explained in the CP,[24] for access to a scheme of financial relief to be justified, it may be thought necessary to demonstrate that there was an established relationship between the parties that was more than merely fleeting or temporary.[25]

---

[20] Department of Work and Pensions, *Decision Makers Guide,* vol 3, ch 11, para 11040 and following, available at http://www.dwp.gov.uk/publications/dwp/dmg/ (last visited 3 July 2007).

[21] This factor is, of course, already covered by our express requirement that the parties share a household: see above paras 3.11 and 3.13.

[22] Even where the presence of particular children in the couple's household would not of itself give rise to eligibility to apply for financial relief (see discussion below at para 3.46 and following), the fact that the parties were together responsible for a child may be indicative that they were a couple.

[23] See Department of Work and Pensions, *Decision Makers Guide,* vol 3, ch 11, para 11053, available at http://www.dwp.gov.uk/publications/dwp/dmg/ (last visited 3 July 2007): the focus there is on the parties' domestic activities in the household.

[24] See generally CP, para 5.41 and following.

[25] See also para 3.29.

3.21 The sexual aspect of the parties' relationship is an important consideration.[26] The present project is concerned with couples as opposed to other home-sharers. A key feature of couples which sets them apart from other home-sharers is the sexual intimacy between the parties. Or rather, as one consultee helpfully put it, it is the absence of a sexual relationship between other home-sharers that distinguishes them from couples, who may or may not have such a relationship.[27] Although inclusion of this factor raises the possibility of intrusive inquiry where this aspect of the parties' relationship is disputed, the courts would be unable to avoid consideration of the issue in some cases.

3.22 How the parties represented their relationship to friends, family and the outside world[28] should also be relevant. In some cases, for example, involving parties to religious marriages or those who are engaged, there is clear evidence that the parties are regarded as a couple. However, like other factors, public recognition should be neither necessary nor sufficient to support a finding that the parties were a couple.[29]

FURTHER ELIGIBILITY REQUIREMENTS

3.23 It may be argued that where two people, who are neither married to each other nor civil partners, have been living as a couple in a joint household, they should be entitled to claim financial relief on separation without satisfying further eligibility requirements. However, most jurisdictions which have enacted legislation conferring financial remedies on the separation of cohabitants have imposed additional criteria, for example requiring the parties to have lived together for a specified duration (a "minimum duration requirement"). The question that we now address is whether we should recommend the imposition of a minimum duration requirement in all or any cases, or whether the presence of children should be relevant to the eligibility of cohabitants to claim.

3.24 In the discussion that follows, we address three sets of circumstances:

(1) cohabitants who have children together – where the parties to the relationship are as a matter of law the joint parents of a child or children;

(2) other cohabitants with children – where the parties shared their household with a child or children none of whom are as a matter of law the children of both parties (for example, cases involving step-parents); and

(3) cohabitants without children – couples who do not fall within either of the previous categories.

3.25 In the discussion which follows, we deal with (1), then (3) and finally (2).

[26] See Re J (Income Support: Cohabitation) [1995] 1 FLR 660, 666.

[27] Dr Stephen Cretney.

[28] See Department of Work and Pensions, Decision Makers Guide, vol 3, ch 11, para 11060, available at http://www.dwp.gov.uk/publications/dwp/dmg/ (last visited 3 July 2007).

[29] Some consultees were concerned that a requirement of public acknowledgement could, in particular, disadvantage some same-sex couples and couples in some minority ethnic communities.

Cohabitants who have children together

3.26 In the CP we provisionally proposed that cohabitants[30] who are (as a matter of law)[31] joint parents of a child born before, during or following their cohabitation should be able to apply for relief on separation without having to satisfy any minimum duration requirement.[32] Most consultees who considered this provisional proposal supported it.

3.27 The Chancery Bar Association and the Family Law Bar Association, although in principle in favour of reform, were amongst the minority who disagreed with our proposal.[33] Between them, they raised both practical and substantive concerns. It was argued that if no minimum duration were required it would be difficult to distinguish between those parents who had cohabited and those who had not. That distinction was considered important as a matter of principle in so far as it could be said to differentiate between those who had made a commitment to each other and those who had had only "transient, relatively temporary" relationships.[34] Where there was no true cohabitation between the parents, it was felt that their disputes should continue to be governed simply by Schedule 1 to the Children Act 1989.[35] It was acknowledged that incorporating a minimum duration requirement could allow a party wishing to avoid responsibility under the scheme to do so by leaving before the required period had elapsed. But this, it was argued, would be a "small price to pay" for preserving a clear distinction.[36]

3.28 We note that the Republic of Ireland's Law Reform Commission recently recommended a minimum duration requirement where cohabitants had children together which was shorter than that which would otherwise apply (two years and three years respectively).[37] But they also recommended that the court should be entitled to dispense with either requirement on an application for financial relief where serious injustice would otherwise arise.[38] As we explain below, we do not generally favour discretions to dispense with eligibility requirements, as they

---

[30] "Cohabitants" here only includes those who satisfy the concept of cohabitants that we recommend at para 3.13.

[31] This includes parties who become parents via adoption, assisted reproduction or pursuant to a parental order following a surrogacy arrangement.

[32] CP, para 9.67.

[33] Several of that minority were largely against any reform. One other consultee raised concerns about the possible detrimental effects on children of their presence being key to the availability of remedies, in particular about paternity tests being called for. It seems to us that such disputes are likely already to arise in relation to child support, and that reform of this nature would not add to that existing problem.

[34] Chancery Bar Association.

[35] Conversely, some consultees (eg One Parent Families) considered that reform should extend generally to all parents, regardless of whether they had cohabited.

[36] Family Law Bar Association.

[37] It should be noted that this recommendation was made in the context of a project which dealt with issues extending beyond the private law relationship between the parties, creating a status for various purposes in relation to the State. It could be argued that in that context there is greater need for a minimum duration requirement, even in cases with children.

[38] Rights and Duties of Cohabitants (2006) Law Reform Commission of the Republic of Ireland LRC 82-2006, paras 2.16 to 2.18 and 2.27 to 2.28.

would detract substantially from the certainty that the basic rule would seek to achieve.

3.29 We agree with the Chancery Bar and Family Law Bar Associations that, in line with our terms of reference, cohabitation is an essential part of our recommended scheme. It would therefore be necessary in all cases to prove that the parties had been cohabiting. However, we do not accept that this necessitates the universal application of a minimum duration requirement. Cohabitation, in so far as it requires the establishment of a joint household, does not connote a mere fleeting relationship. It connotes a continuing state of affairs. Where there is doubt about whether the parties had been cohabiting, most likely because it is questionable whether they had shared a joint household, then those doubts would not be allayed simply by the passage of time. Either they were cohabiting or they were not.

3.30 Some individual consultees highlighted difficult cases where conception was not wanted by both parents, or was even engineered by one against the known wishes of the other. The courts have declined to give any weight to such arguments in the context of claims for the benefit of the child.[39] Different considerations may be felt to apply where the issue is provision for the benefit of the cohabiting adult. But accommodating such considerations directly within the eligibility requirements of the scheme would open the door to highly acrimonious argument. For similar reasons, Parliament and the courts have made the conduct of the parties of very limited relevance to the determination of ancillary relief on divorce.[40]

3.31 **We recommend that cohabitants who are by law the parents of a child born before, during or following their cohabitation ("cohabitants who have a child together") ought to be eligible to apply for financial relief on separation.**

Cohabitants without children

3.32 In the CP, we did not make a provisional proposal about such cases. Instead, we invited the views of consultees: if cohabitants without children were to be covered by a new scheme at all,[41] on what basis should they be eligible? In particular, should there be a minimum duration requirement in such cases?[42]

Should there be a minimum duration requirement?

3.33 A minority of consultees opposed the imposition of a minimum duration requirement. We note that this is the Scottish approach,[43] and that it can be supported on the grounds that remedies based on an evaluation of contributions would be self-limiting so that no further eligibility requirements would be needed: if no relevant contribution had been made, or if parties' contributions had been

---

[39] *J v C (Child: Financial Provision)* [1999] 1 FLR 152, 154, Hale J (as she then was).

[40] See recently *Miller v Miller; McFarlane v McFarlane* [2006] UKHL 24, [2006] 2 AC 618, esp at [64] and [145].

[41] We discuss that basic issue in Part 2.

[42] CP, para 9.114.

[43] Family Law (Scotland) Act 2006, s 28.

equal, then no remedy would be forthcoming. Some of the consultees who took this view argued that requiring proof of duration would compound the problem of proving cohabitation, and could generate arbitrary results.[44] One consultee suggested that this could impact disproportionately on same-sex couples and on opposite-sex couples who cohabit later in life, since they are less likely to have children together.

3.34 Others highlighted possible adverse consequences of a minimum duration requirement. Would such a requirement create a "threshold effect", inducing one party to leave as the relevant anniversary approached in order to avoid liability; or conversely, to remain in an unsatisfactory, even violent, relationship to ensure that the key date was reached and access to the remedies thereby secured? Might a minimum duration requirement generate new myths surrounding cohabitation, akin to the "common law marriage" myth, encouraging people to think that they had far greater legal entitlements than they actually did? Given this last possibility, the Mission and Public Affairs Council of the Church of England[45] suggested that instead of a minimum duration requirement it would be better to have a threshold of "substantial injustice". The Association of Muslim Lawyers drew attention to the position of parties to religious marriages not recognised by the law of England and Wales. They argued that, since those couples have clearly demonstrated their mutual commitment, they should not have to satisfy a minimum duration requirement before becoming eligible to claim financial relief.

3.35 However, most consultees who addressed this question considered that a minimum duration requirement should apply to cases of cohabitants without children. Some who opposed reform indicated that, if reform were to extend to cohabitants without children, a minimum duration requirement would be essential in order to identify those relationships with sufficient stability, interdependence and commitment to warrant access to a remedial scheme.

3.36 We take seriously the concerns raised by the minority. However, we think that several factors support the inclusion of a minimum duration requirement and accordingly recommend that such a requirement be adopted.

3.37 There is some attraction in using "substantial injustice" as an eligibility criterion. It clearly indicates that merely cohabiting with another person should not, of itself, merit access to financial relief.[46] However, we think that the practical difficulties likely to be encountered in applying such a test would be formidable. While it may not always be agreed by the parties whether a minimum duration requirement had been satisfied, it would generally be easier to establish whether an objective test based on length of cohabitation had been met than an inherently subjective test based on the existence of injustice.

3.38 Education and information would, as now, be necessary to maximise public understanding of what legal remedies might be available between cohabitants

---

[44] See also R Tennant, J Taylor and J Lewis, *Separating from cohabitation: making arrangements for finances and parenting* (2006) Department for Constitutional Affairs Research Report 7/2006, p 145.

[45] The Council is the body responsible for overseeing research and comment on social and political issues on behalf of the Church.

[46] See discussion in CP, Part 5, esp paras 5.74 to 5.86.

who separate. It would be particularly important to emphasise that, although the parties would be able to apply for financial relief once the relationship passed the minimum duration, the grant of remedies would be by no means guaranteed.

3.39 Most importantly, a minimum duration requirement would, albeit somewhat crudely, serve as a mechanism for identifying those relationships likely to entail commitment of a level meriting specific legal protection. Large-scale attitude surveys indicate that length of relationship is a key factor affecting public opinion about whether and when remedies should be available between cohabitants without children.[47]

3.40 A minimum duration requirement would help to reduce the prospect of nuisance claims being brought by unmeritorious applicants. Although it would, inevitably, prevent many couples from applying for relief at all,[48] we do not think, on balance, that this would be a bad outcome.

3.41 Couples without children who have only lived together for a short period are intrinsically less likely to have combined their lives and finances in a way, or to an extent, that merits access to special remedies. Where couples in short-term, childless relationships have invested in property together, the general law of property and trusts will often provide an adequate remedy. Where they have made an express declaration of trust, their position is very straightforward.[49] As we discussed in Part 2, changes to conveyancing practice and the relevant Land Registry forms might help improve parties' understanding of the financial arrangements that they enter into on purchasing property together, and so enhance the prospects of those arrangements being fair.[50] Matters may be more complex where parties have not expressly stipulated their beneficial entitlements or one simply moves into the other's home, and the general law deals rather better with financial contributions than financial sacrifices.[51] However, parties to short-term cohabiting relationships without children are less likely to make substantial sacrifices of a sort that are difficult to recover and which would therefore merit financial relief under a statutory scheme.

---

[47] See CP, para 5.86, and recently A Park et al, *British Social Attitudes. The 24th Report* (forthcoming, January 2008).

[48] See n 53 below.

[49] *Goodman v Gallant* [1986] Fam 106.

[50] Notably in relation to conveyancing practice and advice: see G Douglas, J Pearce, H Woodward, *A Failure of Trust: Resolving Property Disputes on Cohabitation Breakdown* (2007) paras 10.28 to 10.31, available at http://www.law.cf.ac.uk/researchpapers/papers/1.pdf or http://www.bris.ac.uk/law/research/centres-themes/cohabit/cohabit-rep.pdf (last visited 3 July 2007). The researchers indicated to us in their consultation response that one of the team took the view that, if their suggested conveyancing reforms were introduced, a minimum duration requirement of five years should be considered, but that without such reforms, two years would be appropriate.

[51] The relevance of indirect financial contributions remains unclear (see paras 2.13 and A.35, and CP, paras 4.12 and 4.13) but, when made over only a short period of time, are unlikely to be sufficiently substantial to merit special relief. The relevance of domestic contributions is likewise doubtful, notwithstanding *Stack v Dowden* [2007] UKHL 17, [2007] 2 WLR 831.

Where should a minimum duration requirement be set?

3.42 Our consultees made various suggestions about where a minimum duration requirement should be set. The option attracting the most support was two years, the period already used by the Inheritance (Provision for Family and Dependants) Act 1975 to determine cohabitants' eligibility to apply for family provision on death.[52] Almost as many consultees advocated periods of three years or more, a handful of those advocating ten years or more. Only a small number proposed periods of a year or less, some expressly describing this as a means of ensuring that the parties had cohabited, rather than perceiving it as a distinctive additional requirement.

3.43 We think that it is difficult to identify any principled basis on which to select a minimum duration. Consultees tended to see a minimum duration requirement as a measure of the degree of interdependence, mutuality, commitment and stability warranting access to a regime of financial relief. To this list we might add a concern to protect adult autonomy or to identify the time over which couples tend to become sufficiently economically interdependent that special remedies are warranted. But none of these considerations themselves suggests a particular period, and we do not have detailed research data in this jurisdiction that provide a basis on which to make a selection on these grounds.

3.44 Demographic data indicate that the median and mean lengths of cohabiting relationships in this jurisdiction are increasing over time.[53] However, since many cohabiting relationships end relatively early (whether by separation or by the parties marrying or becoming civil partners), a higher requirement would self-evidently reduce the number of relationships to which the scheme might apply. But we think it would be inappropriate to set the requirement so high that it excludes most relationships, as that would be to deprive reform of any significant practical effect.

3.45 While we think that there should be a minimum duration requirement for cohabitants without children, we have taken the view that it is not for us to recommend a specific period. There is clearly a wide range of considerations that are potentially relevant to determining that question, including issues concerning the administration of justice, in light of which an essentially political judgement may be required. We think that various periods of minimum duration could reasonably be defended, and we are not in a position to say that any one period would be uniquely correct. We have set out the considerations which policy-makers may wish to bear in mind when coming to a decision. Clearly, consistency with existing legislation was a key consideration for those of our consultees who advocated the two-year period. It seems to us that this would provide a sound basis for selection, and it may already have some public

---

[52] See also the Fatal Accidents Act 1976.

[53] The data reported by K Kiernan, "Cohabitation and Childbearing Outside Marriage" (2001) 15 *International Journal of Law, Policy and the Family* 1, table 2, indicating the proportion of cohabiting relationships that end (by marriage or separation) after two and five years respectively, is now over ten years old. See further data discussed in CP, paras 2.35 to 2.40; and in relation to cohabitants with children, emerging data from the Millennium Cohort Study: plenary paper by K Kiernan, "Partnership and Parenthood in the UK" at the Family and Parenting Institute's Parent Child 2006 Conference, London, November 2006.

currency.[54] Our research of overseas jurisdictions indicates that the highest period adopted anywhere in relation to cohabitants is five years.[55] We therefore recommend that a selection be made from within the range of two to five years.

Other cohabitants with children

3.46 We now consider those cohabitants who do not have children together, but who have or have had a dependent child living in their household whom they have treated as a child of their family. This is a difficult area, covering a wide range of circumstances. The most common example is step-parenthood. But we should also include private foster parents,[56] and cohabitants who begin a family by means of assisted reproduction techniques or surrogacy but who do not (under the current law) thereby become joint parents.[57]

3.47 We invited consultees' views on whether such cohabitants should be automatically eligible to apply for financial relief, or whether a minimum duration requirement should apply.[58] We are not concerned here with liability to support the child in these cases: that is the exclusive responsibility of the parents.[59] The issue is when the adults should be eligible to apply for financial relief for their own benefit under our recommended scheme.

3.48 Consultees focused on cases of step-parenthood. A majority of those who addressed this question said that such couples should not be automatically eligible. Most focused on the step-parent as potential respondent, faced with a claim by the parent relating to care for the latter's own child. They contended that step-parents take on a significant commitment and may regard themselves as having more than discharged their moral obligations by supporting their partner and their partner's child during the relationship. Cohabitation might be discouraged if the step-parent could become liable to provide financial relief for the parent should the relationship end relatively quickly. Only a few consultees addressed the converse case where the step-parent who has cared for the respondent's child wished to apply under the scheme.[60]

---

[54] It commonly appears in media discussion of reform.

[55] In all Canadian and Australian jurisdictions where claims between cohabitants can be made, the minimum duration requirement for claims on separation is two or three years. A five-year requirement is adopted only in South Australia, and then in the context of entitlement on intestacy: Administration and Probate Act 1919 (South Australia), s 4 and Family Relationships Act 1975 (South Australia), s 11(1) for the definition of a "putative spouse".

[56] We exclude local authority foster parents from this category, by analogy with MCA, s 52 and in line with the policy at work in that provision, which is to ensure that couples who foster for a local authority are not receiving the foster child as a member of their own family.

[57] See para 3.50.

[58] CP, para 9.68.

[59] Child Support Act 1991; Children Act 1989, sch 1. We are not recommending that liability under the latter Act for a child other than that of the respondent should be extended to cases of cohabitants: see para 4.108.

[60] See CP, para 7.46, Example 4.

3.49 We think that a principled answer to this issue turns on why the presence of children should affect eligibility between the adults. Where the child is a child of both parties, the child is relevant to eligibility because:

(1) the fact that the parties have had a child together might indicate something of the nature of their relationship, furthermore it gives rise to shared responsibilities and specific economic consequences, thereby justifying special remedies; and

(2) the child would benefit indirectly from remedies for the primary carer.

3.50 The second point would apply equally in step-parent cases. But primary responsibility for supporting children lies with the parents, not with a parent's new partner.[61] The first point is clearly inapplicable in many cases under consideration here. While the decision to become a step-parent is often hugely significant, it is not invariably so; nor does it necessarily connote any immediate assumption of long-term responsibility in the way that becoming joint parents may be said to do. However, the same cannot be said of couples who begin a family by means of assisted reproduction or surrogacy but who are currently unable thereby to become joint parents. For example, the female partner of a woman who gives birth to a child following assisted reproduction cannot become a parent in the way that a male partner currently can;[62] and neither opposite-sex nor same-sex cohabitants can apply for parental orders following surrogacy.[63] However, if reforms contained in the Human Tissue and Embryos (Draft) Bill[64] were enacted, couples using those techniques in future would be able to become joint parents as a matter of law, and so become automatically eligible under our recommended scheme.

3.51 That would then leave cases where a couple lives with a child of whom neither party is the parent – for example, a young relative, or a child of friends – where the legal parents may or may not still be alive. This child might have been taken in by the couple together, or on the initiative of one of them (whether before or after the relationship began). Such an arrangement might be one that the local authority has a duty to oversee,[65] and it might be accompanied by financial arrangements made with the child's parents. It might say little or nothing about the relationship of the couple.

3.52 It is important to ensure that the eligibility criteria for our recommended scheme are straightforward, not least to facilitate public understanding of the law. That consideration deters us from seeking to sub-categorise these cases in order to provide different eligibility criteria for, say, claims by step-parents and claims against step-parents; or to deal discretely with some or all cases of private fostering.

---

[61] See n 59.

[62] See Human Fertilisation and Embryology Act 1990, s 28.

[63] Nor, at present, can civil partners: see Human Fertilisation and Embryology Act 1990, s 30.

[64] Published by the Department of Health in May 2007; see Part 3 of the Bill, available at http://www.dh.gov.uk/prod_consum_dh/idcplg?IdcService=GET_FILE&dID=140183&Rendi tion=Web (last visited 3 July 2007).

[65] Children Act 1989, sch 8.

3.53 We think that the focus should be on providing appropriately for the most common case – step-parenthood – and the potential for claims based on economic disadvantage arising from care given to the children. We need to consider separately the possibility of claims being made by the step-parent who had cared for his or her partner's child; and claims being made against the step-parent by the parent him or herself. But an examination of both possibilities suggests that a minimum duration requirement may be appropriately applied.

3.54 Cases in which a step-parent had acted as a primary carer for the other party's child during the relationship can readily be imagined. But it seems to us highly unlikely that that individual would continue to be the primary carer for the child following the parties' separation where the relationship had only lasted for a short period. Any continuing economic disadvantage flowing from that care would therefore be likely to be transitory or might be readily mitigated.

3.55 The case of a parent wishing to bring a claim against a step-parent in relation to economic disadvantage incurred from caring for the parent's own child would seem to involve formidable problems in establishing that the economic disadvantage was caused by the parent's contributions to this relationship, rather than a consequence of the earlier relationship with the child's other parent.[66] Again, cases in which a sufficient causal connection could be found between the care given and the parties' relationship might tend to involve longer relationships.

3.56 We therefore consider that it would be appropriate to subject the case of cohabitants with other children to a minimum duration requirement. But the precise response to these cases should depend on what minimum duration requirement is selected for cohabitants who do not have children together. If a two-year period were adopted, then these cases should also be subjected to that requirement. By contrast, if a longer minimum duration requirement were selected, then we would strongly encourage Parliament to permit the courts to dispense with the minimum duration requirement in such cases, where it was in the interests of justice to do so.[67]

A discretion to dispense with the minimum duration requirement?

3.57 A small number of consultees addressed the question whether there are any circumstances in which the court should have the power to dispense with a minimum duration requirement. Opinions were evenly divided.[68] While those advocating a discretion were concerned about the hard case, opponents emphasised the importance of certainty and of precluding any possibility of very short relationships generating litigation.

3.58 We think that the case for permitting the minimum duration requirement to be dispensed with depends in part on how high that requirement is set. The longer the duration, the greater the chances of unfairness in individual cases and so the stronger the case for mitigating the hardship that might otherwise arise from rigid

---

[66] See Part 4, n 36.

[67] See para 3.58, and for the approach of the Law Reform Commission of the Republic of Ireland, see para 3.28.

[68] Two further consultees offered observations on the point without coming down firmly on either side.

adherence to the requirement. This would be particularly important where cohabitants have been living with children who are not the children of both parties. By contrast, a shorter minimum duration requirement would be likely to generate fewer hard cases, and so greater weight could be given to the importance of maintaining a clear rule that would remove scope for dispute in large numbers of cases and give parties a clearer sense of where they stand.[69]

Breaks in continuity

3.59 A cohabiting relationship may continue notwithstanding that one party is temporarily absent from the shared home, for example as a result of hospitalisation or employment.[70] Such periods would therefore count towards satisfaction of a minimum duration requirement. However, in other cases, the relationship may break down, apparently irretrievably, only for the parties some time later to commence a new relationship together. The question therefore arises how a minimum duration requirement should apply in such circumstances. This is an issue that would only affect couples who did not have children together.

3.60 There are various ways in which this issue might arise. Consider, by way of example, a relationship of over twenty years, towards the end of which the parties separated for eighteen months. They were then reconciled, and lived together once more, but only for six months before the relationship finally ended. The "second relationship" would clearly not have been long enough by itself to satisfy the minimum duration requirement, and it might now to be too late to bring any claim in relation to the "first relationship", the limitation period having expired.[71] Another, rather different, example would involve a couple whose relationship had been intermittent, being composed of successive periods of cohabitation punctuated by separations, none of which periods individually satisfied the minimum duration requirement.

3.61 Only a small number of consultees addressed this issue, and there seemed to be a slight preference among them for allowing some means of satisfying the minimum duration requirement cumulatively, rather than by reference to an unbroken period.

3.62 However, we have concluded that, in the interests of clarity and to reduce the prospect of nuisance claims, it should not be possible for applicants to satisfy the minimum duration requirement in such a way. A continuous period of cohabitation should be required. This is currently the position under both the Inheritance (Provision for Family and Dependants) Act 1975 and the Fatal Accidents Act 1976. In Part 4, we recommend that in exceptional circumstances the court should have the power to dispense with the normal limitation period applicable to claims for financial relief on separation.[72] The first example we gave above is the

---

[69] Although there is no discretion to dispense with the minimum duration requirement applicable to cohabitants under the Inheritance (Provision for Family and Dependants) Act 1975, some individuals can bring claims as "dependants".

[70] See also circumstances such as those in *Gully v Dix* [2004] EWCA Civ 139, [2004] 1 WLR 1399.

[71] See para 4.151.

[72] Para 4.155.

very kind of case in which that power might appropriately be exercised, in order to enable the court to take account of the parties' earlier relationship.

3.63 **We recommend that:**

(1) **save where cohabitants have a child together, they should not be eligible to apply for financial relief on separation unless they have lived as a couple in a joint household for a duration specified by statute (the "minimum duration requirement");**

(2) **any such minimum duration requirement should be set by statute within a range of two to five years;**

(3) **if the minimum duration requirement is set at two years, then the court should have no discretion to dispense with the requirement; but**

(4) **if the requirement is set at a period longer than two years, then consideration should be given to allowing the court to dispense with the requirement, including in particular cases where, although cohabitants do not have a child together, they treated a child who was living with them in their joint household as a child of their family; and**

(5) **any minimum duration requirement should be satisfied only by a continuous period of cohabitation.**

SPECIAL CASES

3.64 The CP sought consultees' views on whether parties should be eligible to claim where one or both was at any material time a minor; where they are related within the prohibited degrees for marriage and civil partnership; or where one or both are or were party to a concurrent relationship.[73] In all these cases, it would be necessary to demonstrate that the parties otherwise fulfilled the eligibility requirements to qualify as "cohabitants".[74] The only issue, therefore, is whether the presence of the additional factor should operate to disqualify them from eligibility to apply for relief. No existing legislation applicable to cohabitants deals expressly with these issues.[75]

Minors and relatives

3.65 The issues of eligibility of minors[76] and cohabitants related within the prohibited degrees attracted a wide range of responses from the small number of consultees who addressed them. Some would exclude them entirely on grounds

---

[73] CP, paras 9.135 and 9.161.

[74] In particular, blood relatives who simply share a home would not be eligible.

[75] See CP, para 9.125 and following.

[76] That is, persons under the age of eighteen.

of public policy,[77] some would include them without qualification, and others took a middle course.[78] Case law under existing legislation applicable to cohabitants has not, to our knowledge, addressed these issues.

3.66 Other consultees drew an analogy with the law relating to nullity of marriage and civil partnership. Where one or both parties to a marriage or civil partnership are minors, or the parties are related within the prohibited degrees, the union is void. Nevertheless, the court is empowered to grant financial relief as if the marriage or civil partnership had been dissolved.[79] Such relief is available even if sexual activity between the parties would have constituted a criminal offence. These consultees observed that the applicant in such a case might well be in a vulnerable position, and that to deprive such individuals of financial relief might compound their difficulties.

3.67 Whilst it is tempting to draw that analogy, we have concluded that we should recommend the exclusion from our scheme of couples between whom sexual activity would constitute an offence.[80] Whether spouses or civil partners had a sexual relationship is entirely irrelevant to the question of whether their marriage or civil partnership was void. In order to establish that parties were living as a couple, proof of a sexual relationship would not be necessary, though it would usually be an aspect of their relationship.[81] However, where one party was a minor or the parties were related by family ties, it would effectively become necessary for the applicant to prove that the parties were engaged in a sexual relationship in order to rebut what must otherwise be the very strong presumption, given their ages or family relationship, that they were not a couple. In all but relatively unusual circumstances,[82] this would involve proving the commission of a criminal offence, and often entail self-incrimination by the applicant. It seems to us undesirable to grant access to a scheme of financial relief on that basis.

Concurrent relationships

3.68 The question about parties to concurrent relationships attracted a more uniform response. The small number of consultees who addressed it were largely in favour of inclusion. The fact that one cohabitant is the spouse or civil partner of someone else does not, as a matter of law, preclude a finding that the parties were cohabiting for the purposes of the Inheritance (Provision for Family and

[77] Largely by reference to the law of sexual offences, which we suggested in the CP should be determinative: para 9.128. One consultee suggested drawing the line at cases where sexual relations would be criminal but including others who fall within the prohibited degrees; some other consultees would exclude all prohibited degree relationships.

[78] Notably in relation to minors, drawing various lines at sixteen, the age at which no criminal offence will ordinarily be committed by the parties having a sexual relationship: see the Sexual Offences Act 2003, ss 16 to 29, though a "marriage exception" is available: ss 23 and 28.

[79] MCA, Part 2, and equivalent provisions of the Civil Partnership Act 2004 applicable on dissolution.

[80] Sexual Offences Act 2003, ss 5 to 29 and 64 to 65. Note that the range of prohibited degrees for marriage and civil partnership is slightly wider than the criminal prohibition.

[81] See paras 3.19 and 3.21.

[82] For example, where one or both parties reasonably had no idea that one or both were minors or that they were related, and so lacked mens rea for the relevant offence.

Dependants) Act 1975 ("the 1975 Act").[83] There should be no difficulty in making such a finding of fact where the concurrent relationship was a moribund marriage or civil partnership.[84] More factually difficult would be cases where the party's other relationship, whether a marriage, civil partnership or cohabitation, was continuing. Here it would be necessary to determine whether the individual who was a party to both relationships was sufficiently involved in either household for one or both to amount to cohabitation at all.[85]

3.69　Clearly where concurrent relationships end simultaneously, whether by the death of one party or otherwise, claims brought against one individual (or that individual's estate) by two parties should be addressed together. This situation already arises under the 1975 Act, where the court is able, within its statutory discretion, to accommodate competing claims. We realise that the prospect of simultaneous proceedings consequent, for example, upon a divorce and the separation of cohabitants might raise particular difficulties. Those who move on to new relationships without first addressing the financial consequences of earlier, undissolved marriages might find themselves in difficulty. But even if they did not wish to dissolve that first relationship (perhaps out of sensitivity to the other spouse or civil partner's position), there would be no reason for not making a financial settlement with that individual pursuant to a judicial separation. We do not think that such circumstances should shape our recommendations.

3.70　**We recommend that persons should not be eligible as "cohabitants" where sexual activity between them would constitute a criminal offence owing to the age of either party or to the fact that the parties are relatives.**

3.71　**We recommend that cohabitants should not be disqualified from claiming financial relief on separation on the grounds that one or both of them are or were at any relevant time married to, or civil partners of, or cohabiting with, another party.**

APPLICATION OF THE SCHEME TO EXISTING RELATIONSHIPS

3.72　There is no question of the scheme applying to relationships that ended prior to its legislative implementation.[86] But beyond that, how if at all should a new scheme apply to relationships already existing at the date on which legislation introducing a new scheme came into force? What impact might different modes of implementation and transitional provisions have on such relationships?

3.73　We have concluded that the most appropriate response is that adopted by other jurisdictions which have introduced legislation in this field.[87] Accordingly, we recommend that the scheme should apply to any relationship which is continuing at the date on which the legislation is implemented, as well as to those which

---

[83]　For example, *Churchill v Roach* [2002] EWHC 3230 (Ch), [2004] 2 FLR 989.

[84]　That is, the relationship has broken down and the cohabitant has separated from his or her spouse or civil partner.

[85]　The basic question about whether the parties were living as a couple in a joint household would apply even if the individuals concerned were parties to a polygamous marriage not recognised by the law of England and Wales.

[86]　A few individual consultees hoped that this might be possible.

[87]　Including, most recently, Scotland: Family Law (Scotland) Act 2006.

commence after that date, but that parties to existing relationships should be given ample time before the scheme comes into force to consider whether they wish to make an agreement opting out of the scheme. We think that this would achieve a proper balance between the need to protect vulnerable individuals in existing relationships and the need to respect parties' autonomy. We explain in the following paragraphs our reasons for rejecting alternative options, and our conclusions on the compatibility of our recommended approach with the European Convention on Human Rights.

3.74 Most consultees accepted that the scheme should apply to some degree to existing relationships. But it is necessary to be cautious. It is difficult to predict how people might respond to the incentives and potential constraints created by a new scheme. Any degree of retrospective effect could potentially threaten existing relationships, even if parties would only become eligible if they satisfied a minimum duration requirement (or had a child) following implementation.[88] Parties who could not agree whether to remain within the scope of the scheme or to opt out of it might reach an impasse that resulted in the end of their relationship. However, research suggests that the law has a relatively marginal impact on people's behaviour and decisions regarding relationships.[89] Relationships that falter at that point might already be fragile; though that is not to say that we take the possibility of any relationship breakdown lightly.

3.75 There are various alternatives to applying the scheme to existing relationships on the same basis as new ones. The most extreme option, denying eligibility to claim altogether to those whose relationships began before implementation, would deprive large numbers of people of the legal protection that the scheme would be intended to provide. A handful of consultees advocated unilateral opt-outs for parties to existing relationships, allowing either party the right to exclude the operation of the scheme by giving due notice to the other. Another possibility would be to apply the scheme to existing relationships only where the parties had expressly opted in.

3.76 We are not attracted to any of these options. The existence of any form of transitional provisions[90] would place immense pressure on pinpointing the date on which the relationship began. For example, suppose the rule were that parties to existing relationships had to satisfy a minimum duration requirement of two years exclusively by reference to cohabitation post-implementation. A minimum duration requirement could in itself generate disputes about dates. But requiring that the relationship lasted at least two years from a particular date, the date of implementation, would exacerbate that potential.[91] Indeed, in order to identify which relationships were subject to them, the implementation of any type of transitional arrangements would require a finding as to whether the given relationship existed immediately prior to the date of implementation.

---

[88] This approach appears to have been adopted by the Catalan legislator for same-sex, but not opposite-sex, relationships: Act 10/1998 of 15 July, regarding stable pair relationships.

[89] C Smart and P Stevens, *Cohabitation Breakdown* (2000) p 50; and other sources cited at para 2.42.

[90] That is, rules that treat relationships in existence immediately before implementation differently from new ones.

[91] These problems would be further compounded were the scheme only to apply to parties in existing relationships where a child was conceived following implementation.

3.77 We have explained in Part 2 why we are not recommending that a new scheme take the form of an opt-in regime, whereby parties would have to register their relationships or otherwise reach a formal agreement to be eligible to apply for financial relief. Opt-in regimes might be felt to offer better protection to parties' autonomy, a factor which carries particular force in relation to parties to existing relationships. However, we remain of the view that greater weight should attach to the need to offer protection to those who would not, for whatever reason, take that step. Setting up a registration system for these transitional cases would not only seriously risk public confusion regarding the basic nature of the scheme, it would also have additional resource implications.

3.78 Nor are we attracted to unilateral opt-outs. It was suggested to us that unilateral opt-outs were necessary to ensure the continuation of existing relationships post-implementation, where one party did not wish to be subject to the scheme. But enabling one party unilaterally to deprive the other of access to financial relief at any point in the future would itself be extremely threatening to the relationship, not least because that opt-out would have to be communicated in writing to the other party, in order to ensure that that party was aware of his or her legal position.[92] We are of the view that there are considerable advantages to instituting a scheme that encourages couples to act together, and to discuss and agree the basis on which they cohabit.

3.79 We have considered whether a recommendation that the scheme should apply to relationships existing at the date of legislative implementation would be compatible with the European Convention on Human Rights. We have concluded that no incompatibility with either Article 1 of Protocol 1, or Article 8, would arise.[93]

3.80 Article 1 of Protocol 1 to the Convention protects the right to peaceful enjoyment of possessions. In our view, any potential deprivation of property pursuant to a court order following the end of a relationship which began before implementation would readily be justified on the basis that it struck a fair balance between the relevant parties' interests and was in the public interest. We would anticipate that a court would find that the scheme could be justified on the basis that it promoted social and economic justice between separating cohabitants.[94]

3.81 Nor do we think that there would be any breach of the Article 8 right to respect for private and family life.[95] Laws which specifically prohibit a "private life" activity[96] or which permit a public authority to interfere directly with the exercise of private life

---

[92] Indeed, in order to avoid dispute about whether the notice had been received and understood, it would at least be necessary for the recipient to confirm receipt by signature.

[93] No problem of compatibility has been raised in relation to the schemes operating in Sweden or Scotland, or the Irish Law Reform Commission's recent recommendations: see para 1.45.

[94] Compare, in rather different contexts, *James v UK* (1986) 8 EHRR 123; *Burrows v UK* (App No 27558/95).

[95] One individual consultee argued that not to permit unilateral opt-outs would violate the ECHR by making some individuals feel compelled to break up their family before legislative implementation, with serious repercussions for any children.

[96] See *Dudgeon v UK* (1982) 4 EHRR 149; *Norris v Ireland* (1991) 13 EHRR 186.

(for example, by monitoring correspondence)[97] may interfere with Article 8. But our recommended scheme – a private law remedy that might, in the absence of an opt-out agreement, be invoked by either party if the couple separate – would have no direct impact on the parties' relationship. Its impact would be altogether more remote, and dependent upon choices made by the parties in light of the new legal context in which their relationship would continue. Even were an interference to be found, we anticipate that it would be justified by reference to the policy considerations that support a new scheme of general application and that protect the rights and freedoms of others, by ensuring a fair distribution on separation of the economic consequences of parties' contributions to cohabiting relationships.[98]

3.82 Legal change often takes effect in a way that impacts on existing arrangements. Individuals cannot expect the law to stand still, and both statutory reform and developments in case law change the conditions under which they live and work. Our clear preference is therefore to apply the scheme to existing relationships. However, there was some support amongst our consultees for the position adopted in New Zealand, providing a one-year "lead-in" time prior to full implementation. This would give parties to existing relationships the opportunity to discuss the possible effects of the new law before it came into operation. They would have ample time, prompted by a wide public information campaign about the new remedial scheme, to consider whether and on what basis they wished to fall within it and to make an opt-out agreement if they saw fit. We make a recommendation to this effect in Part 5.[99]

3.83 We conclude by emphasising the importance of public information and education about any reform, not least for parties to existing relationships. It is essential that the general public should understand that our recommended scheme would not result in either party automatically being required to give away half of their hard-earned wealth to a former partner. Whether any financial relief would be granted would depend entirely upon whether the applicant had made qualifying contributions giving rise to a retained benefit or economic disadvantage, and then upon the exercise of the court's discretion to decide what, if any, relief to grant.[100] Parties to existing relationships therefore need not fear that they would, overnight, automatically stand to lose a portion of their wealth. But they would need clear information about how, if they wished to do so, they could agree to disapply the scheme, and so be free to reach their own financial arrangements.

3.84 **We recommend that:**

(1) **the scheme**

(a) **should not apply to any relationship which ended prior to implementing legislation coming into force; but**

---

[97] *Campbell v UK* (1993) 15 EHRR 137; *Klass v Germany* (1979-80) 2 EHRR 214.

[98] We were unable to find any case law under Art 8 bearing directly on this point. But we do consider it likely that the European Court of Human Rights would grant states a wide margin of appreciation in any area such as this: *James v UK* (1986) 8 EHRR 123, at [46].

[99] See para 5.72.

[100] See Part 4.

(b) should be capable of applying to any relationship which exists at that date; and

(2) in seeking to establish that they satisfy the eligibility criteria, parties to such relationships should be able to rely on periods of cohabitation and the birth of children prior to implementation.

PART 4
FINANCIAL RELIEF ON SEPARATION

INTRODUCTION

4.1 In this Report, we are recommending that legislation should provide for the possibility of financial relief on separation between cohabiting couples who satisfy specified eligibility criteria. In this Part, we consider the principles upon which financial relief should be granted, the orders which should be available to the courts, and the procedural implications of the introduction of a new statutory scheme.

4.2 As we have explained in Part 2, the current law does not provide satisfactory outcomes for many cohabitants, and there is a powerful case for reform. But, as we explain in this Part, there is a strong argument that a simple extension to cohabitants of the existing regime which applies following divorce is inappropriate, because cohabitants have not given each other the legal commitment, or accepted the status, of marriage or civil partnership. We therefore believe that it is necessary to find a middle ground between, on the one hand, the law that currently applies to cohabitants and, on the other, the law that applies to spouses and civil partners. It follows that there should be a new statutory scheme of specific application to cohabitants on their separation.

4.3 Reform must produce principled outcomes, and must combine some flexibility with certainty and consistency.[1] The law must be capable of being operated by separating cohabitants without litigation, although they may have the help of lawyers and mediators. Results must be predictable, not with mathematical precision but with some degree of confidence.

THE AVAILABLE OPTIONS

4.4 In the CP we discussed some of the options available.[2] There was a wide range of consultation responses. While it was not possible to identify a consensus, many consultees considered that the law should respond more effectively to the needs of the parties and their children on separation, giving appropriate weight to the contributions that each had made in the course of their relationship. We discuss in this Part the conclusions that we have reached in the light of those responses. A more detailed discussion of possible schemes that we have rejected is contained in Appendix C.

Extension or modification for cohabitants of the Matrimonial Causes Act 1973[3]

4.5 The MCA governs the award of ancillary relief on divorce. The statute confers wide discretionary powers on the court to make orders for property adjustment

---

[1] CP, para 6.24.

[2] CP Part 6, Overview Part 3.

[3] We shall refer to Part 2 of the Matrimonial Causes Act 1973 (titled "Financial relief for parties to marriage and children of family") as "the MCA". References to the MCA and financial relief between spouses should be taken to refer also to the equivalent provisions for financial relief between civil partners under the Civil Partnership Act 2004.

and financial provision, reallocating the spouses' capital and income resources having regard to all the circumstances of the case, with particular reference to a list of matters to which it is to have regard. The court exercises these powers primarily on the basis of need. In most cases, the assets available are not sufficient to meet, or are only just sufficient to meet, the needs of both parties and any children of the family. Where the available assets do exceed those needs, the House of Lords' decision in *White v White*[4] establishes the "yardstick of equality" approach whereby the surplus (at least in so far as it was generated during the marriage) will normally be divided equally between the parties.[5]

4.6 Some jurisdictions have applied all or part of their divorce regimes to certain cohabiting relationships.[6] Extension of the MCA to cohabitants could be seen as a straightforward option in this jurisdiction because it would simply involve the application of tried and tested principles to a wider range of relationships. Many people, including some district judges who operate the MCA, feel that it works efficiently and predictably in most cases. But many would disagree with that view. Several of our consultees expressed dissatisfaction with the MCA. They pointed in particular to the lack of a statutory objective underpinning the exercise of discretion, the theoretical and practical difficulties in applying its principles to so-called "big money" cases, and the lack of predictability of outcome.[7]

4.7 In the CP we provisionally rejected the option of extending the MCA to cohabitants.[8] As one consultee observed:

> Some account should be taken of the decision of the parties not to marry: it is one thing to relieve the unequal impact of the relationship, but quite another to treat the parties as if they actually had married.[9]

4.8 Applying the MCA would impose an equivalence with marriage which many people would find inappropriate, and some consultees suggested that it is unlikely that a scheme which equated cohabitation with marriage in this way would be politically attainable.

4.9 Recent research[10] has indicated that, in particular situations, a majority of the public would like to see couples with children, whether married or unmarried, treated in the same way on separation, whatever that treatment might be. It also seems that a majority would support financial relief being granted between couples without children, at least following a long relationship, and in light of such

---

[4] [2001] AC 596; affirmed in *Miller v Miller; McFarlane v McFarlane* [2006] UKHL 24, [2006] 2 AC 618.

[5] *Miller v Miller; McFarlane v McFarlane* [2006] UKHL 24, [2006] 2 AC 618; *Charman v Charman* [2007] EWCA Civ 503, [2007] 2 FCR 217, at [73].

[6] Including New Zealand, and certain Australian states and Canadian provinces: see CP, para 6.16.

[7] Including the Law Society, *Financial Provision on Divorce: clarity and fairness* (2003). See also the comments of Potter P in *Charman v Charman* [2007] EWCA Civ 503, [2007] 2 FCR 217, from [106] to the end; and A Greensmith (National Chair, Resolution), "Let's play Ancillary Relief" (2007) 37 *Family Law* 203.

[8] CP, para 6.239.

[9] Rebecca Probert.

[10] A Park et al, *British Social Attitudes. The 24th Report* (forthcoming, January 2008).

factors as their contributions to the relationship. However, it is by no means clear that all the members of that majority would support the specific application of the MCA regime to cohabitants with children, let alone to those without. Cohabiting relationships differ widely in terms of duration, commitment and degree of economic interdependence.[11] Case law on the MCA has advocated the treatment of a divorcing couple as a "partnership of equals"[12] to which the yardstick of equality may be applied.[13] This approach may generate enormous awards even after very short marriages,[14] and we believe that there would be significant public disquiet if cohabitants were to be treated similarly.

4.10 Most consultees were in agreement with our provisional view, with only a handful disagreeing. Some consultees suggested modifications to the MCA specifically for cohabitants, or for cohabitants with children. Although we discuss these in Appendix C, our view is that these suggestions would not be workable. Accordingly, we reject the option of extending or modifying the MCA for cohabitants.

A rule-based or formulaic approach

4.11 One way of stepping back from the MCA, and devising a specific scheme for cohabitants, would be to adopt a formulaic, rather than a discretionary, approach. The most obvious way to do this would be to define a pool of property and split it equally. For example, in Sweden, when cohabitants have acquired a home and household effects for their joint use, the value of those assets is divided equally between them on separation.[15]

4.12 Community of property regimes[16] apply to married couples throughout most of Europe (but not in this jurisdiction, nor in Scotland or the Republic of Ireland), and in many Commonwealth countries and some of the American States. They are examples of rule-based systems. So too is the current statutory formulation of the obligation to maintain one's children in the Child Support Act 1991 as amended. As we pointed out in the CP, the disadvantage of a rule-based approach is that it may give rise to individual injustice.[17] The great advantage of such systems is

---

[11] CP, para 6.15 and following.

[12] *Miller v Miller; McFarlane v McFarlane* [2006] UKHL 24, [2006] 2 AC 618, at [16] and [17].

[13] *White v White* [2001] AC 596. The "yardstick" approach arises from concerns about discrimination in the context of marriage and it is not clear that this argument can be easily translated into the context of cohabitation, where the parties have not made a formal commitment to each other.

[14] For example, *Miller v Miller; McFarlane v McFarlane* [2006] UKHL 24, [2006] 2 AC 618.

[15] Cohabitees Act 2003 (Sweden).

[16] These rule-based systems determine the ownership of property during marriage and on divorce (but not the incidence of maintenance obligations). For an account of many European regimes see C Hamilton and A Perry, *Family Law in Europe* (2002); and E Cooke, A Barlow and T Callus, *Community of Property: a regime for England and Wales?* (2006); see para 5.18 and following.

[17] CP, para 6.36; and, of course, attempts to remedy individual unfairness by developing the rules catering for different situations are likely to encounter the problems of excessive complexity seen in the child support legislation as originally enacted.

their predictability. The community of property systems appear to work well in the jurisdictions where they operate, and to be publicly acceptable.[18]

4.13 In the CP we rejected rule-based approaches on the basis of their inflexibility. Cohabitation arrangements vary widely and one size cannot fit all. While it might be argued that a community of property approach, and its underlying assumptions of partnership and sharing, may be appropriate for spouses and civil partners, it is highly questionable whether it is suitable for cohabitants at all.[19] Moreover, it would seem particularly difficult, and possibly contentious, to introduce community of property for cohabitants in this jurisdiction, where it does not apply to spouses and civil partners.

4.14 A majority of consultees who addressed the issue agreed with our rejection of fixed rules. A handful disagreed, the Legal Services Commission attaching particular importance to predictability. We believe that this concern can largely be met by devising a regime for cohabitants which, although discretionary, operates predictably and in a principled way. Accordingly, we reject a system of fixed rules for property division.

A principled discretion

4.15 The alternative to rules is discretion, and discretion is a broad concept accommodating a range of levels of flexibility. The CP proposed a principled discretion, whereby the court would be given distinct objectives and some leeway in how they were to be achieved. Outcomes would be predictable within a range of possibilities and settlement would thereby be facilitated. Most consultation responses supported this proposal.

4.16 Another way to describe such a scheme is as a relatively "weak" rather than a "strong" discretion.[20] The MCA discretion is "strong" because the statute does not say what is to be achieved. Discretion in our recommended scheme would be weaker because the statute would determine the pre-conditions for relief and its objectives. We regard it as particularly important that the court should not be presented with a "menu" that simply invites the judge to "have regard to" a wide range of considerations without any prioritisation in deciding what relief is appropriate to the circumstances of the case. Those using the scheme need to know what principles will be applied in the determination of their claim.

4.17 **We recommend that the courts should be given a discretion structured by principles which determine the basis on which any financial relief is to be granted on separation.**

---

[18] E Cooke, A Barlow and T Callus, *Community of Property: a regime for England and Wales?* (2006) ch 3.

[19] CP, para 6.38.

[20] See S Gardner, "The Remedial Discretion in Proprietary Estoppel" (1999) 115 *Law Quarterly Review* 438, at 461: strong discretion is where "the judge is at liberty to arrive at the order by taking into account whatever factors, and attaching to them whatever normative significance, he or she thinks fit".

Need as the guiding principle for discretion?

4.18 A major reason for the reference of this issue to the Law Commission was the perception that the ending of cohabitation can result in hardship.[21] Should legislation, therefore, simply direct the courts to exercise their discretion in order to meet the needs of separating cohabitants and their children?

4.19 The initial difficulty with this approach is defining what precisely is meant by "need". Need, as it is operated by the courts under the MCA, is not absolute, but relative, varying according to the standard of living that the spouses had enjoyed during the marriage. It follows that, for MCA purposes, the "needs" of a millionaire's former spouse may be entirely different from those of people with average or low incomes.

4.20 Even if we could define need satisfactorily, it is difficult to find a principled justification for an individual's needs to be met by a former cohabitant rather than by other means.[22] Cohabitants, unlike spouses and civil partners, have not made any legal commitment to provide for each other, and currently are under no legal obligation to maintain each other during their relationship.[23]

4.21 Consultees' views about the significance of the parties' needs in a new scheme were wide-ranging. It was not possible to discern a majority view; some thought that needs alone were insufficient as a basis for relief, some thought that they should be one of a number of factors, or a predominant factor; some thought that they should be entirely irrelevant. But by and large consultees did not suggest a definition of "needs" or offer a principled justification for needs-based relief.

4.22 One response to this difficulty would be to develop a scheme that would provide needs-based relief defined at subsistence level.[24] Such a scheme would be relatively straightforward (except for the awkward question: for how long after the parties' separation should support be given?). But it would be very limited and of no help to those whose own means would raise them above subsistence level. We prefer a scheme that would be of wider application, and which would seek to recognise the contributions made by each cohabitant to the relationship and the economic consequences of those contributions.

4.23 An alternative approach would be to focus specifically upon needs that arise from the cohabiting relationship. A number of consultees distinguished such needs from absolute need. Some highlighted circumstances where an "expectation of

---

[21] The Law Commission: Ninth Programme of Law Reform (2005) Law Com No 293, para 3.6.

[22] Cf American Law Institute, *Principles of Family Dissolution: Analysis and Recommendations* (2002) p 789.

[23] There is no such obligation in either private or public law, although social security law assumes that cohabitants do in fact support each other for the purposes of assessing means-tested benefits.

[24] This may be close to the scheme envisaged in the Options Paper published in Ireland by the Working Group on Domestic Partnership set up by the Minister for Justice, Equality and Law Reform. In addition, the Irish Law Reform Commission's recently published Report, Rights and Duties of Cohabitants (2006) LRC 82-2006, would appear to give relief on the basis of needs, since eligibility depends upon proof of economic dependency.

support has been created and accepted"[25] (for example where one partner has given up work in order to look after the children or a disabled partner or relative), and where separation therefore gives rise to considerable cost.

4.24 We consider that, while respondents should not have responsibility to meet all categories of need, it is appropriate to recommend a scheme that would respond to needs arising from the parties' contributions to the relationship. However, as we explained in the CP,[26] we consider that such needs are better viewed as a sub-set of a wider principle, focusing on the economic impact of the parties' contributions to the relationship.[27] We have therefore framed our recommended scheme in terms of "retained benefit" and "economic disadvantage" rather than "need". We use the term economic disadvantage in order to indicate that the loss arising from the relationship may encompass matters that would not usually be described as need. However, given the substantial overlap between needs as a general term and economic disadvantage, we do envisage and intend that awards based on economic disadvantage would often have the practical effect of responding to the applicant's basic needs.

4.25 Accordingly, although we reject need as the guiding principle for financial relief for cohabitants, we do think that it is important to respond to needs arising from the parties' contributions to the relationship. However, we do not think that a scheme defined simply in those terms would go far enough, hence our recommended scheme, to which we now turn.

OUR RECOMMENDED APPROACH

The scheme in outline

4.26 In the CP[28] we discussed a scheme based on the economic impact of cohabitation. We argued that hardship following separation often arises because the gains and losses arising from the parties' contributions to the relationship have not been shared fairly. Decisions taken during the relationship about the allocation of the parties' resources or of their respective roles may leave one party in need on separation, or, if not actually in need, at least bearing an unequal share of the costs of the relationship. Equally, one party may be left with an economic gain from the relationship. While there may often be "need" in consequence, it is likely to be only part of the problem.

4.27 The CP provisionally proposed a scheme that would seek to identify the contributions made by each party to the relationship and to assess the economic consequences of those contributions for the parties following their separation. The approach that we now recommend is a development (and, where possible, a simplification) of the scheme discussed in the CP.

[25] This wording was adopted by Craig Lind.

[26] See CP, para 6.67 and following.

[27] We note that the House of Lords have said that compensation for relationship-generated disadvantage following divorce will often overlap with the applicant's needs, at least in so far as they were generated by the relationship, though the compensation "strand" has the potential to go further: *Miller v Miller; McFarlane v McFarlane* [2006] UKHL 24, [2006] 2 AC 618, at [15], Lord Nicholls, and [140], Baroness Hale.

[28] CP, para 6.71.

4.28   We should emphasise that we are not advocating a scheme whereby contributions are enumerated and their value, once quantified, simply reimbursed.[29] We called that sort of exercise "global accounting" in the CP and we rejected it because of its evidential complexity and the impossibility of attributing a value to many contributions, in particular those that are not financial. This is why it would not be practicable to recommend a scheme whose single guiding principle was, simply, "contributions".[30] Instead, our recommended scheme would examine the lasting economic effect of the parties' contributions to the relationship.

4.29   The use of principles focusing on the economic impact of the relationship attracted support from consultees, although (perhaps unsurprisingly) our question about the basis of relief[31] prompted such a huge variety of opinions that it was impossible to distil any consensus. A number of concerns were expressed about our proposed scheme, and in particular its potential complexity. Consultees emphasised the importance of proportionate case management, particularly where assets are limited.

4.30   We take all these concerns seriously and have endeavoured to eliminate some of the complexity of our provisional proposals. We attempt in this Report to explain in more practical terms than the CP how the scheme should operate. We hope that this will alleviate some of the concerns raised.[32]

4.31   We now set out an outline of our recommended scheme. We then discuss various aspects of the scheme, in the light of consultees' views.[33]

4.32   **We recommend that financial relief on separation should be granted in accordance with a statutory scheme based upon the economic impact of cohabitation, to the following effect.**

4.33   **An eligible cohabitant applying for relief following separation ("the applicant") must prove that:**

   (1)   **the respondent has a retained benefit; or**

   (2)   **the applicant has an economic disadvantage;**

   as a result of qualifying contributions the applicant has made.

4.34   **A qualifying contribution is any contribution arising from the cohabiting relationship which is made to the parties' shared lives or to the welfare of members of their families. Contributions are not limited to financial**

---

[29]   See CP, paras 6.115 to 6.127.

[30]   See para C.19.

[31]   CP, para 6.238.

[32]   On procedure and costs, see paras 4.109 and 4.120 and following.

[33]   The principles that we are recommending are similar to those recently enacted for claims between cohabitants in Scotland: Family Law (Scotland) Act 2006, s 28. However, we have sought to develop these principles in our own terms. Our discussion of them may therefore differ in some respects from a Scottish analysis of the issues.

contributions, and include future contributions, in particular to the care of the parties' children following separation.

4.35 A retained benefit may take the form of capital, income or earning capacity that has been acquired, retained or enhanced.

4.36 An economic disadvantage is a present or future loss. It may include a diminution in current savings as a result of expenditure or of earnings lost during the relationship, lost future earnings, or the future cost of paid child-care.

4.37 The court may make an order to adjust the retained benefit, if any, by reversing it in so far as that is reasonable and practicable having regard to the discretionary factors listed below. If, after the reversal of any retained benefit, the applicant would still bear an economic disadvantage, the court may make an order sharing that loss equally between the parties, in so far as it is reasonable and practicable to do so, having regard to the discretionary factors.

4.38 The discretionary factors are:

(1) the welfare while a minor of any child of both parties who has not attained the age of eighteen;

(2) the financial needs and obligations of both parties;

(3) the extent and nature of the financial resources which each party has or is likely to have in the foreseeable future;

(4) the welfare of any children who live with, or might reasonably be expected to live with, either party; and

(5) the conduct of each party, defined restrictively[34] but so as to include cases where a qualifying contribution can be shown to have been made despite the express disagreement of the other party.

Of these discretionary factors, item (1) above shall be the court's first consideration.

4.39 In making an order to share economic disadvantage, the court shall not place the applicant, for the foreseeable future, in a stronger economic position than the respondent.

4.40 The following range of orders should be available to the court:

(1) lump sums, including payment by instalment, secured lump sums, lump sums paid by way of pensions attachment, and interim payments;

(2) property transfers;

---

[34] To reflect the approach of the courts under the MCA.

75

(3)   **property settlements;**

(4)   **orders for sale; and**

(5)   **pension sharing.**

Unlike on divorce, periodical payments should not generally be available.[35]

4.41   **In so far as the scheme is engaged, it should apply between the parties to the exclusion of the general law of implied trusts, estoppel and contract.**

4.42   **Procedural and costs rules must be carefully framed to protect the parties from oppressive litigation and to preserve court time and resources. In particular, the rules must prevent parties who are eligible cohabitants from bringing claims under the general law of implied trusts, estoppel and contract on the basis of facts which constitute qualifying contributions under the scheme.**

Qualifying contributions

4.43   The key to our recommended scheme is that it would respond to the economic consequences of particular contributions made by one or both cohabitants. It therefore follows:

(1)   that contributions themselves would not have to be precisely valued (thus avoiding a global accounting approach); but

(2)   that it would be necessary for there to be a causal relationship between the contribution alleged and the benefit or disadvantage asserted. This must follow from our rejection of an all-encompassing "MCA-style" discretion and our view that cohabitants should not be required to meet each other's needs unless they are caused by their contributions to the cohabiting relationship.

Examples of qualifying contributions

4.44   Our description of "qualifying contribution" at paragraph 4.34 encapsulates the idea that it would be something that arises from the cohabiting relationship; and that it would be any contribution made to the parties' shared lives, or to the welfare of members of their families. Qualifying contributions would include:

(1)   care for children of both parties, both during and after the relationship;

(2)   care for other members of their families, including children who are not children of both parties and elderly relatives[36] (whether or not they are members of the parties' joint household);[37]

---

[35]   We discuss, at para 4.101 and following, one circumstance (child-care costs) where that type of order, on an unsecured or secured basis, should be available.

(3)   financial support of the family;

(4)   activities (whether financial or non-financial)[38] which enhance the value of, or enable the respondent to acquire or retain, capital assets, including savings and investments;

(5)   unpaid work in the respondent's business;[39]

(6)   funding professional and other training; and

(7)   giving up secure accommodation in order to commence cohabitation.

4.45   We reiterate that financial relief should not be available simply because an applicant could establish that he or she made a qualifying contribution. Qualifying contributions would only give rise to relief where they had resulted in a retained benefit or an economic disadvantage. For example, carrying out routine maintenance work on property in one's spare time, without adding to its value, would not give rise to relief. Nor would buying groceries where the respondent was able to pay the mortgage without that contribution being made.

Domestic contributions

4.46   The current law of implied trusts is relatively unresponsive to domestic contributions,[40] and one of our objectives in this project is to improve upon that aspect of the current law. Although domestic contributions are difficult to value, their precise valuation would not be necessary, as our scheme would respond not to their value but to their lasting economic impact on the parties.

4.47   Accordingly, where the applicant had given up work to look after the parties' children, his or her claim would be for any economic disadvantage incurred as a result. That disadvantage could include the fact that pension contributions and savings had not been made, as well as the effect upon the applicant's future earning capacity. However, it would not include those earnings which have

---

[36]   CP, para 7.57, Example 6. We do not think that care for children or relatives who are the applicant's and not the respondent's should normally suffice, though there might be some cases in which that would be appropriate. Most consultees who clearly addressed the question posed (CP, para 6.215) wanted all cases to be considered for relief, though others expressed concern. See also findings of R Tennant, J Taylor and J Lewis, *Separating from cohabitation: making arrangements for finances and parenting* (2006) Department for Constitutional Affairs Research Report 7/2006, pp 118 to 119 regarding the hardship that can be suffered in such cases.

[37]   For example, the child who stays for regular, staying contact visits; the elderly relative who lives elsewhere but is given day-to-day care by one party.

[38]   For example, direct or indirect financial contributions to the payment of a mortgage: CP, para 7.72, Example 8A; and substantial renovation of the respondent's property: CP, para 7.69, Example 8.

[39]   CP, para 7.63, Example 7.

[40]   *Burns v Burns* [1984] Ch 317.

already been lost, except in so far as such loss of earnings could be shown to have produced lasting disadvantage of the nature just described.[41]

4.48 It would theoretically be possible for an applicant to claim that his or her domestic contributions have conferred a retained benefit on the respondent in the form of savings or increased earning capacity. The applicant might, for example, contend that, by looking after the family, he or she had enabled the respondent to build up savings or to advance a career. However, such a contention would be very difficult to uphold because of the need to establish causation.[42] The applicant would have to prove what the respondent would have achieved had the applicant not made his or her contribution. This would be extremely difficult as there are so many variables: for example, the respondent could argue that he or she would have been able to deal with household tasks by engaging professional domestic help.[43] Accordingly, it would only be in exceptional circumstances that domestic contributions could be shown to have conferred a retained benefit, and we expect that they would more often give rise to claims of economic disadvantage.

Future contributions

4.49 It is important that the concept of qualifying contributions should also cover some categories of future contribution. In particular, the primary carer of the cohabitants' children will often suffer economic disadvantage following separation, not only as a result of child-care undertaken during the relationship, but also in so far as child-care obligations continue to inhibit that party's ability to engage in paid employment. In unusual cases, continuing to care for other dependants, such as children of the respondent, following separation might also constitute a qualifying contribution.

Joint decision-making

4.50 In the CP we noted that qualifying contributions would normally arise from decisions jointly made by the parties. This goes without saying in most households where joint decisions, spoken or unspoken, underpin the parties' choices as to who is to undertake different responsibilities.[44] It is fundamental to our recommended scheme that the consequences of the parties' joint decisions should be apportioned fairly between them.

---

[41] Data discussed by K Rake (ed), *Women's Incomes over the Lifetime* (2000) exposes the huge losses suffered by women in terms of lost earnings as a result of child-care responsibilities. However, it would not be realistic for any scheme of relief for cohabitants simply to seek to reimburse that loss. A scheme that did so would have to enter upon a complex accounting exercise, in order to avoid over-compensation. It would have to subtract from those lost earnings what the applicant gained in terms of free accommodation and living expenses during the relationship. We have rejected this "global accounting" approach. Instead our recommended scheme looks at the present and the future, and responds to the current and future economic effect of the contributions that cohabitants, whether male or female, have made to their shared lives.

[42] See also paras 4.43(2) and 4.56.

[43] See, generally, the observations of Charles J in *H v H* [2007] EWHC 459 (Fam), at [130] on the difficulties entailed in such a claim in the context of ancillary relief following divorce.

[44] CP, para 6.154.

4.51 We have not recommended that there be a specific requirement of proof of a joint decision. The difficulties of such proof would be considerable.[45] However, there may be cases where cohabitants have manifestly not been in agreement, and a qualifying contribution (such as giving up work to look after the children) has been made in the face of the other party's clearly expressed disagreement. Such cases are likely to be rare. Proof of such conduct would be difficult, but when it could be established, it should nevertheless be a factor in the exercise of the court's discretion to quantify and fashion any relief to be granted.[46]

Retained benefit

4.52 In some cases retained benefit would be readily identifiable. The most obvious example is where the family home is registered in the name of one party only, rather than in the parties' joint names, but the other has made a financial contribution to its purchase or its retention by a payment of capital, by making mortgage repayments (whether of interest or of capital), or by paying household bills without which the other party would not have been able to pay the mortgage. In each of these cases it would not be difficult to identify the capital fruits of that contribution.[47]

4.53 In many other cohabitation cases the family home is in joint names, but the contributions made by the respective owners are not fairly reflected in their respective beneficial interests. Where one party paid all of the purchase price of a house which the cohabitants hold as beneficial joint tenants and the relationship breaks down, the fact that the non-paying party has a half share in the equity might well be regarded as a retained benefit.[48]

4.54 Other possible retained benefits include investments funded by the other party; an increase in the value of one party's property as a result of improvements made by the other; business profits arising from the cohabitant's work or financial investment; savings generated by a career for which training was funded by the other party; or exceptionally the future earnings from such a career.[49]

4.55 In all these cases a contribution has been made (and a benefit conferred) in the expectation that the relationship would continue. On the ending of the relationship, our scheme would seek to reverse that benefit rather than leaving it

---

[45] Proof of intention has caused notorious difficulties in the context of the general law of implied trusts, and was a major issue in *Stack v Dowden* [2007] UKHL 17, [2007] 2 WLR 831.

[46] See para 4.38(5).

[47] Contrast the case where the non-owning party had looked after the children of the family so as to enable the homeowner to stay in work or to work longer hours. We have argued above, at para 4.48, that it is extremely unlikely that the applicant would be able to show that work done in the home had been a cause of a retained benefit in the other party's hands. In such a case the applicant's claim would be better framed in terms of economic disadvantage.

[48] This might be the case where the beneficial interest had been expressly declared by the parties. Where it has not, and the house is purchased in joint names, it is clear from *Stack v Dowden* [2007] UKHL 17, [2007] 2 WLR 831 that there is a presumption that the parties are beneficial joint tenants; again, our recommended scheme would be able to respond to the fact that this might not be a fair reflection of qualifying contributions.

[49] But see para 4.56 for a discussion of the difficulties of a retained benefit claim based on such contributions

where it lies. However, its reversal would be subject to the discretionary factors. The remedy under our scheme would not be as clear-cut as it is where a resulting trust claim can be brought. That is because our scheme is based upon discretion and it would therefore be necessary to take account of wider considerations. For example, where the applicant worked on the respondent's property and increased its value, the fact that the respondent has children living with him or her might often lead the court not to make an order that would force an immediate sale of the respondent's property.

Benefit dependent on the respondent's input

4.56　In some circumstances, while it would be clear that the applicant had contributed to the respondent's retained benefit, the extent of the effect of that contribution might not be ascertainable, in particular where the benefit was dependent upon the respondent's own input, in terms of talent and effort. Where, for example, the applicant has paid the respondent's medical school fees, it is impossible to assess how much of the respondent's future earnings as a consultant surgeon have been generated by the applicant's contribution. We accept that professional training is costly and the payment of fees is likely to have been a considerable investment. However, the funding of training is only one of the pre-requisites for success in building a career.

Gifts

4.57　We would expect litigation over gifts, such as small birthday presents, to be heavily penalised in costs. It must be inappropriate to allow the unscrambling of gifts of this nature, which might well have been given regardless of the cohabitation or its continuation. But gifts may be of high value and jewellery, in particular, may be viewed as an investment as well as a pleasure. Attitudes may differ in different cultures and in different families. There are difficult issues here as to whether such gifts should be treated as qualifying contributions; whether a gift is seen as small or large may be very much a subjective matter; and there is considerable scope for argument in drawing the lines between different types of gift.

4.58　We believe that it is necessary to adopt a robust approach to discourage argument of this nature. The basic rule should be that goods[50] given by one cohabitant to the other should not comprise a retained benefit (nor should giving such gifts amount to an economic disadvantage) save where it can be proved by the donor that the gift was conditional upon the relationship continuing and that it should therefore have been returned following its breakdown. We do not anticipate that such a conditional intent will be easily proved. However, it may be possible to show that jewellery, for example, was given primarily as an investment on the understanding that the parties would continue to share their lives. Proof of this sort of intention would not be relevant in cases other than these.

4.59　**We recommend that goods given to one party by the other should not comprise a retained benefit, nor should it be possible to mount a claim for economic disadvantage on the basis of making such gifts, unless it can be**

---

[50] "Goods" is a sub-category of chattels encompassing only physical objects, and excluding money: Sale of Goods Act 1979, s 61(1).

proved by the donor that the gift was conditional upon the cohabiting relationship continuing.

Economic disadvantage

Examples of economic disadvantage

4.60 The economic disadvantage principle would be capable of accommodating claims in respect of various losses arising from qualifying contributions, including:

(1) loss of future earnings and earning capacity, typically as a result of paid employment being limited by caring responsibilities (during or after the relationship), but also as a result of promotion, relocation, or other employment opportunities having been forgone;

(2) failure to secure future pension provision, owing to past and future inability to make contributions to a pension fund; and

(3) failure to make other savings or investments.

4.61 The CP had discounted (3) and similar claims[51] on the basis that there could be said to be a difference between electing to spend existing resources in a particular way, and making contributions which prevented the party in question from accumulating financial resources at all (as in (1)). On further reflection, we accept the views of those consultees who argued that this distinction was false. We should not rule out such claims. However, they are by definition speculative and so should not succeed unless supported by clear evidence. For example, the applicant might be able to show that a regular savings pattern had been interrupted.

4.62 None of these heads of claim is akin to the problematic tort concept of "loss of a chance" (where the only head of actionable loss claimed is the reduction of a chance): all should be susceptible to proof of an actual loss on the balance of probabilities. In so far as proof of such issues entails an element of speculation, it does not appear to us that that speculation is considerably greater here than in the context of tort claims in which damages are designed to cover loss of future earnings (save that the application for relief based on (1) may be being brought many years after the applicant originally gave up work).

4.63 In all cases applicants would be expected to "mitigate" their loss, by making the best of their existing resources and minimising any economic disadvantage as far as reasonable and possible. A claim that earning capacity had been lost should be supported by evidence of the applicant's own efforts to get back into the labour market (at an equivalent level to previous employment, or, if that is unobtainable, at a lower level) and to maintain his or her expertise. A contention that savings had been forgone should not be accepted unless the applicant can show that he or she had been prudent and economical with those resources that were available.

---

[51] CP, paras 6.170 to 6.171.

Determining the extent of economic disadvantage

4.64 It is important to realise that the quantification of economic disadvantage would be only a first step in the evaluation of the claim.

4.65 Moreover, the extent of the disadvantage would not itself dictate the value of the award to be made under the scheme. A number of other factors would impact on the amount of relief:

(1) the economic equality ceiling (that is, the fact that in making an order to share economic disadvantage, the court shall not place the applicant, for the foreseeable future, in a stronger economic position than the respondent);[52] and

(2) the discretionary factors (which bear on the value of the relief and the form in which it is to be granted).

4.66 This first step in quantification would necessarily involve a hypothesis: what was the impact of the cohabitation on the applicant's economic position, or what would the applicant have had but for making the qualifying contribution? There are several sources of assistance available in making that assessment. One is the developing case law on the concept of "compensation" or "relationship-generated disadvantage" under the MCA.[53] Guidance may also be derived from case law from other jurisdictions in which a similar inquiry is required,[54] although considerable care must always be taken in drawing analogies with the operation of the laws of other jurisdictions, where the nature of the question to be asked, and the wider statutory context of that inquiry, may be different from that required here. Likewise, litigation in tort is very different in nature from the sort of discretionary family law regime that this Report recommends. However, the considerable experience acquired in tort cases in relation to the calculation of damages for loss of future earnings and loss of earning capacity may be of assistance. Reference material, such as *At a Glance*,[55] official statistics relating to the labour market,[56] and information from employment agencies, may also provide a useful starting point.

4.67 It is inevitable that a principled scheme which responds to the economic impact of parties' contributions to the relationship will at times involve some difficult areas

---

[52] Paras 4.39 and 4.72 and following.

[53] Following *Miller v Miller; McFarlane v McFarlane* [2006] UKHL 24, [2006] 2 AC 618.

[54] Notably Scotland, where a principle of economic disadvantage operates both between divorcing spouses and civil partners, and now between separating cohabitants: Family Law (Scotland) Acts 1985 and 2006. See also New Zealand, where courts are called upon to consider economic disparity between the parties on separation arising from the division of functions during the relationship: Property (Relationships) Act 1976 (New Zealand), s 15.

[55] A set of tables and references used in connection with ancillary relief. Among its contents are sample salaries for various occupations.

[56] Including the Office for National Statistics publication *Annual Survey of Hours and Earnings*, which reports data by sector and by gender (some of which is drawn on by *At a Glance*), and the *Labour Force Survey*.

of proof, particularly in relation to loss and causation.[57] While we regard this as a necessary element of our scheme as a consequence of the variety of cohabiting relationships, we stress the importance of rigorous procedural rules and robust case management to maintain a proportionate approach.

4.68　A fuller discussion of quantifying economic disadvantage may be found in Appendix B to this Report.

Sharing the loss

4.69　We have said that economic disadvantage must be shared fairly, and that this would normally involve halving it, subject to an economic equality ceiling.

4.70　An economic disadvantage is a continuing cost of the relationship – such as child-care expenses or lost earning capacity – for which there may be no corresponding retained benefit that could form the subject of a claim in itself and which should be shared rather than borne by one party alone. We are not here addressing losses that have been caused by the wrongdoing of one party against the other. By contrast, economic disadvantage encompasses losses which have been borne exclusively by one party when they should be shared. It would therefore be clearly inappropriate to find that the applicant had suffered a loss and then to reverse it, simply transferring the burden to the shoulders of the other party.

4.71　At first sight, it might seem strange that economic disadvantage is shared while retained benefit is reversed. But there is good reason for the different treatment of the two sorts of claim. A retained benefit is wealth generated by a contribution made by one party to the cohabitants' shared lives and which lies in the hands of the other party at separation. Assume that A and B have both made deposits in a bank account held in A's sole name. The benefit conferred on A is the balance in the account arising from B's contributions. Just as there can be no argument, based solely on the history of transfers into the account, that B should be granted outright ownership of the mixed funds, so it is not right that A should be able to retain the full balance of the account. A retained benefit is therefore not something that should be shared between the couple, but rather something that should be restored to its contributor.

The economic equality ceiling

4.72　We have recommended that, in sharing economic disadvantage, the court should not place the applicant, for the foreseeable future, in an economically stronger position than the respondent. We refer to this component of our scheme as the "economic equality ceiling".

---

[57] An approach recognising needs arising from the relationship must at some stage involve proof of an element of causation, and therefore some detailed fact-finding; but that would seem to be an inevitable consequence of promoting a principled approach that is specifically designed for cohabitants.

4.73 "Economic equality" is a more subtle concept than that of mere arithmetical equality represented by a halving of the parties' assets.[58] In order to apply the equality ceiling, it would first be necessary to carry out a holistic, "in the round", assessment of the parties' economic positions. This would involve taking account of the parties' income and earning capacity, the value and liquidity of particular assets, and the risks associated with particular activities or investments. It might be that, in light of such factors, the applicant would receive more than half of the capital currently available to the parties.

4.74 Economic equality would not be a goal. It would simply set an upper limit on economic disadvantage claims. In cases where the extent of the applicant's economic disadvantage was relatively small, or the respondent was affluent, the ceiling might not be reached. In those cases, the ceiling would have no effect on the sharing of the loss. Elsewhere, the ceiling would operate to cap the total award that could be made.

4.75 The equality ceiling would operate so as to prevent either party from claiming economic disadvantage when the two parties are in broadly equivalent economic positions at the end of the relationship (no matter what those positions might have been had qualifying contributions not been made). And where the parties were in unequal economic positions, the economically stronger party would be unable to pursue an economic disadvantage claim, even to the extent of setting such a claim off against the applicant's claim (although claims by that party in relation to a retained benefit would remain possible).

4.76 Although it is a necessary corollary of the economic equality ceiling, the second of these effects may seem particularly controversial. It is undoubtedly the case that both parties' economic positions might have deteriorated as a result of contributions made to the relationship. The economically stronger party might have declined a lucrative offer of employment because it would not be possible to accept it while sustaining the relationship. Moreover, the increase in that party's outgoings consequent upon supporting a family might often have reduced his or her ability to accumulate capital savings. These sacrifices would not be entirely ignored by the scheme, because the respondent's reduced circumstances would lower the economic equality ceiling. We do not consider that it should be the function of the scheme to provide further redress in such cases.

4.77 In our view, the arguments in favour of adopting an economic equality ceiling outweigh concerns about the hard results that it might appear to generate in some cases. By preventing the court from making an award that would put the applicant in a stronger economic position than the respondent, the ceiling would recognise an element of partnership that arises from the parties having shared their lives. Precluding the economically stronger party from bringing a claim based on economic disadvantage would reflect an underlying concern of that principle to respond to needs arising from parties' contributions to the

---

[58] It is implicit in the New Zealand legislation, though there it has a somewhat different function: see Property (Relationships) Act 1976 (New Zealand), s 15. In s 15 cases, the equal sharing of "relationship property" may be adjusted where there remains an economic disparity between the parties, having regard to their income and living standards, which has been generated by the division of functions during their relationship.

relationship.[59] It would not seem to us appropriate for a claim to be permitted in circumstances where the grant of relief would further impair the position of the less affluent party, for whom relationship breakdown may already have caused significant economic hardship.

4.78 We think that different considerations apply in relation to claims based on retained benefit. When we discussed the equality ceiling in the CP, we made it clear that it should not apply to claims based on what we now call retained benefit. Where the applicant was the economically stronger party on separation, the effect of applying the ceiling to retained benefit claims would be to "gift" all or part of that benefit to the respondent, thereby denying that applicant any claim. As discussed above, retained benefit claims relate to wealth in the respondent's hands which has been generated by the applicant's contributions, is still in existence on separation and so can be transferred to the applicant. Contrast a claim based on economic disadvantage which can be characterised as a loss generated by the relationship, the sharing of which is essential but should be limited by the equality ceiling. Any party who has enhanced the value of the other's property should therefore be able to claim for the full transfer of benefits retained, subject to the operation of the discretionary factors and to the possible existence of a countervailing retained benefit or economic disadvantage claim from the other party.

The discretionary factors

4.79 In the CP we asked what factors should guide the exercise of the court's discretion in quantifying the award and deciding what orders to make, having first determined in broad terms the extent of the retained benefit or economic disadvantage.[60] In response, some consultees proposed a very long list of factors.

4.80 It is important to emphasise that our scheme, unlike the MCA, would not confer on the court a "strong" discretion to make whatever order it considered just, having regard to "all the circumstances of the case".[61] We have recommended that it should be a principled discretion determining the basis upon which relief should be granted. Consistent with this approach, we have concluded that the list of factors should be tightly drawn. We note that a number of consultees advocated a wider range of factors,[62] but we believe that a long list would detract from the focus of the scheme.[63]

4.81 We asked consultees whether they favoured the inclusion on the list of the needs of both parties and of children living with them, and the financial resources of each party. Most consultees agreed, and we have framed our recommended discretionary factors accordingly. But we stress that meeting need should not be the objective of the scheme, and that the role of need would be very much to determine the types of order to be used to give effect to the award. It should

---

[59] See para 4.18 and following.

[60] CP, para 6.241 and 6.263.

[61] MCA 1973, s 25(1), and see para 4.16.

[62] In answer to CP, para 6.241.

[63] See also discussion in Appendix C.

never be a factor that increases an award, nor should it substantially impinge on the reversal of a retained benefit. We anticipate that the courts would be alert to the danger of the discretionary factors being used to subvert the principles on which the scheme is based.

4.82 The discretionary factors would perform two tasks. They would assist the court in determining:

(1) the amount of relief; and

(2) the form of the order to be made.

In practice these two functions would not always be sharply differentiated, either in the parties' minds or by the courts.

The welfare of children

4.83 In the CP we asked consultees how the welfare of children ought to be taken into account in the provision of financial relief between cohabitants.[64] It would be possible, for example, for the welfare of the parties' children to be one of the discretionary factors; or it could be given some priority. And which children should these be – the joint children of the couple, or any children who live with them?

4.84 Generally consultees were very concerned that children should be given priority, although only one consultee thought that their welfare should be paramount. We think the latter view is impracticable since our recommended scheme is firmly grounded in the contributions made by adults and is intended to supplement, but not to replace, the existing law relating to financial provision for children.[65]

4.85 We have taken the view that the welfare of the parties' joint children should be the court's first consideration, by analogy with the provision in section 25 of the MCA, and we have so recommended.[66]

4.86 We have not recommended, however, that the welfare of "children of the family", who are not the parties' joint children, should be the first consideration.[67] It is important to bear in mind that neither party bears responsibility for children who are not their own.[68] However, such children cannot in practice be ignored. The presence of children in the respondent's home might well persuade the court not to make an immediate order for its sale; but it should not move the court to make an order which is otherwise less favourable to the applicant. Equally, the respondent should not ordinarily be held responsible for the applicant's inability to mitigate economic disadvantage in so far as it arises from the applicant having to look after children who are not the respondent's. Accordingly we have recommended that the discretionary factors should include the welfare of any

---

[64] CP, para 6.264.

[65] We note that children's welfare is only the first consideration under the MCA, and that the welfare principle in the Children Act 1989, s 1, is inapplicable to claims under sch 1.

[66] Para 4.38.

[67] Contrast MCA, s 25(1); see concept of cohabitants who have children together in para 3.26.

[68] See para 4.108.

children who live with, or might reasonably be expected to live with, either party. However, the welfare of such children should not be the first consideration for the court.

4.87 The discretionary factors would be important in framing an order in the most constructive manner so as to take account of the parties' current and future responsibilities. One of the criticisms of the current law that we highlighted in the CP is that it is often not possible in practice to settle property for the benefit of the children under Schedule 1 to the Children Act 1989. Where the parties have relatively modest means, the respondent may not be able to afford a house for the children free of mortgage. The court cannot order the respondent to make periodical payments for the benefit of the children (owing to the general prohibition on doing so contained in the Child Support Act 1991). Nor can the court make any provision for the parent with whom those children live in his or her own right. It may therefore not be possible for such a house to be adequately financed.

4.88 Equally, even if a house can be afforded, an order made under Schedule 1 is likely in practice to render the parent with whom the children live homeless when the children leave home. This may very well deter that parent from accepting such provision for the children in the first place. Indeed, we have been told that that parent may well be advised to apply for local authority housing: he or she would have a "priority need" while the children were dependent, but would have no priority need later when the children were no longer dependent.[69]

4.89 The possibility of a claim under our recommended scheme would make it practicable in both these instances to make a workable order for the provision of a house for the children. We illustrate this, and other options that might be available in a case where there were still dependent children, in Example 2 in Appendix B.

4.90 The CP invited the views of consultees as to how existing remedies for children of cohabitants should interact with any new statutory scheme. The issue here principally concerns Schedule 1 to the Children Act 1989, since child support is outside our terms of reference and not ordinarily a matter for the courts.[70] Very few consultees addressed this question specifically, and those who did expressed divergent views as to how our recommended scheme might interact with Schedule 1. Members of the Association of District Judges have since suggested to us that the provisions of Schedule 1 might usefully be incorporated within a new statute governing claims for financial relief between cohabitants; but some consultees wanted to keep remedies for adults distinct from provision for children.

4.91 We make no recommendation as to whether Schedule 1 should be so incorporated. But it would obviously be important that the claims for financial relief and under Schedule 1 were heard together so that the court could make an order dealing effectively with the overall justice of the case, with a view particularly to making appropriate housing provision for children.

---

[69] See para 2.66 and following.

[70] Save as a consent order: see generally Child Support Act 1991, s 8.

The relevance of conduct

4.92   In the CP we said[71] that we did not consider it appropriate that fault or conduct generally should play a significant part in a new scheme for financial relief on separation, except where one party's behaviour had been such that it would be manifestly unfair to disregard it. An example of such behaviour would be financial or litigation misconduct, where one party had deliberately wasted assets[72] or had incurred large legal costs without good cause.

4.93   This is a very difficult area. It has a well-established background in the context of ancillary relief on divorce, where section 25 of the MCA directs the court to have regard to conduct only where it would be inequitable to disregard it. The courts have taken a very narrow view of what it would be inequitable to disregard. Serious criminal behaviour may be reflected in the substantive award made under section 25; financial or litigation misconduct may also be taken into account, although such conduct often results in costs penalties rather than having any effect on the substantive award of financial relief.

4.94   The majority of consultees who addressed the issue agreed with our provisional proposal in the CP.[73] Many were aware of the reasons why such a narrow range of conduct is relevant in ancillary relief: the difficulty of adjudication, the increased costs, and the fact that making such allegations, as one consultee put it, "raise[s] the temperature dramatically" to the detriment of all involved, including children. A few consultees were unhappy about excluding most forms of conduct from consideration, preferring to think in terms of innocent and guilty parties. But we agree with that majority of consultees that this is not only inappropriate but also unrealistic.

4.95   We have therefore framed our recommendation by analogy with the MCA wording.[74] We make specific reference, however, to one form of behaviour that would be relevant particularly to proceedings under our recommended scheme, namely the fact that qualifying contributions had been made despite the express disagreement of the other party. This is important, and at the heart of our recommended scheme.[75] Contributions such as giving up work to look after the children are normally the result of a joint decision by the parents, although such an agreement may not necessarily be put into words. We do not want to encourage fraught disputes following separation about the true motives of such decisions nor to solicit claims, easily made and difficult to refute, that one party's actions had not been expressly agreed by the other. But it is important that if disagreement to a course of conduct was expressed at the time and was clearly known to both parties, that should be a relevant consideration in assessing what relief, if any, should be granted in relation to it.

---

[71]   CP, para 6.233.

[72]   See, for example, the case discussed in CP, para 6.219, where the respondent had transferred assets to the applicant during the relationships in recognition of economic disadvantage being incurred but the applicant had squandered the money.

[73]   CP, para 6.245.

[74]   Para 4.38(5).

[75]   See paras 4.50 to 4.51.

No requirement of manifest unfairness

4.96 In the CP we invited the views of consultees on whether awards should only be made where it would be substantially or manifestly unfair not to do so.[76] Responses were almost equally divided. The objective of such a requirement would be to emphasise the discretionary nature of the exercise and to discourage weak applications. But we take the view that an additional threshold on claims, such as manifest or substantial unfairness, would increase forensic complexity and merely provide one further issue for parties to argue about. Of course, the court should not entertain trivial or far-fetched claims, which would in any event be discouraged by costs and procedural rules.

The available orders and the clean break

4.97 The MCA requires the court to consider whether it would be appropriate to exercise its powers so that divorcing spouses' mutual dependency is terminated as soon after the grant of decree absolute as the court considers just and reasonable.[77] The "clean break" is neither a goal nor an objective which the court must strive to achieve, but merely something which the court is required to consider as a possibility.[78]

4.98 By contrast, the clean break would be a substantive objective of our recommended scheme.[79] The arguments in favour of a clean break which apply to divorcing couples are even stronger for separating cohabitants, who have not entered into any legal commitment to support each other financially.[80] This has implications for the types of order that the courts should be able to make. Orders for periodical payments keep parties in a continuing economic relationship following their separation, potentially indefinitely. We do not think that this would be appropriate between parties who had not made a formal commitment to each other. Instead, we think that it is desirable that once the dispute has been determined (whether by consent or following contested litigation), the "paying" party should know exactly what the extent of his or her liability is to be. As we discuss below, that is not to say that orders would have to be complied with immediately. But we do not think that courts should be able to make open-ended orders, allowing parties subsequently to seek variation of the order in light of

---

[76] CP, para 6.244.

[77] Principally in MCA, s 25A.

[78] This was strongly affirmed by *Miller v Miller; McFarlane v McFarlane* [2006] UKHL 24, [2006] 2 AC 618.

[79] Although consultees were rather divided in their responses to our question (CP, para 6.272). Some consultees stated or implied that the clean break should be given the same weight as on divorce. Others indicated that the clean break should have greater weight between cohabitants, or otherwise advocated a strong presumption in favour of the clean break with restrictions being placed on the use of periodical payments, should they be available at all.

[80] See *The Financial Consequences of Divorce* (1980) Law Com No 103 and (1981) Law Com No 112.

changed circumstances.[81] Once the parties' cohabiting relationship has ended, so too should their financial ties.[82]

4.99 We therefore consider that the court should not be entitled to make orders for periodical payments under our recommended scheme, save in the case of child-care costs, discussed below.[83] However, the court would be able to order the payment of a lump sum by instalments, a method of disposition that may be particularly useful where there is insufficient capital to achieve an immediate clean break. But that would be a commitment limited in amount and in time (subject only to later variation of the timetable for payments).[84]

4.100 We also consider that the court should be entitled, on application being made, to order interim payment of a lump sum, provided that eligibility has been established and that a *prima facie* case for relief has been made out.[85] This would be particularly useful where the applicant needed urgent access to funds for housing.[86] We realise that interim lump sums are not currently available in ancillary relief proceedings, as the provisions conferring power on the courts to make such orders have not yet been brought into force.[87]

Child-care costs

4.101 As we discussed in the CP, the issue of child-care costs raises questions about the interaction of financial remedies between the cohabitants themselves and existing remedies for the benefit of children. They exemplify the difficulty of treating children and their parents as separate economic entities, rather than as a unit.

4.102 It is important first to appreciate the entirely separate function of child support.[88] Payments made under the Child Support Act 1991 are intended to cover half the

---

[81] For a recent example in the matrimonial context, see *N v N* [2006] EWHC 3269 (Fam), [2007] 1 FCR 749.

[82] Save in relation to financial support for their children.

[83] Paras 4.101 to 4.105.

[84] And, in exceptional circumstances, of quantum: *Westbury v Sampson* [2001] EWCA Civ 407, [2002] 1 FLR 166.

[85] Our intention here is that the courts should have interim powers that are (in very broad terms) analogous to their power to order maintenance pending suit and thereafter interim orders in proceedings under the MCA (see Family Proceedings Rules 1991, r 2.64(2)). Since we are not recommending a needs-based scheme or periodical payments, interim awards would take effect as capital orders (including lump sums payable by instalments) and be quantified in light of the applicant's likely award under the scheme.

[86] The scheme does not, of course, have the objective of meeting need. But the sharing of economic disadvantage and the reversal of retained benefit will often go towards meeting needs arising from the applicant's contributions to the relationship (see para 4.18 and following). And needs are among the discretionary factors (see para 4.38(2)) which may influence the timing of payments awarded, and could lead the court to make an order for an interim lump sum.

[87] Family Law Act 1996, s 15 and sch 2, para 3, inserting MCA, s 22A(4).

[88] Our discussion of this issue is based on the existing law of child support, but we note the reforms proposed in the Child Maintenance and Other Payments Bill 2007, which we do not think have a direct bearing on this issue, save in so far as more parents would be free to make their own arrangements for child support.

cost of raising the child.[89] The basic cost of bringing up a child is therefore already shared by the child support legislation, and neither child support payments nor the cost of caring for the child at home would be regarded as economic disadvantage. Nor would the receipt of child support payments by the primary carer constitute a retained benefit, though the child support obligation would be relevant as a discretionary factor.[90]

4.103   However, where the parent with whom a child lives is in paid employment, that individual is likely to incur some child-care costs. Indeed, unless the children are at school and the employment is restricted to school hours, such payments may be necessary to enable that parent to work at all and so mitigate any economic disadvantage. The court's powers under Schedule 1 to the Children Act 1989 do not provide a solution (save in cases where the court does, exceptionally, have jurisdiction – principally in high value cases).[91] Moreover, it would seem that the costs of paid child-care are not encompassed in the child support system but are regarded as a separate matter, dealt with to some extent by way of tax credits.[92] But in so far as tax credits do not cover the costs of child-care, such costs should be viewed as a form of economic disadvantage arising from the cohabitants' shared lives which should, subject to the discretionary factors, be shared.[93]

4.104   This is a case where an order for periodical payments is obviously apt. Child-care arrangements are so variable that it is important to share the expense in a way that can vary with the costs. It would, of course, remain open to the court in appropriate cases to capitalise the award and to order payment of a lump sum in lieu of periodical payments.

4.105   Some consultees suggested that this reform is one that should not be made specifically in the context of cohabitation reform, but would be better effected by reform of Schedule 1 to the Children Act 1989. It might be argued that there is no logical reason for restricting the availability of periodical payments for child-care costs to former cohabitants, in so far as it can be characterised as a cost relating to the child, rather than (exclusively) for the benefit of the parent. We see the force in this argument, but the point falls outside our terms of reference. If such a change were to be made, then we accept that the reform relating to child-care costs which we recommend might more rationally be contained in an amendment to Schedule 1 to the Children Act 1989, so as to be available between all parents.

The effect of finding a new partner

4.106   Despite the narrow role which we are recommending for periodical payments, we must address the effect on such an order of the recipient forming a new relationship, whether a marriage, civil partnership or cohabitation. We invited the

---

[89]   Department of Social Security, *A new contract for welfare: children's rights and parents' responsibilities* (1999) para 2.5.

[90]   Relating to the parties' financial needs and obligations.

[91]   See CP, paras 6.201 to 6.202.

[92]   Availability of tax credits would form part of the "financial resources" to which the court would have regard in deciding what, if any, order to make in respect of this cost. See Working Tax Credit (Entitlement and Maximum Rate) Regs 2002, SI 2002/2005, r 20(3), as amended.

[93]   See n 36 on which children would be relevant for such a claim.

views of consultees on this point.[94] The view that emerged from those who addressed the issue was that, while marriage or civil partnership should result in the automatic termination of periodical payments, a new cohabiting relationship should not trigger automatic termination. Instead, it should be a relevant circumstance to be considered on an application to court to vary or terminate the periodical payments order. A couple of consultees suggested that no application for a periodical payments order should be possible where the applicant had already married or formed a civil partnership with a third party, or had commenced a cohabiting relationship which had become "eligible" under the scheme.

4.107 We see the logic of the argument that, given the compensatory basis on which periodical payments would be payable under our recommended scheme, the inception of any new relationship should have no bearing on the continuation of periodical payments.[95] However, in light of the well-established position that applies under the MCA,[96] we see considerable difficulty in following that logic through in this context. In particular, we do not think that liability under a periodical payments order should survive a subsequent marriage or civil partnership.

Liability under Schedule 1 to the Children Act 1989

4.108 We invited the views of consultees on whether the liability under Schedule 1 to the Children Act 1989 of those who are not parents of a child, but who have treated that child as a child of the family (most commonly, as step-parents), should be extended from cases involving spouses and civil partners to cover cohabitants.[97] The opinions of the small number of consultees who addressed this question were evenly divided. We have concluded that it would be inappropriate to recommend any extension of liability. Consultation provided no firm support in favour of reform, and, while there are some cases in which such liability might justly be imposed,[98] we are concerned that any prospect of liability in such cases might have the undesirable effect of deterring individuals from taking on the responsibility of step-parenthood.

COURTS, PROCEDURE AND ENFORCEMENT

4.109 Above all, a new scheme of financial relief must be accompanied by procedures and rules that require parties to take a proportionate approach to the resolution of disputes that might arise on separation.

---

[94] CP, para 6.277.

[95] This view might be particularly strongly held in relation to costs of child-care. Were the issue characterised as a form of provision for the benefit of the child, and so payable under the Children Act 1989, sch 1, a new relationship of the primary carer would not automatically impact on the other parent's responsibility to contribute towards those costs.

[96] Where marriage or civil partnership precludes any application and automatically terminates periodical payments: MCA, s 28 and Civil Partnership Act 2004, sch 5, para 47.

[97] CP, para 6.297.

[98] For example, where the other parent had died, and the step-parent had had a long relationship with the child.

Civil courts or family courts?

4.110 Most consultees agreed with our provisional proposal in the CP that cases under a new scheme of financial relief on separation should be heard in the county court or the High Court.[99] The county court would deal with the majority of first instance claims, but applicants should be able to commence high-value or particularly complex claims in the High Court.

4.111 At county court level, where the vast majority of claims are likely to be heard, the characterisation of proceedings would only affect which rules applied to the conduct of the claim. In the High Court, the additional question of allocation between Divisions arises, as the High Court has separate Chancery, Family and Queen's Bench Divisions. The CP suggested that claims under the scheme should be treated as family (rather than civil) proceedings and should be heard by family judges,[100] which in the case of the High Court would mean the Family Division.

4.112 The CP's primary concern was that procedure under a new scheme should be governed by the Family Proceedings Rules. It highlighted the overriding objective of those Rules to deal with ancillary relief cases justly, and more specifically: to ensure that parties are on an equal footing; to save expense; to deal with the case proportionately; to ensure that it is dealt with expeditiously and fairly; and to allot to it an appropriate share of the court's resources.[101] The CP argued that a claim under the new scheme would place similar demands on the court.[102] The family courts' practices with regard to case management, the disclosure of financial information, the admission of evidence, the valuation of assets, opportunities for diversion to mediation, the use of first appointments and financial dispute resolution hearings, and their general informality, would be entirely appropriate for a new scheme of financial relief operating between cohabitants.

4.113 The CP also referred to the unnecessary duplication of work that can currently arise when family disputes form the subject matter of several different cases heard in different courts. It suggested that, in the event that a new scheme were introduced for separating cohabitants, there would be many cases where an applicant would bring proceedings for relief under both the separation scheme and under Schedule 1 to the Children Act 1989, and such proceedings should be joined and heard together.[103] Were there to be a concurrent jurisdiction for a number of Divisions, there would be similar risks of duplication of work. In addition, there would be a danger of the different Divisions developing diverging interpretations of the scheme, thereby complicating matters for litigants.[104]

---

[99] CP, para 11.16.

[100] CP, paras 11.4 and 11.21.

[101] CP, para 11.7.

[102] CP, paras 11.18 to 11.24.

[103] CP, para 11.15.

[104] See the suggestion that the Family and Chancery Divisions have developed distinctive approaches under the Inheritance (Provision for Family and Dependants) Act 1975: F Cownie and A Bradley, "Divided justice, different voices: inheritance and family provision" (2003) 23 *Legal Studies* 566.

4.114 Almost all of the consultees who commented on the CP's provisional proposal thought that the family courts should have exclusive jurisdiction to hear claims under any new separation scheme.[105]

4.115 The most notable dissent from that view came from the Chancery Bar Association ("CBA"), which was the only consultee positively to promote a role for the Chancery Division. The CBA suggested that a more suitable division of work might be for all cases involving children to be family proceedings, while cases between cohabitants without children might be dealt with as chancery proceedings. The CBA took this view in large part because it considered that the general law of contract, property and trusts would still have a substantial role to play in the determination of such cases, and because of the nature of the concepts underpinning the proposed scheme.

4.116 We do not agree that cases between cohabitants without children would be more appropriately conducted as chancery proceedings. This Report recommends that it should not be possible to bring prior or concurrent claims under the general law of implied trusts, estoppel or contract where the scheme is invoked.[106] The exercise that would be carried out by the court under our recommended scheme would be based on an assessment of the economic impact of the parties' contributions to the relationship. This would not involve a determination of the parties' contractual, property or trust interests. The presence of a child would be relevant to eligibility to apply for relief. But once cohabitants were eligible, the claim would be assessed on the same grounds in all cases, the only difference being the need to consider the interests of children where they were present. We therefore do not support the view that the allocation of, and procedure for, cases should depend on the presence or absence of children.

4.117 It could be argued that it would be inconsistent to give the Family Division exclusive jurisdiction to hear claims for financial relief on separation where there is dual jurisdiction for claims for family provision on death.[107] The Law Commission's 1974 Report,[108] implemented as the 1975 Act, recommended that all claims on death in the High Court should be heard in the Family Division. Government rejected that argument and granted concurrent jurisdiction to the Chancery and the Family Divisions. However, it should be noted that, prior to 1974, jurisdiction to hear family provision claims was the exclusive preserve of the Chancery Division,[109] and so the Commission's recommendation would have entailed a marked shift from the status quo. It should also be borne in mind that, under current practice, a marriage or civil partnership that ends in death may be subject to the jurisdiction of the Chancery or Family Divisions whereas only the Family Division may hear a claim for ancillary relief following divorce. In other

---

[105] Including two senior members of the judiciary; Wall LJ (formerly of the Family Division) and Lloyd LJ (formerly of the Chancery Division).

[106] See para 4.41 and para 4.132 and following.

[107] The CP suggested that claims on death should continue to be subject to the procedural and other rules applying to claims under the Inheritance (Provision for Family and Dependants) Act 1975: CP, Part 11, n 1.

[108] Second Report on Family Property: Family Provision on Death (1974) Law Com No 61.

[109] Other than claims under the Matrimonial Causes Act 1965 by former spouses who were receiving maintenance from their now-deceased former spouse.

words, the potential for different Divisions to hear claims depending on the cause of the termination of the relationship would not be new.

4.118 We remain of the view that, although we have clearly rejected the MCA as a technical basis for our recommended scheme, the type of dispute that would be dealt with under our scheme is of a character similar to applications for ancillary relief. Claims would often be emotionally charged and might prompt diverging evidence about the details of family life. The court hearing such claims would have to take account of not only the principles of retained benefit and economic disadvantage, but also factors such as the respective needs of the family members, the nature and (often limited) extent of available assets and the types of order available.[110] In our view, the family courts therefore provide the more appropriate forum for the optimal disposal of claims.

4.119 However, we do not make any recommendation as to whether exclusive jurisdiction should be granted to the family courts. The allocation of court business is a matter entirely for Government as the body responsible for the proper deployment of judicial resources. We understand that the starting point in such deliberations is that there should be equal jurisdiction for all divisions of the High Court. We have explained why we consider that the established practices of the Family Division would offer distinct advantages in the conduct of claims under our scheme. However, there is no reason in theory why, for example, the Chancery Division could not adopt specific Family Proceedings Rules in respect of separation claims[111] or create its own procedures closely mirroring the rules of the Family Division. It would be for Government to decide what is most appropriate, taking into account the interests of litigants, the taxpayer and the overall administration of justice.

Costs

4.120 We consider that the costs rules for a new regime should:

(1) be appropriate to the nature of the dispute between the parties;

(2) provide incentives for proportionate case management and alternative dispute resolution, with costs penalties where appropriate; and

(3) be able to operate alongside any other relevant costs regime.

4.121 In the CP, we asked consultees what costs regime they thought should apply to proceedings under a new scheme. Very few consultees addressed this point; most of those who did thought that the costs rules applicable to proceedings for ancillary relief on divorce should apply here too.

4.122 While it is tempting to draw that analogy, we wonder whether it is appropriate. The respondent to ancillary relief proceedings only very rarely has legitimate grounds on which to object in principle to those proceedings being brought. By

---

[110] The complex issue of pension sharing is, in particular, currently unique to the matrimonial jurisdiction.

[111] The Family Division uses the Civil Procedure Rules when hearing claims under the Inheritance (Provision for Family and Dependants) Act 1975 and the Trusts of Land and Appointment of Trustees Act 1996.

contrast, a respondent to a claim under a new scheme between cohabitants might more often (a) dispute that the parties had had an eligible relationship and (b) contest the substantive claim in its entirety. To that extent, proceedings under a new scheme for cohabitants would seem more akin to those under the Trusts of Land and Appointment of Trustees Act 1996 ("TOLATA"), where the normal civil costs rules apply. It is also significant that our recommended scheme would not – as ancillary relief now does – operate to dispose of all the couple's property between them.

4.123   In relation to point (3) identified above, we understand that there may be difficulties currently where proceedings under TOLATA are joined with proceedings under Schedule 1 to the Children Act 1989, to which quite different costs regimes apply. We sense from recent discussion of this point with practitioners that there may be some uncertainty about how these rules should operate together.

4.124   We do not make any positive recommendation regarding costs rules, which we think would better be considered, in conjunction with development of new procedural rules, by the relevant committee. We would emphasise that we think it important that procedural and costs rules be developed in tandem to ensure that the objectives of each are consistent and mutually supporting.

Public funding

4.125   In the CP we invited the views of consultees as to the public funding of cohabitants' claims and as to accessibility for litigants in person.[112] The question elicited responses emphasising the importance not only of proper public funding, but also of clear, concise and accessible law, forms, information and so on (and not just for the sake of the litigant in person). However, as we said in the CP, it is for Government to make decisions as to public funding and we make no recommendation about this.

Mediation

4.126   It is well-established that where parties arrive at an agreement that they have devised themselves there are greater chances of that agreement "sticking". Mediation, and the developing discipline of collaborative law, would have an important role to play in the operation of our scheme, as would the more traditional lawyer-led negotiation. Parties must be encouraged to participate in mediation; in the event that public funding is available for the scheme, parties should be required to attempt mediation unless their advisers certify that the case is not suitable, as is currently the practice for ancillary relief on divorce.

4.127   **We recommend that the promotion of mediation as an alternative to court proceedings be facilitated wherever possible by the rules.**

Anti-avoidance and enforcement

4.128   Issues as to anti-avoidance and enforcement under our recommended scheme would arise in very much the same way as they do between spouses and civil partners in the course of ancillary relief proceedings. There would need to be

---

[112] CP, para 11.39.

statutory provision to restrain the respondent from disposing of assets in anticipation of a claim, and to set aside dispositions already made with the intention of preventing (or reducing) financial relief being awarded under the scheme.[113] In the CP[114] we provisionally proposed that measures be introduced similar to those currently available in relation to ancillary relief, and nearly all consultees agreed.

4.129 **We recommend that the scheme should include anti-avoidance provisions modelled upon section 37 of the Matrimonial Causes Act 1973, and similar provisions for the enforcement of orders.**

Interaction with Schedule 1 to the Children Act 1989

4.130 One of the issues discussed above has been the interaction of our recommended scheme with the financial provision available for children under Schedule 1 to the Children Act 1989. In many cases, claims between cohabitants would be made concurrently with Schedule 1 claims. It is obvious that the two sets of proceedings should be disposed of together, not only for the sake of minimising costs and bringing litigation to a close, but also because the two sets of claims would have a bearing on each other.[115]

Taxation and social security

4.131 Tax and social security fall outside our terms of reference. We simply observe, however, that consideration would need to be given to steps that might be taken in order to ensure that the transfer of assets under the scheme did not attract fiscal and welfare benefit consequences which would undermine the scheme's objectives.

THE INTERACTION OF THE SCHEME WITH THE LAW OF IMPLIED TRUSTS AND ESTOPPEL

4.132 Self-evidently, when parties have made contractual arrangements as to what is to happen in the event of separation, those contractual arrangements would be overridden by our recommended scheme, unless the parties had entered into a valid opt-out agreement.[116]

4.133 The parties might also have made arrangements as to the ownership of assets. Property disputes between cohabitants can at present only be resolved using equitable principles developed by the courts over many years. The law relating to implied trusts and the law of estoppel[117] may give a former cohabitant an interest in the other's property or determine the shares in which jointly owned property is held. But some aspects of these areas of law were not designed for relationship

---

[113] The Association of District Judges observed that the lack of such a power in the county court in cases under the Children Act 1989, sch 1, is extremely inconvenient. The current solution is to transfer such cases to the High Court, causing delay and additional cost to the parties.

[114] CP, para 11.41.

[115] See para 4.83 and following.

[116] See Part 5.

[117] See Appendix A.

breakdown, which is why we are recommending a tailor-made jurisdiction that is sensitive to family situations.

4.134 Our scheme would not abolish implied trusts and estoppel; these principles (which we call the "general law") would remain important in many contexts.[118] So we have to determine what would happen in cases where it appeared that a claim could be made under both our recommended scheme and the general law. Since general law claims arise most frequently in relation to claims to land, typically the formerly shared home, and arise from different kinds of contribution to property, there could be an overlap in a number of cases.

4.135 The few responses to the CP question about the interaction issue[119] were inconclusive, with a number of views expressed. Recent research suggests that practitioners find using the general law in these cases problematic for a number of reasons.[120] We are especially concerned that for parties to plead the new law and the general law together would be a disaster in terms of complexity and costs. It is necessary to recommend a scheme that would replace, rather than merely supplement, the general law in these cases.

Illustrating the interaction problem

4.136 It may help to give an example of the difficulties that might arise if the general law remained relevant. Let us suppose that A and B have bought a house together. They are joint registered proprietors; they contributed one quarter and three-quarters of the deposit respectively, and they continue to make the mortgage payments in those proportions. Later their relationship breaks down and they want to sell the house and divide the proceeds.

4.137 As joint legal owners, A and B hold the house upon trust.[121] They have not executed a declaration of trust,[122] nor have they had any discussion about the

---

[118] For example, on death, in disputes with third parties and where cohabitants are not eligible under the scheme.

[119] CP, para 6.288.

[120] See G Douglas, J Pearce, H Woodward, *A Failure of Trust: Resolving Property Disputes on Cohabitation Breakdown* (2007), available at http://www.law.cf.ac.uk/researchpapers/papers/1.pdf or http://www.bris.ac.uk/law/research/centres-themes/cohabit/cohabit-rep.pdf (last visited 3 July 2007); see "Dealing with Property Issues on Cohabitation Breakdown" (2007) 37 *Family Law* 36. The desirability of having an overarching scheme, and the problems created by the multiple applications required by the current law, were also flagged by some solicitors interviewed by R Tennant, J Taylor and J Lewis, *Separating from cohabitation: making arrangements for finances and parenting* (2006) Department for Constitutional Affairs Research Report 7/2006, p 128.

[121] Law of Property Act 1925, s 34(2).

[122] Had they done so, that would have been conclusive as to the extent of their beneficial interests: *Goodman v Gallant* [1986] Fam 106; see paras A.10 to A.16 and Appendix A generally on this area of the law. Under our recommended scheme, their express beneficial interests would provide the starting point from which one party might bring a claim under the scheme. In particular, one might argue that the other's share was a retained benefit to the extent that the first had in fact provided more of the purchase price or mortgage payments; such an argument based on mortgage payments would not be tenable where the other had discharged other household bills of equal value.

proportions in which they own the house.[123] How then is their beneficial interest held? The starting point is that they hold upon trust for themselves as beneficial joint tenants,[124] but B, who has contributed three-quarters of the value of the house, may not be content with this. If B wishes to show that the beneficial interests were different, then B must establish that this is an "very unusual" case.[125]

4.138 Whether B succeeds will depend upon how A and B's relationship is viewed by the court[126] and in particular the extent to which it appears that they have pooled their resources. The case will probably not be an "very unusual" one, and it is likely that B will not be able to displace the presumption of beneficial joint tenancy under the general law.

4.139 However, if the matter were examined under our recommended scheme, it might be that a different result would be reached. The scheme would not involve the determination of beneficial ownership in property. The court should not consider whether the presumption of joint beneficial ownership should be rebutted. The scheme would require the court to assess whether that presumption left either party with a retained benefit or an economic disadvantage in the event of separation.[127] B's greater financial contribution would point to As having a retained benefit and, subject to the operation of the discretionary factors, it is likely that A would have to repay that benefit to B.

4.140 If B were able to prove under the general law that the case was unusual and that beneficial ownership should mirror the parties' contributions, then B would have no incentive to invoke our recommended scheme. A, by contrast, might wish to invoke the scheme in order to determine whether the retained benefit might be held to be somewhat smaller in the light of the discretionary factors, and to enable the court to look at other matters and in particular at economic disadvantage.

4.141 It can be seen that the general law governing beneficial entitlement to property might yield, for either party, results different from those generated by our recommended scheme.

Conclusions

4.142 There are two questions to be answered. First, what should be the relationship between the scheme and the general law: which should take priority? And

---

[123] An expression of common intention, upon which the parties have relied (by investing in the house), will determine the extent of a beneficial interest in property held upon constructive trust following *Lloyds Bank plc v Rosset* [1991] 1 AC 107. The precise status of that principle is unclear following *Stack v Dowden* [2007] UKHL 17, [2007] 2 WLR 831, but it is consistent with the House of Lords' view expressed in that case (at [61]) that the court must ascertain "what the parties must, in view of their conduct, be taken to have intended".

[124] *Stack v Dowden* [2007] UKHL 17, [2007] 2 WLR 831, at [56].

[125] *Stack v* Dowden [2007] UKHL 17, [2007] 2 WLR 831, at [69]. The House of Lords held in that case that it is not appropriate to use resulting trust reasoning in the domestic context.

[126] See para 2.8 and following.

[127] Our scheme would also operate in place of the remedy of equitable accounting: see *Stack v Dowden* [2007] UKHL 17, [2007] 2 WLR 831, at [150]; *Wilcox v Tait* [2006] EWCA Civ 1867.

second, given that priority, should it still be possible for litigants to plead both the new scheme and the general law in the alternative, despite the risk of complexity and costs referred to above?

4.143 Taking the first question, it is clear that the law must make priority clear. Our recommended scheme and the general law might give similar results in some cases; they would give different results in others. Parties need to know on what basis to negotiate in order to settle their disputes; courts need to know on what basis to make orders for financial relief. It is equally clear that our recommended scheme must "trump" the general law.

4.144 Once that priority has been determined, it is clear that the second question is determined at least as a matter of logic: even if permitted to do so, the parties would merely waste costs if they brought a concurrent general law claim as between each other, because the general law's attribution of the parties' equitable interests would be superseded by the adjustive powers of the scheme.[128]

4.145 However, even though this is clear as a matter of logic, parties might try to bring alternative claims unless explicitly prevented. Moreover, it is very important that parties – particularly those for whom expense is no object – should be prevented from bringing multiple claims. It is clear from meetings we have had with family law practitioners that this will happen unless the rules make it clear that it must not. Hence our recommendation.[129]

4.146 Our recommendation in this respect would make the interaction between the general law and our scheme no different from that which arises when the MCA is invoked. It is well-established that in proceedings between separated or divorcing spouses where ancillary relief is available under the MCA, proceedings under the general law are not permitted. The position of civil partners is identical. Nevertheless, the rights of spouses and civil partners under the general law (and those of their creditors) are not otherwise affected and indeed they may need to litigate under the general law where third parties are involved.[130] The position is well-understood by family practitioners.

THE LIMITATION PERIOD

4.147 It is important for people to be able to get on with their lives and to start afresh after the end of a relationship. Potential respondents need to know when there is no further possibility of claims being made against them by a former cohabitant. Potential applicants need to be aware that at some point they can no longer bring a claim and must rely on their own resources.

---

[128] As it will also adjust the parties' expressly declared beneficial interests; see para 5.62 and following.

[129] See paras 4.41 and 4.42.

[130] For example, *G v G (Matrimonial Property: Rights of Extended Family)* [2005] EWHC 1560 (Fam), [2006] 1 FLR 62; *TL v ML and others (Ancillary relief: claim against assets of extended family)* [2005] EWHC 2860 (Fam), [2006] 1 FLR 1263. See also issues raised in *Mountney v Treharne* [2002] EWCA Civ 1174, [2003] Ch 135; *Ram v Ram (no 2)* [2004] EWCA Civ 1684, [2005] 2 FLR 75; *Hill v Haines* [2007] EWHC 1012 (Ch), [2007] NPC 58; *X v X (Crown Prosecution Service Intervening)* [2005] EWHC 296 (Fam), [2005] 2 FLR 487; see also CP, paras 6.298 to 6.301 in relation to debt.

4.148   Limitation rules are intended to provide certainty. The CP argued for a relatively short limitation period of one year from the date of separation, so as to enable people to draw a line as soon as possible under the relationship that has ended. Most of our consultees agreed with that view.

4.149   However, the evidence gathered in a recent research project[131] convinces us that one year would be too restrictive, allowing insufficient time for parties to take advice and to attempt negotiation before feeling the need to issue proceedings. The break-up of a family, particularly where there are children, is typically too complex and chaotic to be "tidied up" so swiftly.

4.150   We note that two years is the limitation period adopted in most Australian states[132] and proposed for Ireland.[133]

4.151   **We recommend that claims for financial relief should be brought within two years of the parties' separation.**

4.152   Should the two-year period be capable of extension in any circumstances? There are many advantages to fixed rules, even though they inevitably generate some hard cases. For example, we have recommended that if the minimum duration requirement (for couples who do not have children together to be eligible under the scheme) is set at two years, it should not be possible to dispense with that requirement. A limitation period which cannot be extended or dispensed with could be said to be compatible with that approach.

4.153   Most consultees felt that there should be a general discretion to extend the limitation period; but that view was expressed in the context of the proposal of a one-year limitation period. Arguments for a discretion to extend are weaker if the limitation period is longer.[134]

4.154   However, we remain concerned about four cases in particular:

(1)   Where the potential respondent voluntarily supported the potential applicant financially following separation, but ceased to do so on or shortly after the expiry of the limitation period. There may be a remedy for the applicant within the law of estoppel or of contract, but such an

---

[131]   G Douglas, J Pearce, H Woodward, *A Failure of Trust: Resolving Property Disputes on Cohabitation Breakdown* (2007), available at http://www.law.cf.ac.uk/researchpapers/papers/1.pdf or http://www.bris.ac.uk/law/research/centres-themes/cohabit/cohabit-rep.pdf (last visited 3 July 2007); see "Dealing with Property Issues on Cohabitation Breakdown" (2007) 37 *Family Law* 36.

[132]   Note that in all Australian states there is a discretion to extend the limitation period, usually on a "balance of hardship" test (that is, on the basis of the court's assessment as to whether the limitation of the action would cause greater hardship to the applicant than extending the period would cause to the respondent).

[133]   Rights and Duties of Cohabitants (2006) Law Reform Commission of the Republic of Ireland LRC 82-2006, para 7.07. Contrast Family Law (Scotland) Act 2006, which does adopt a one-year period: s 28.

[134]   Clearly unnecessary now is our proposal in the CP (at para 11.78(1)) that the period be extended to one year beyond the birth of a child to the applicant where, at the time of separation, she was pregnant with the respondent's child.

answer is necessarily an uncertain one and it would be better to leave the door open for the court to extend the limitation period.

(2)   Where neither party thought it worth making a claim initially, but circumstances significantly changed after the expiry of the limitation period. The case which concerns us most is where a child develops a serious disability. Schedule 1 to the Children Act 1989 will respond to the child's needs, but not to the consequent economic disadvantage of the former cohabitant with whom the child lives (who might have to give up work to care for the child, and therefore be out of the labour market for much longer than had previously been anticipated).

(3)   Where a claim is brought under the general law of trusts after the expiry of the scheme's limitation period. The limitation period for trusts claims is six years from the date of the breach of trust, save that there is no limitation period for an action brought by a beneficiary against a trustee in possession of the trust property.[135] One of our objectives, as explained above, is to replace the law of implied trusts with a family-focused scheme applicable to separating cohabitants. We do not think it would be right to allow parties to wait for the expiry of the limitation period under our recommended scheme so that they might then bring a trusts claim with the aim of defeating their former partner's claim for financial relief.

(4)   Where the parties had had more than one cohabiting relationship together, and it would be inequitable to deny the applicant any possibility of bringing a claim in respect of the earlier relationship following the final separation. See, for example, the case discussed at paragraph 3.60. The putative applicant might have declined to bring any proceedings following the first separation because he or she was seeking a reconciliation with the other party. We think that it would be undesirable to impede such efforts by that party feeling under pressure to protect his or her position by bringing proceedings at such a time. It could be deeply inequitable to deprive the applicant of a claim in such circumstances, particularly if the second cohabitation was not long enough to satisfy the minimum duration requirement. Where the second cohabitation was itself long enough to satisfy the minimum duration requirement, the court would then be able to examine both periods in a composite claim. But the longer the intervening separation, the less strong may be the case for granting an extension of the limitation period in relation to the first cohabitation.

4.155   **We recommend that there be a general discretion vested in the court to extend the two-year limitation period for making a claim, to be exercised in exceptional circumstances only.**

---

[135] Limitation Act 1980, s 21(1) and (3).

PART 5
COHABITATION CONTRACTS AND OPT-OUT AGREEMENTS

INTRODUCTION

5.1 In Parts 3 and 4 of this Report, we have recommended a new statutory scheme of financial relief for eligible cohabitants on separation. We have explained why it would not be an opt-in scheme, but rather a scheme of general application which would allow cohabitants to make their own financial arrangements which would be enforceable on separation.

5.2 In this Part, we make recommendations for the ways in which cohabitants might make, and the courts enforce, opt-out agreements, leaving the parties free to make their own financial agreements for separation. We consider, as a preliminary, the validity under the current law of cohabitation contracts that deal with the couple's property or financial arrangements. We then discuss the extent to which parties should be able to make and enforce their arrangements on separation, and make recommendations in relation to:

   (1)   the nature and effect of opt-out agreements;

   (2)   the qualifying criteria for such agreements;

   (3)   who is capable of entering into such agreements; and

   (4)   the circumstances in which the court may set such agreements aside.

   We then discuss whether express declarations of trust should, without more, be regarded as opt-out agreements. Finally, we consider three related issues.

5.3 It is important to emphasise that it is not possible to opt out of the responsibility to provide for one's children either under the Child Support Act 1991 or under Schedule 1 to the Children Act 1989.[1] Nothing that we are recommending would change that.

5.4 Some consultees queried whether it should ever be possible for the parties to disapply the statutory scheme, leaving the parties free to make their own financial arrangements for separation, where there are children. We think that it should, because the presence of children should not detract from the parties' autonomy. But it will be seen that our recommendations would incorporate safeguards intended to meet these concerns.[2]

---

[1]   CP, para 10.3. Note also Children Act 1989, sch 1, para 10; and see *Morgan v Hill* [2006] EWCA Civ 1602, [2007] 1 WLR 855.

[2]   See paras 5.56 to 5.61.

COHABITATION CONTRACTS

5.5 Most of this Part addresses the nature and effect of opt-out agreements in the context of a new statutory scheme. However, we begin by making a separate recommendation.

5.6 Currently, some cohabitants make agreements, commonly referred to as "cohabitation contracts", to govern their financial arrangements during the cohabitation and in the event of the parties separating. There is some lingering doubt as to whether such contracts might be unenforceable for reasons of public policy. Such doubts may have had substance in the days before cohabitation outside marriage was publicly acceptable, but today they should no longer be warranted.[3]

5.7 We argued in the CP that statute should affirm that cohabitation contracts are no longer unenforceable for that reason.[4] Responses to consultation revealed considerable support for this view.

5.8 **We recommend that legislation should provide, for the avoidance of doubt, that, in so far as a contract ("a cohabitation contract") governs the financial arrangements of a cohabiting couple during their cohabitation or following their separation, it should not be regarded as contrary to public policy.**

5.9 This recommendation is self-standing, and could be usefully implemented in its own right, even if no scheme for financial relief on separation were introduced.

5.10 Implementation of this recommendation would also complement our recommended scheme for financial relief on separation. It would confirm that such contracts, in so far as they deal with the couple's finances during cohabitation, would not be contrary to public policy. But where the contract made provision for what would happen on separation, and the couple would be eligible to apply for financial relief under the scheme, it would be enforceable only in so far as the couple had executed a valid opt-out agreement, which we discuss below.

OPT-OUT AGREEMENTS

5.11 We use the term "opt-out agreement" to refer to an agreement between cohabitants, which provides that the statute providing financial relief for cohabitants on separation shall not apply to the parties.[5] Such an agreement might be made before or during the parties' cohabitation, or after it had ended.

5.12 Such an agreement might simply disapply the statute, without more; or it might go further and make positive provision for financial arrangements on separation.[6] In the latter case it might deal comprehensively with all of the parties' respective financial resources or it might be of more limited effect, for example, exempting

---

[3] See paras A.18 to A.22.

[4] CP, para 10.9.

[5] We discuss in Part 6 the rather different considerations relevant when a cohabiting relationship ends by the death of one party.

[6] CP, paras 10.32 to 10.43.

one or more assets which have particular financial or sentimental value from the scheme.[7]

5.13 Not all arrangements between cohabitants about their property would be opt-out agreements. A number of qualifying criteria, discussed below,[8] would have to be satisfied in order for an agreement to constitute an opt-out. An agreement that did not satisfy these requirements might, however, be a cohabitation contract. Such contracts would be binding on the parties, subject to the general law of contract, but would not disapply our recommended scheme on separation where that scheme was invoked by either party. We discuss later in this Part the effect of express declarations of trust.[9]

5.14 Our recommended scheme would incorporate important protections for separating cohabitants and would significantly improve upon the shortcomings of the current law. It is important, therefore, to establish the circumstances in which cohabitants should be able to opt out of it. What should be the criteria for the validity of an opt-out agreement? What should be the effect of a valid agreement? Should it be inviolable, or are there circumstances where the court should be able to set it aside?

Objectives

5.15 Many of our consultees were anxious to preserve the freedom of cohabitants to make their own arrangements to deal with the financial consequences of separation. We accept not only that this principle should be respected, but also that cohabitants should be encouraged to make such arrangements. To achieve the latter, it is important that opt-out agreements should not lightly be set aside. At the same time, there must be safeguards. The courts should be able to respond to circumstances where enforcing the parties' agreement would give rise to serious injustice, in order:

(1) to protect parties who had been treated unfairly at the time the agreement was made; and

(2) to accommodate those cases where circumstances had changed in a way that was not foreseen when the agreement was made.

5.16 In formulating our recommendations on the nature and effect of opt-out agreements, we are mindful of the fact that it is not currently possible to opt out of specialist statutory family law provisions so as to exclude the court's jurisdiction entirely. Separation agreements made between spouses and civil partners, and pre- or post-nuptial contracts, do not prevent an application to the court for ancillary relief on divorce. Nevertheless, the idea of private ordering is gaining currency. The courts are likely to follow the terms of separation agreements on divorce, provided that they were made after full disclosure and independent advice.[10] Pre-nuptial agreements are being given increasing weight by the

---

[7] See further para 5.55.

[8] Para 5.30 and following.

[9] Para 5.62 and following.

[10] CP, paras 10.87 to 10.89.

courts,[11] and there are calls for the enforceability of such agreements to be reviewed.[12]

5.17   In making our recommendations we have taken into account:

(1)   the need to protect the autonomy of individuals and of couples;

(2)   the need to protect the vulnerable, including those susceptible to pressure and those who have assets that are precious to them (for whatever reason) and that they are anxious to protect;

(3)   the desirability of certainty, so that people know where they stand; and

(4)   the potential legal costs, both of making and of challenging agreements.

Other jurisdictions

5.18   Throughout Europe, it is the norm for married couples to be able to change their matrimonial property regime[13] by agreement.[14] In a number of jurisdictions there is no question of the court being entitled to set aside such agreements for unfairness; in others, in particular the Nordic countries, the court has a wide discretion to set them aside. In all but the Nordic countries such agreements are notarised, which means that a notary advises both parties with respect to the interests of the family and the interests of each individual.

5.19   From the perspective of most European jurisdictions, therefore, our reluctance to allow parties to live with the consequences of the agreement they have made on the basis of legal advice is something of an English eccentricity. Moreover, as we pointed out in the CP, the arguments for private ordering for cohabitants are stronger than those for married couples and civil partners.[15]

5.20   In the CP we described the statutory requirements for making alternative arrangements in other jurisdictions which have introduced financial remedies between cohabitants on separation. In New Zealand, the formality requirements are heavy: the agreement must be in signed writing, the parties must have independent advice, and a lawyer must witness each party's signature.[16] The court has jurisdiction to set aside agreements only if they cause "serious

---

[11]   See CP, para 10.87, n 35.

[12]   *Charman v Charman* [2007] EWCA Civ 503, [2007] 2 FCR 217, at [122] to [124], at least in the context of a wider review of ancillary relief.

[13]   These are the rule-based systems operated throughout continental Europe to determine the ownership of property during marriage and on divorce (but not the incidence of maintenance obligations).

[14]   The Asser Institute Report for the European Commission on Matrimonial Property Regimes states that all member states of the European Union which have a matrimonial property regime allow this, except Slovakia: section 1, para 1.1.3 (p 26) and section 2, para 1.3.3 (p 85) and following; available at: http://www.asser.nl/ipr/documents/cms_ipr_6_1_Final%20Report%20EU%20Commission%20030703.pdf (last visited 3 July 2007). Different considerations may apply to post-divorce maintenance. See generally J Scherpe, "A Comparative View of Pre-Nuptial Agreements" [2007] *International Family Law* 18.

[15]   CP, paras 10.90 to 10.91.

[16]   Property (Relationships) Act 1976 (New Zealand), s 21F.

injustice", a requirement which is strictly interpreted.[17] In Sweden, by contrast, the requirement is simply for signed writing with, again, a jurisdiction to set aside.[18] In Australia there are different formality requirements in different states; those in New South Wales are almost as comprehensive as those in New Zealand, and the jurisdiction for setting aside is, as in New Zealand, quite limited.[19]

Correlation between qualifying criteria and jurisdiction to set aside

5.21 Formalities have an important protective function: the need to comply with formalities encourages people to be clear about what they are doing and to think before deciding, and a formally constituted agreement helps to avoid evidential disputes.[20] We discussed in the CP the range of possible requirements, from simple writing without more to the other extreme of requiring writing, witnessing, financial disclosure and independent legal advice.[21]

5.22 At the same time, entering into opt-out agreements may have a range of possible consequences. The agreement could be no more than a consideration for the court to take into account in the exercise of its discretion, or it could be binding on the parties, subject to challenge only under the general law of contract where there is fraud, duress, misrepresentation, mistake or undue influence.[22] A middle course would be for the agreement to be binding, subject to a discretion vested in the court to set it aside on specific statutory grounds.

5.23 A clear message that we take from the international comparisons we have referred to above is that there is a correlation between the formalities prescribed for opt-out agreements and the potential for such agreements to be set aside.[23] In general, the higher the level of formalities prescribed, the more restricted should be the court's ability to set the agreement aside.

5.24 Consultation responses reflected a particularly wide spectrum of opinion on the relationship between qualifying criteria and grounds for setting aside. Most of those who addressed the issue favoured the imposition of qualifying criteria, but opinions varied as to what they should be. Opinions also varied on the effect of agreements and the extent to which they should be subject to challenge. We remain of the view that it is important to retain a correlation between the strength of the qualifying criteria and the difficulty of setting agreements aside. It would be most unsatisfactory for parties to go to the trouble and expense of complying with onerous formal requirements only to find that their agreement could be relatively easily set aside by the court.

---

[17] Property (Relationships) Act 1976 (New Zealand), s 21J(1); *C v S* [2004] NZFLR 546; *Harrison v Harrison* [2005] NZFLR 252.

[18] Cohabitees Act 2003 (Sweden), s 9.

[19] Property (Relationships) Act 1984 (New South Wales), s 49(1).

[20] P Critchley, "Taking formalities seriously" in Bright and Dewar (eds) *Land Law, Themes and Perspectives* (1998) pp 507 to 528.

[21] CP, paras 10.55 to 10.79.

[22] It is important to note that it would not be possible to put agreements wholly beyond challenge as the general law of contract would require them to be unravelled on these grounds.

[23] CP, para 10.46.

5.25 Parties who had met whatever qualifying criteria were imposed should be entitled to have confidence that their agreement will be enforceable, subject to the general law of contract. As will be seen, it would not be possible to guarantee this in absolute terms.[24] But the grounds for setting aside agreements should be strictly limited. The mere fact that an agreement yielded a different result from that which the statute would provide should not be a ground for setting it aside. In general, it ought not to be possible to challenge agreements which have been fairly negotiated except where circumstances have arisen which were not foreseen by either party when the agreement was made.

5.26 In view of the range of possibilities,[25] we contemplated making available different levels of financial agreement. There is a precedent for a "two-tier" system in Australia, where all the states except Victoria have a system of "basic" agreements (which, if one party applies to court, will simply be a relevant factor for the exercise of the court's discretion) and "formal" agreements which are much more difficult to set aside.[26]

5.27 We think that certainty is valuable, and we were attracted to the idea of a formal ("cast-iron") agreement which could only be challenged under the general law of contract. But, having discussed this idea with practitioners, we have decided not to pursue it further.

5.28 We believe that it would only be acceptable for an agreement to have cast-iron status if it complied with an extremely high level of qualifying criteria, including independent legal advice for each party, together with full financial disclosure. The imposition of such requirements would be very expensive, possibly costing several thousand pounds for the couple. This would render the facility available only to the rich. Clearly some couples would take legal advice together before making and signing an opt-out agreement; some would take advice independently of each other. But we do not think that taking advice should be made a pre-condition for the validity of such agreements. There would be no way of ensuring that both parties received comparable legal advice, in terms of detail and of time spent with the adviser. In the circumstances, we do not think it is appropriate to make such a recommendation.

5.29 We therefore return to the question of how best to provide the protection of affordable formal requirements together with an acceptable degree of certainty about the effectiveness of agreements that comply with them.

Qualifying criteria

Formalities

5.30 A requirement of writing, signed by both parties, would seem a necessary level of protection, both cautionary and evidential. We therefore consider that the opt-out

---

[24] Not least because of the operation of the general law: see n 22.

[25] Para 5.22.

[26] For example, Property (Relationships) Act 1984 (New South Wales), Part 4; Domestic Relationships Act 1994 (Australian Capital Territory), Part 4; Relationships Act 2003 (Tasmania), Part 6; De Facto Relationships Act 1991 (Northern Territory), Part 3.

agreement should be written and signed.[27] By "writing" we mean a written paper document rather than any other form of writing such as email.[28] An exchange of letters would be sufficient for this purpose.

5.31 Given the protective function of formalities, we do not consider that an agreement that falls short of our qualifying criteria should be of any legal effect. We accept that this means that some genuine agreements between cohabitants which have not been committed to writing should remain unenforceable to the extent that they purport to disapply a new statutory scheme. But if we are to encourage a culture of private ordering, we must encourage a culture that embraces the formalities requirements that we are recommending.[29]

5.32 Nor do we consider that an agreement signed by only one party should be effective to disapply the statute, even if it is signed only by the party against whom it is raised in litigation. We want to encourage parties to engage in a process of discussion in which both participate, and an "agreement" that amounted only to a unilateral waiver of rights would not meet that objective.

Consideration

5.33 Opt-out agreements would, of course, be contracts. They would be subject to the normal requirements of agreement, intention to create legal relations, and so on. In particular, they would have to be supported by consideration. Normally this would not give rise to problems. Opt-out agreements would involve both parties giving up their rights under the statutory scheme, and would therefore involve an element of mutual promise which would readily constitute consideration. But for the avoidance of doubt, we think that there should be express statutory provision to cover the point.[30]

5.34 **We recommend that statute provide that opt-out agreements shall be taken to have been made for valuable consideration.**

Capacity

5.35 In the CP we provisionally proposed that parties should be able to enter into an opt-out agreement whether or not they were at the time cohabitants who were eligible to apply for financial relief under the new statutory scheme.[31] Almost all consultees who answered this question agreed with our provisional proposal.

5.36 We discussed in particular whether it should be possible for a minor to enter into an opt-out agreement.[32] We observed that as the law of contract stands, such agreements would be voidable at the instance of a party who was a minor when

---

[27] It would not be sufficient for an agreement to be *evidenced* in writing; this is too uncertain and would bring with it too much ancient case law.

[28] CP, para 10.57.

[29] Compare the degree of common knowledge about the necessary formalities for making a will.

[30] The New Zealand statute, the Property (Relationships) Act 1976, s 21K makes similar provision.

[31] CP, para 10.26.

[32] CP, paras 10.20 to 10.27.

the contract was made;[33] and that some jurisdictions have legislated specifically to ensure that such agreements could not be avoided for that reason.[34]

5.37 We invited views about this issue in the CP.[35] A handful of consultees commented, with a mixture of views. Resolution observed that some jurisdictions require the consent of a parent or guardian for an opt-out agreement made by a minor to be valid. However, we would prefer to rely on the law which already exists to protect minors from the consequences of entering into imprudent bargains.

Full financial disclosure?

5.38 We have considered whether parties to an opt-out agreement should be obliged to make full mutual disclosure of their financial affairs. We take the view that such a requirement would be neither necessary nor desirable. As we have explained, financial relief would be awarded under our recommended scheme in order to address the financial consequences of cohabitation, rather than to redistribute the parties' entire resources. The court would not, therefore, need to know the full extent of the parties' finances. That being the case, cohabitants should be entitled to keep their financial affairs private if they wish.[36]

Mandatory terms, model agreements and pro formas

5.39 We have considered whether opt-out agreements should be required to contain particular terms. We explained above that an opt-out agreement is one which disapplied the new statute and would have effect in the event of the parties' separation. We asked in the CP whether such an agreement must in terms disapply the statute (that is, with specific reference to the statute by its title). Of the handful of responses to this question, most thought it should. We accept that it must be clear on the face of the agreement that the parties are aware that they are disapplying a statutory regime and thereby giving up rights. However, we do not think it would be appropriate to insist that any particular form of words, such as a reference to the title of the statute, be used.

5.40 In the CP we invited the views of consultees on the use of model agreements.[37] Responses were very mixed, a majority favouring such agreements being made available. But concern was expressed that comprehensive "off the shelf" agreements containing a number of model clauses would be inappropriate. We

---

[33] Under the law of England and Wales, the only contracts which are binding on a minor are "contracts for necessaries", that is clothes, food, medicine and lodging, and contracts for apprenticeship, education and services. Subject to these exceptions, contracts with a minor are voidable at the minor's option, but can be enforced against any party who was not a minor at the time that the contract was made. See *Chitty on Contracts* (29th ed 2004) para 8-004.

[34] For example, Property (Relationships) Act 1976 (New Zealand), s 21I; court approval of such agreements is required if the child is under the age of 18 and is not, and has not been, married or in a civil union.

[35] CP, para 10.27.

[36] The so-called "millionaires' defence" could therefore apply: *Thyssen-Bornesmisza* [1985] 2 FLR 670; see, generally, S Cretney, J Masson and R Bailey-Harris, *Principles of Family Law* (7th ed 2003) para 14-047.

[37] CP, para 10.84.

think that this concern is important, and that the adoption of model clauses could lead to arguments that such agreements should be set aside (on the basis that they might not have been properly considered or fully understood).

5.41 However, we think that it would be useful for parties to have the opportunity to use pro forma agreements which did not make any suggestions of alternative financial arrangements. The forms would contain wording to make clear that the parties knew that they were disapplying the statute. Such forms could provide guidance about the scheme of financial relief and about the effect of opting out, suggest those matters the parties might wish to consider in deciding whether to enter into such an agreement, and explain the qualifying criteria. The use of such forms would enable parties (and their legal advisers) to be sure that they had made an effective agreement. We see the use of such a form as worthwhile, in that it might save the parties legal costs and assist couples to create binding opt-out agreements.[38]

5.42 We have also considered whether agreements should be required by law to include "sunset clauses" to the effect that the agreement would automatically cease to have effect after a certain period of time. But other jurisdictions do not seem to use this mechanism, and they are not imposed upon wills, powers of attorney or any comparable instrument. As consultees did not support the imposition of sunset clauses, we do not consider that there should be any such legal requirement.

The scope of the qualifying criteria

5.43 We said in paragraph 5.12 that an opt-out agreement might simply disapply the statute, or might also make positive provision for financial arrangements. We anticipate that in many cases one document would both disapply the statute and also make positive provision. Equally, the parties might have other arrangements on foot. They might have already made express declarations of trust in relation to land or personalty, which they would intend to take effect on their separation in place of the statutory scheme. They might make such arrangements later in the knowledge that they had opted out of the statutory scheme. So the arrangements made by a couple to take effect on their separation might be found in a range of agreements and documents.

5.44 Should the qualifying criteria set out in paragraphs 5.30 and 5.39 apply to all of the couple's contractual arrangements, or only to the one agreement that disapplies the statute?

5.45 In a number of Australian jurisdictions the equivalent qualifying criteria apply across the board to the whole provision made by the couple.[39] The purpose of such a requirement is to ensure that the couple know what they are doing and have clear evidence of what they have done.[40]

---

[38] Such a form might also include space in which parties could make their own financial arrangements, having opted out of the scheme.

[39] See, for example, Property (Relationships) Act 1984 (New South Wales), Part 4.

[40] See para 5.21.

5.46 However, we do not think that this requirement should be imposed. The Australian statutes require the parties to obtain legal advice; but we are recommending that it be possible to opt out of our recommended scheme without incurring that expense. As a result, the parties could execute a valid opt-out agreement, but might fail to re-execute existing contractual arrangements or express declarations of trust. In that event, the parties would have opted out of the statutory scheme but their other arrangements would be rendered invalid and could not take effect upon their separation. Moreover, having once executed a valid opt-out agreement, we think that if the parties subsequently executed a declaration of trust of property or made another contractual arrangement they should not have to re-state their intention to disapply the statutory scheme.

5.47 Accordingly we take the view that the opt-out agreement, disapplying the statutory scheme, should comply with our qualifying criteria. But other financial arrangements made by the parties need not do so.[41]

Effect of an opt-out agreement

5.48 We are not offering cast-iron certainty, for the reasons discussed above. Equally, we do not think that it would be satisfactory for the existence of an opt-out agreement, in signed writing, to be simply one of the factors for the court to bear in mind when exercising its discretion.[42] It would be highly undesirable to place the parties in a position whereby their agreement was neither enforceable nor irrelevant.[43] Moreover, the existence of such an agreement would not sit comfortably alongside the other factors pertinent to the court's discretion to grant relief.[44] The other factors would be there to modify the effect of an award under the scheme, whereas the agreement would be relevant to a different question, namely whether or not the statutory scheme should apply at all.

5.49 An alternative is to make an opt-out agreement binding, subject to carefully defined grounds on which the court may set it aside. Potential advantages to making these agreements binding include:

(1) reducing litigation by discouraging challenge; and

(2) putting the onus on the party seeking to challenge the agreement, rather than requiring the other party both to defend the substance of the claim under the scheme and to argue that the agreement should be upheld. If the challenge to the agreement were unsuccessful, there would be no need to invoke the statutory scheme.

5.50 Accordingly, we take the view that where cohabitants had made an opt-out agreement that met the criteria that we recommend for validity, it should be enforceable, subject only to challenge on tightly defined grounds. We discuss what these grounds should be next.

---

[41] The normal rules of validity and formality applicable, as the case may be, to contracts, property and trusts would still apply to such arrangements.

[42] Para 5.22.

[43] See the comment in *Pounds v Pounds* [1994] 1 WLR 1535, 1550, Hoffman LJ (as he then was).

[44] Para 4.38, and 4.79 and following.

The grounds for setting opt-out agreements aside

5.51 We take the view that agreements should not lightly be set aside. Accordingly, we consider that agreements should only be set aside if their enforcement would give rise to manifest unfairness. Manifest unfairness would not be a free-standing criterion but could only be established in the light of certain circumstances, which we discuss below. Equally, the occurrence of those circumstances would not amount to grounds for setting the agreement aside unless it could also be shown that the agreement was manifestly unfair as a result.

5.52 Manifest unfairness might be established having regard to the circumstances at the time the agreement was made. It might be that, although both parties signed the agreement, it could be shown that one of them did not understand its effect. In consequence, those couples who take legal advice would be more likely to have their agreement upheld by the court, as are those who had participated in full mutual disclosure of their financial affairs. It would therefore be in the interests of each party to see that the other had proper information and, where it could be afforded, legal advice.

5.53 Manifest unfairness might also be established where there are circumstances at the time that the agreement is being enforced that were not foreseen at the time that the opt-out agreement was made or in the course of the making of their other contractual arrangements and which, if foreseen, would have had a material effect upon the parties' arrangements. For instance, the birth of a child might be such a circumstance if it appeared that the parties did not contemplate it in making arrangements for what would happen in the event of separation, and if their arrangements are inadequate as a result of the birth. So would unforeseen events such as the bankruptcy of one of the parties, or a large inheritance, a significant change of career or the onset of disability. However, the passage of time would not in itself be sufficient; nor would the mere fact that the agreement yields results different from those that would be generated by the scheme.

5.54 In some cases the parties to an opt-out agreement will get married to each other or become civil partners. We do not think it necessary for the scheme to make specific provision for the agreement to cease to be binding in that event. If the parties subsequently divorced, or dissolved their civil partnership, and one party wanted to raise the agreement, the court might decide to have regard to it as a pre-nuptial agreement.[45]

5.55 We noted in the CP the need to give further thought to the effect of opt-out agreements relating to some but not all of the couple's assets.[46] We take the view now that the effect of such agreements would be a matter of interpretation. An agreement that stated that a particular asset – say, a grand piano – was to belong to one party if the couple were to separate, and made no other provision,

---

[45] See para 5.16.

[46] CP, para 10.43. We have in mind a situation where one party wanted to protect a specific asset, for example an heirloom, or perhaps wanted to make sure that a gift to the other party could not later be reversed.

would mean that the piano could not be regarded as a retained benefit, whatever its origins, and therefore that the scheme should operate without reference to it.[47]

5.56 **We recommend that an agreement which is in writing, is signed by the parties, and makes clear the parties' intention to disapply the statute, should be enforceable as an opt-out agreement in place of our recommended scheme.**

5.57 **We recommend that agreements that purport to disapply the statute but do not comply with these qualifying criteria should be of no effect when the statutory scheme is invoked.**

5.58 **We recommend that pro forma agreements be made available for the use of cohabitants who wish to make opt-out agreements.**

5.59 **We recommend that parties should be able to enter into an opt-out agreement whether or not they are eligible cohabitants at the time that the agreement is made.**

5.60 **We recommend that minors should be capable of entering into opt-out agreements, but that such contracts should be voidable (in accordance with the general principles of contract law) at the instance of a party who was a minor at the time that the agreement was made.**

5.61 **We recommend that a court should be entitled to set aside an opt-out agreement if its enforcement would cause manifest unfairness having regard to:**

(1) **the circumstances at the time the agreement was made; or**

(2) **circumstances at the time the agreement comes to be enforced which were unforeseen when the agreement was made.**

Express declarations of trust and other financial arrangements

5.62 In the CP we asked whether an express declaration of trust in relation to land or other property should be regarded either as an opt-out from the scheme as a whole, or as an opt-out as regards that particular asset. Discussion of this issue concentrated on trusts of land, but declarations as to the ownership of other assets, such as shares, bank accounts or business assets (for example in a partnership deed) may also be relevant.

5.63 An express declaration of ownership is a form of self-regulation. As such, it should be encouraged, and under the current law it is encouraged, by the courts' firm insistence that a declaration of an express trust of land is conclusive in the face of any claim to the benefit of an implied trust.[48] However, there are

---

[47] Whether that attribution of ownership might be regarded as sharing, in whole or in part, economic disadvantage would depend upon the circumstances and the terms of the agreement; as would the question whether it would be taken into account for the purpose of assessing the economic equality ceiling: see para 4.72 and following.

[48] *Goodman v Gallant* [1986] Fam 106; *Stack v Dowden* [2007] UKHL 17, [2007] 2 WLR 831, at [49]. As one consultee pointed out, express declarations can be considered to be an opt-out agreement from the law of implied trusts.

difficulties, which we expressed in the CP, in treating all such declarations of trust as opt-out agreements. They might not have been made with separation in mind. Parties often elect to become beneficial joint tenants so that when one dies the other becomes sole beneficial owner by virtue of survivorship.[49] They might not necessarily appreciate, at least without legal advice, that in the event of separation they would be treated as each having one half of the beneficial interest irrespective of their financial contributions to the acquisition of the property.[50]

5.64   In the CP we had not, of course, formulated policy on the questions that we raised about the nature and content of opt-out agreements. However, we have now concluded that opt-out agreements must make it clear that the parties intend to disapply, and to give up their rights under, the new legislative scheme. It must follow from this that an express declaration of the ownership of any asset should not, without more, be treated as an opt-out agreement.[51] For the reasons explained in the previous paragraph, we believe that it is, if anything, even more important that this be the position where trusts of land are concerned. We do not think that there is any need to make any separate recommendation about this. Although we do not consider that an express declaration of trust should be regarded as an opt-out agreement, it would be prudent for couples when they buy a house together to consider whether they should make such an agreement. Indeed, those advising them on the purchase should alert them to the advantages of taking such a course of action.[52]

Certain religious marriages

5.65   We have had discussions with the Association of Muslim Lawyers, who highlighted the potential benefits of any new scheme for those who have contracted a religious marriage, but whose marriage is not recognised by the law of England and Wales.[53]

5.66   In order for there to be a valid marriage for the purposes of Shari'a law, one of the essential requirements is that the marriage contract (Nikah) must make provision for a payment of money (the Mahr). The contract will stipulate that this is to be paid at the time of the marriage, in the event of divorce or at some other time, for example, when a child is born.

---

[49] See para A.81.

[50] See G Douglas, J Pearce, H Woodward, *A Failure of Trust: Resolving Property Disputes on Cohabitation Breakdown* (2007), available at http://www.law.cf.ac.uk/researchpapers/papers/1.pdf or http://www.bris.ac.uk/law/research/centres-themes/cohabit/cohabit-rep.pdf (last visited 3 July 2007); see also "Dealing with Property Issues on Cohabitation Breakdown" (2007) 37 *Family Law* 36, discussed from para 2.18. Compare *Stack v Dowden* [2007] UKHL 17, [2007] 2 WLR 831, at [62], Baroness Hale.

[51] And therefore the declarations provided for in Land Registry forms of transfer, TR1 and FR1 (see para 2.18), cannot of themselves amount to opt-out agreements.

[52] See generally para 2.17 and following. Parties might wish to execute a partial opt-out agreement to exclude any retained benefit argument being made in relation to their shares of the beneficial interest.

[53] Even as a void marriage: see paras 2.101 and 3.6.

5.67 A Nikah contract written and signed by the parties,[54] which contemplated and provided for the eventuality of separation (in particular by providing for the Mahr to be paid on divorce), would go some way to satisfying the requirements for an opt-out agreement. However, it would not constitute an opt-out agreement, preventing an application for financial relief under our scheme, unless it indicated an intention to disapply the statute.[55]

5.68 If and in so far as the Nikah did meet this requirement, making it clear that the parties were giving up their rights under the scheme, it would amount to an opt-out agreement. As such, it would be enforceable but, like any other opt-out agreement, it would be open to either party to claim that to enforce the contract would cause manifest unfairness having regard to the circumstances at the time the agreement was made, or at the time the agreement was being enforced.

The effect of implementation on existing cohabitants

5.69 In Part 3 of this Report we recommended that the scheme should apply to couples who are cohabiting at the date when new legislation comes into force.

5.70 We anticipate that some such couples would be opposed to the application of the scheme to their relationship. Some would prefer to make their own arrangements, and they should be encouraged to do so. It would of course be open to such couples to make an opt-out agreement; and it is important that the publicity given to the new scheme before it comes into force should give them ample notice of the need to do so.

5.71 We note that when legislation came into force in New Zealand, a year's "lead-in" time was provided during which couples currently living together could make a valid opt-out agreement before the scheme itself came into force.[56] There is merit in such an arrangement, because it gives space to reflect. However, we take the view that agreements entered into before the enactment of legislation should not be capable of being valid opt-out agreements because parties should be able to take this step only in full knowledge of the terms of the legislation.

5.72 **We recommend that there should be a period between the legislation being enacted and implementation of the scheme for financial relief during which cohabitants should be able to make an opt-out agreement.**

Opting in by agreement?

5.73 In the CP we invited views on whether cohabitants who would otherwise not be eligible to apply under the scheme (because they had no children and did not satisfy any minimum duration requirement) should nevertheless be allowed to opt into the scheme by agreement. Such an agreement would amount to a cohabitation contract.

---

[54] We have been told by the Association of Muslim Lawyers that such agreements may be entered into by proxy; signature of the Nikah by proxy would not satisfy the formalities requirements recommended here.

[55] See para 5.39.

[56] See CP, para 11.95.

5.74 The views of the consultees who answered this question were evenly split. On balance, we do not consider that it should be open to couples who are not eligible cohabitants to bring themselves within the statutory scheme. In our view, to allow parties to opt in would provide a further unnecessary layer of complexity. Those who were not eligible would be able to make and enforce cohabitation contracts,[57] which would no longer be capable of being challenged as being contrary to public policy.[58]

---

[57] Pursuant to our recommendation at para 5.8.

[58] They would also be able to use other arrangements, for example declarations of trust.

PART 6
SUCCESSION ON DEATH: INTESTACY AND FAMILY PROVISION

INTRODUCTION

6.1 Anyone may leave a will disposing of all or part of his or her estate on death. Where there is no will, the intestacy rules govern the distribution of the estate.[1] The intestacy rules apply automatically, and those who take under the rules are not required to apply to court. The rules are commonly understood to dispose of the estate as it is imagined most individuals would wish to do.[2] Those rules also apply to dispose of the residue where a will does not effectively dispose of the entire estate. However, the disposition of the deceased's estate (whether by will or by the intestacy rules, or by the combined operation of a will and those rules) may be challenged by certain classes of applicant who claim that they have not obtained reasonable financial provision from the deceased's estate and that the court should therefore make an award in their favour. This jurisdiction, contained in the Inheritance (Provision for Family and Dependants) Act 1975 (hereafter "the 1975 Act"), is principally based on meeting the applicant's needs.

6.2 Under the current law, a surviving cohabitant of the deceased is not included among those who will inherit on intestacy, but may apply for provision under the 1975 Act, provided that he or she had been cohabiting with the deceased for the last two years of the deceased's life.[3] We considered the case for reforming the intestacy rules in the CP,[4] and provisionally rejected any inclusion of surviving cohabitants within them. We reviewed the operation of the 1975 Act in relation to cohabitants, and made a number of provisional proposals for its amendment, consequential upon implementation by Parliament of the scheme that we were then provisionally proposing for financial relief on separation.

6.3 In this Part, we first revisit the intestacy rules in light of our consultation exercise, and we conclude that the position of cohabitants on intestacy should not be reformed. We then consider the potential impact of our recommended scheme for financial relief on separation on claims by cohabitants for family provision on death under the 1975 Act, and we make a number of recommendations for its consequential reform. Finally, we discuss, but make no recommendations concerning, certain issues relating to the operation of wills of cohabitants.

6.4 All recommendations for reform of the 1975 Act in this Part are contingent upon the implementation of our recommended scheme of financial relief between cohabitants on separation.

---

[1] Administration of Estates Act 1925; Intestate Estates Act 1952.

[2] C H Sherrin and R C Bonehill, *The Law and Practice of Intestate Succession* (2004) para 1-024. See also Family Law: Distribution on Intestacy (1989) Law Com No 187, para 24.

[3] Inheritance (Provision for Family and Dependants) Act 1975 Act, s 1(1)(ba).

[4] CP, para 8.5 to 8.16.

INTESTACY

6.5 A cohabitant currently has no entitlement to any share of his or her partner's estate on intestacy.[5] There is little doubt that there would be wide public support for the introduction of some intestacy provision for cohabitants. When in the late 1980s the Commission conducted a public opinion survey in the course of a project on intestacy, a majority of respondents were of that view,[6] and the same view has been expressed in more recent surveys.[7] Moreover, recent research has indicated that many people assume that cohabitants inherit as a matter of course on their partner's death.[8] They may therefore fail to make a will providing for them.[9] In so far as the intestacy rules are intended to dispose of the estate in the manner in which, it may reasonably be assumed, the deceased would have wished,[10] they may therefore be said to be inadequate.

6.6 However, as the Commission concluded in its 1989 Intestacy Report[11] and as we explained in the CP,[12] attempting to include cohabitants within the intestacy rules is very difficult. We therefore provisionally rejected reform of the intestacy rules.[13]

6.7 Most consultees who addressed this issue supported our view. The Society of Trust and Estate Practitioners ("STEP") observed that:

> Although we acknowledge that intestacy is intended to reflect an average sort of will someone setting out to make a Will (a testator) would have made, and a reasonable testator might be assumed to be likely to make provision for a co-habitant, we still regard the imposition of automatic rights as too complex.

6.8 The Law Society agreed:

> There are such a variety of possible cohabiting relationships that we do not think it would be equitable to try to impose a standard level of provision on very different types of relationship by using the statutory

---

[5] See para A.85 and following.

[6] Distribution on Intestacy (1989) Law Com No 187, para 58, n 92.

[7] For example, A Barlow, S Duncan, G James and A Park, "Just a piece of paper? Marriage and cohabitation", in A Park, J Curtice, K Thompson, L Jarvis and C Bromley (eds), *British Social Attitudes: Public policy, social ties. The 18th Report* (2001); C Williams, G Potter and G Douglas, Views of members of the public on the intestacy rules relating to cohabitation: a survey conducted by students at Sheffield and Cardiff Universities (2007, unpublished).

[8] For example, A Barlow, S Duncan, G James and A Park, "Just a piece of paper? Marriage and cohabitation", in A Park, J Curtice, K Thompson, L Jarvis and C Bromley (eds), *British Social Attitudes: Public policy, social ties. The 18th Report* (2001).

[9] See low will-making rates amongst cohabitants surveyed in the British Social Attitudes Survey 2001: A Barlow, S Duncan, G James and A Park, "Just a piece of paper? Marriage and cohabitation", in A Park, J Curtice, K Thompson, L Jarvis and C Bromley (eds), *British Social Attitudes: Public policy, social ties. The 18th Report* (2001): only 10% of past and present cohabitants had made a will in light of their cohabitation: p 45.

[10] See n 2.

[11] Distribution on Intestacy (1989) Law Com No 187.

[12] CP, para 8.15.

[13] CP, paras 8.8 to 8.17.

rules. We prefer the flexibility that a system based on the Inheritance (Provision for Family and Dependants) Act 1975 would give.

6.9 We agree that the range of relationships encompassed by cohabitation is too diverse to be appropriately accommodated within the intestacy rules. Moreover, any change in favour of cohabitants would require an appreciation of the overall effect on the intestacy rules as they affect other members of the deceased's family. We consider that any such assessment should be made in the context of a comprehensive review of intestacy.

6.10 We believe that, for the time being at least, the better way of responding to the clear public desire for making provision for cohabitants on death is by means of the 1975 Act. In the meantime, we strongly support continued efforts to educate the public both about the lack of automatic protection for surviving cohabitants on their partner's intestacy, and about the importance of making, and regularly reviewing, a will.

CONSEQUENTIAL REFORM OF THE INHERITANCE (PROVISION FOR FAMILY AND DEPENDANTS) ACT 1975

6.11 Our principal focus is therefore on the 1975 Act. The 1975 Act allows various classes of applicant[14] to apply to the court for an order on the basis that the disposition of a deceased's estate (whether by will, or by the intestacy rules, or by a combination of the two) has failed to give them "reasonable financial provision".

6.12 Most consultees who addressed this issue supported our provisional proposal that the 1975 Act should be amended to achieve a suitable level of correlation between claims brought by cohabitants on separation and claims brought by cohabitants on death.[15]

6.13 It is important, however, not to equate separation and death. Many consultees felt, and we agree, that there is a qualitative difference between a relationship cut short by death and a relationship terminated by separation. On separation, there has ordinarily been a failure of commitment by at least one of the parties. It is, therefore, legitimate when considering the eligibility of separating couples under our recommended scheme to ask whether the length of the relationship indicated that there was, at least at one time, sufficient commitment between the parties to justify bringing the relationship within the scheme. Where a relationship is terminated by death, however, the ending of the relationship does not of itself suggest that there was any lack of commitment on either side. This qualitative difference may well affect what should be regarded as reasonable financial provision on death and who should be eligible to make a claim under the 1975 Act.

---

[14] The classes include: the deceased's spouse or civil partner, former spouses or civil partners (who have not remarried or entered into a subsequent civil partnership), an individual who cohabits with the deceased for the two years immediately prior to his or her death, children of the deceased, children of the family (on which see 06.50 and following) and dependants. There is no requirement for any applicant (save a dependant) to prove that he or she was, at any time, dependent upon the deceased.

[15] CP, para 8.49.

Eligibility to bring a claim on death

6.14 Cohabitants are currently recognised as a distinct class of applicant under the 1975 Act. The Act enables them to bring a claim for financial provision if they were cohabiting with their deceased partner for at least two years immediately before the death. This is so whether or not the couple had children together.[16] An applicant who does not qualify as a "cohabitant" within the statutory definition may nevertheless be able to claim as a "dependant" of the deceased.[17]

The concept of "cohabitant"

6.15 We have recommended that eligibility to apply for financial relief on separation should be based on the parties living as a couple in a joint household, rather than adopting the marriage or civil partnership analogy which currently defines eligibility for cohabitants to apply for provision under the 1975 Act.[18] We recommend here that the 1975 Act should be amended to adopt whatever wording were used for a new scheme of financial relief on separation. It is important to emphasise that we do not intend thereby to alter the range of persons who would be eligible to apply under the 1975 Act and we would not therefore wish to encourage sterile litigation on this point. As we discussed in Part 3,[19] our concerns are that the language used in the statute book should be both consistent and clearly understood by the public, without perpetuating the myth of common law marriage.

6.16 **We recommend that the Inheritance (Provision for Family and Dependants) Act 1975 ("the 1975 Act") be amended so as to provide the same definition of "cohabitant" as that used to define eligibility to apply under the statutory scheme for financial relief on separation.**

Further eligibility requirements: children and duration

6.17 We invited consultees to indicate what amendment, if any, should be made to the existing two-year minimum duration requirement for cohabitants' claims under the 1975 Act.[20] We also asked, in general terms, whether any minimum duration requirement restricting eligibility to bring claims for financial relief on separation should be replicated for claims for family provision on death.[21]

6.18 Of the handful who answered the latter question, most favoured adopting the same minimum duration requirement for separation and death.[22] Those who

---

[16] Inheritance (Provision for Family and Dependants) Act 1975, s 1(1)(ba), inserted by Law Reform (Succession) Act 1995.

[17] Inheritance (Provision for Family and Dependants) Act 1975, s 1(1)(e).

[18] See para 3.13.

[19] See paras 3.9 and 3.12.

[20] CP, para 9.115.

[21] CP, para 9.114(4).

[22] A further five consultees, in answering the question at CP, para 9.115, stated that eligibility should be the same for both types of claim, whether or not that included a minimum duration requirement.

disagreed[23] did so because of what they perceived to be the qualitative difference between a relationship cut short by death rather than by the choice of one party.

6.19 The former question, answered by a larger number of consultees, elicited various opinions. Many consultees differentiated between cases of cohabitants with children and other cases. However, several consultees (a minority) argued that a shorter requirement, or no minimum duration requirement at all, should apply to all claims, not just by those with children. These consultees were guided again by the perceived qualitative difference between death and separation cases, the Society of Trust and Estate Practitioners remarking that the two-year requirement can operate unfairly and arbitrarily. Conversely, a small number of consultees argued for a minimum duration requirement in all cases, whether the relationship ended by separation or by death and whether or not the cohabitants had children together. There was some disagreement about whether the facts pertinent to claims might be easier or harder to establish in the case of death, and so whether a minimum duration requirement for all cases might remain desirable to provide stronger evidence of an eligible relationship.[24]

COHABITANTS WHO HAVE CHILDREN TOGETHER

6.20 Most consultees who dealt with this issue favoured relaxing the current two-year requirement, particularly in cases involving cohabitants with a child. The effect of the majority view would be that, where the cohabiting couple had children together, the eligibility requirements for claiming family provision would be relaxed so that surviving cohabitants would be eligible to claim under the 1975 Act on their partner's death whatever the length of the relationship. We support this approach. It would be unsatisfactory for a cohabitant to be worse off, in terms of financial remedies, in the event of the relationship ending by death rather than by separation. Where the cohabitants had had children together, the survivor should be entitled to apply for family provision on death without having to satisfy any minimum duration requirement.

COHABITANTS WHO DO NOT HAVE CHILDREN TOGETHER

6.21 Similarly, we consider that where the parties do not have children together[25] the eligibility criteria to claim for family provision on death should be no more difficult to satisfy than those applicable to such couples on separation.

6.22 We have recommended that cohabitants who do not have children together should satisfy a minimum duration requirement in order to apply for financial relief

---

[23] The Chancery Bar Association and the Institute of Legal Executives.

[24] Dr Stephen Cretney suggested that the financial facts would be clearer in death cases and so a minimum duration requirement might not be needed. Lloyd LJ suggested that where one party has died, it might be rather harder for third parties to dispute a claim brought by someone claiming to be a cohabitant where there is no minimum duration requirement. Two other consultees advocated adopting, in at least some respects, a more restrictive test than that currently used, to correspond with the tests being proposed by them for cases arising on separation: one would raise the threshold to three years; the other would have no minimum duration requirement for cases with children, but all other cases would be eligible only on an opt-in basis.

[25] Following the recommendations in Part 3, this includes both cohabitants without children and those who have children living in their household who are not, as a matter of law, the children of both of them.

on separation. We have indicated that this should be no less than two years and no more than five years.[26] If Parliament decided that two years was an appropriate minimum duration requirement to impose on cohabitants who do not have children together for the purposes of a claim for financial relief on separation, there would be no need to change the current two-year minimum duration requirement applicable on death.

6.23 However, as we noted above, a minority of consultees argued that the eligibility requirements for claims for family provision by cohabitants who have not had children together should be easier to satisfy. They suggested that the minimum duration requirement should be either reduced or completely removed for all cohabitants in respect of 1975 Act claims.

6.24 We do not think that the case for reducing or removing the two years' minimum duration requirement for cohabitants who do not have children together to claim family provision has been made out. Where the applicant was dependent on the deceased, a claim may already be brought.[27] Otherwise, in the absence of children or of provision by the deceased for the surviving cohabitant in his or her will, we do not consider that the mere fact of cohabitation for less than two years is enough to justify allowing a claim for financial provision to be brought.[28] Parliament might decide that cohabitants who do not have children together should only be eligible to claim financial relief on separation if they satisfy a minimum duration requirement in excess of two years. If that were to happen, we do not think that it should follow that the minimum duration requirement for such cohabitants claiming family provision on death should be increased, so that the two requirements would be the same. On the contrary, we believe that it would be particularly important in such circumstances to maintain a distinction. To do so would reflect the qualitative difference between relationships ended by death and relationships ended by separation, and would have the additional benefit that it would not remove claims which can currently be made from the scope of the 1975 Act.

NO DISCRETION TO DISPENSE WITH THE REQUIREMENTS

6.25 Consistent with our approach to eligibility on separation, we consider that the court should have no discretion to dispense with these requirements. If, contrary to our recommendation, Parliament were to decide upon a minimum duration requirement longer than two years for any claim by a cohabitant under the 1975 Act, serious consideration should be given to providing a limited discretion to dispense with that minimum duration requirement. It is important to note, however, that those who could not satisfy the eligibility criteria for "cohabitants" would still be able to contend that they were maintained by the deceased immediately before the deceased's death, and that they may therefore claim family provision as a "dependant" of the deceased.[29]

---

[26] Para 3.63.

[27] Inheritance (Provision for Family and Dependants) Act 1975, s 1(1)(e).

[28] See general discussion of the function of a minimum duration requirement at para 3.33.

[29] See n 27.

6.26 **We recommend that a person ("the applicant") should be entitled to apply for provision under the 1975 Act as a cohabitant where the applicant was living in the same household as the deceased immediately before the deceased's death and:**

(1) **either:**

(a) **the applicant and the deceased had so lived for a period of two years immediately before the deceased's death,**

or

(b) **the applicant and the deceased had a child together; and**

(2) **that the court should not have discretion to dispense with these requirements.**

Cohabitants who separate shortly before death

6.27 There are certain circumstances, which we outlined in the CP,[30] where rigid insistence on a requirement that the cohabitants were living together immediately before the deceased's death might operate inequitably. These occur where the parties had separated,[31] but one party died before a claim for financial relief was made or determined.

6.28 We do not think that it should be possible for a surviving former partner to make or continue a claim for financial relief under our recommended scheme of financial relief on separation against the deceased's estate.[32] We do, however, think that it should be possible for the surviving former partner to make a claim for family provision against the deceased's estate under the 1975 Act in tightly prescribed circumstances.[33]

6.29 This approach was endorsed by most of the consultees who addressed this question. Those who did not agree were opposed in principle to any reform of the 1975 Act and did not make any criticism of the technical aspects of our proposal.

6.30 It is important to emphasise the strictly limited circumstances in which we consider that a person who was no longer cohabiting with the deceased immediately before his or her death should be able to apply for financial provision. It would have to be established that, immediately before the death, the applicant was entitled to make a claim for financial relief in the event of the parties' separation. This would entail findings that:

---

[30] CP, paras 8.41 to 8.44.

[31] Compare circumstances such as those in *Gully v Dix* [2004] EWCA Civ 139, [2004] 1 WLR 1399 where the relationship was found to be continuing at the point of death.

[32] Nor do we consider that it should be possible for a claim for financial relief on separation to be commenced, or continued, by an estate of a deceased cohabitant. This corresponds with the treatment of outstanding claims for ancillary relief following dissolution of a marriage or civil partnership. See CP, para 8.42.

[33] Of course, it would remain open to all applicants following the death of their partner to bring a claim under the general law of property and trusts to establish that an asset apparently falling within the estate was in fact owned beneficially by the applicant.

(1)   the applicant would have been eligible to apply for financial relief, the parties having had a child together or having satisfied the minimum duration requirement;

(2)   there was no opt-out agreement, or any such agreement should be set aside on the usual grounds; and

(3)   at the date of death, either the limitation period to bring a claim on separation was still running, or the court would have exercised its discretion to extend time.

Therefore, if the applicant would not have been eligible to claim financial relief, or if there was a binding opt-out agreement, or if such an application would have been out of time, the survivor would not be able to make a claim for family provision under the 1975 Act.

6.31   **We recommend that a person ("the applicant") who was no longer cohabiting with the deceased immediately before his or her death should nevertheless be entitled to apply for provision as a cohabitant under the 1975 Act:**

(1)   **if at that date the applicant had made a valid application for financial relief on separation which had not yet been determined; or**

(2)   **although no such application had been made, the applicant was still entitled to make one (if necessary, subject to the court granting permission to extend time for such an application to be made or setting aside an opt-out agreement).**

Basis for financial provision on death

6.32   Where a cohabitant currently applies to the court for an order under the 1975 Act, the court has first to decide whether the disposition of the deceased's estate (by will or under the intestacy rules or by a combination of both) is not such as to make reasonable financial provision for the applicant.[34] In the case of an application by a cohabitant, "reasonable financial provision" means "such financial provision as it would be reasonable in all the circumstances of the case for the applicant to receive for his maintenance".[35] If the court is satisfied that reasonable financial provision has not been made, it may make one of a number of orders against the deceased's estate,[36] having regard to a list of matters set

---

[34] Inheritance (Provision for Family and Dependants) Act 1975, s 1(1).

[35] Inheritance (Provision for Family and Dependants) Act 1975, s 1(2)(b).

[36] Inheritance (Provision for Family and Dependants) Act 1975, s 2.

out in the statute.[37] This test of reasonable financial provision has the effect that awards to cohabitants under the 1975 Act are limited to meeting the applicant's needs.

6.33 Our recommended scheme for financial relief on separation is not principally based on meeting the parties' needs, but engages a different, and potentially wider, range of criteria. If we are to achieve an acceptable degree of consistency between cohabitants' claims for financial relief on separation and for family provision on death, the question arises whether it would be necessary to modify the current 1975 Act test of reasonable financial provision.

General criteria

6.34 In the CP we provisionally proposed the introduction of a "separation analogy" with regard to cohabitants' claims for family provision.[38] This would be to the effect that, in determining such claims, the court should have regard to the provision that the applicant might reasonably have expected to receive in proceedings for financial relief on separation.

6.35 Most consultees who addressed the issue supported the proposition that provision on death should correspond with that on separation. Several consultees were anxious to emphasise, as we had done,[39] that the likely award on separation should be a floor, not a ceiling to provision on death. Some proposed that since, unlike on separation, there is only one partner with future needs, there would be scope for a more generous needs-based award. While this is of course true, it may be that there are other beneficiaries of the estate, as well as other applicants for family provision, whose needs[40] may have to be taken into account.

6.36 It seems to us, having considered our consultation responses and again invoking the qualitative difference between the termination of a cohabiting relationship by separation and by death, that the grant of relief in accordance with needs remains desirable in the 1975 Act context. Although we consider that the principles of our recommended scheme would in many cases help address the applicant's needs, these principles would not directly meet needs that had not been generated by contributions to the relationship. We therefore see merit in requiring the court to continue to have regard to the factors currently listed in the 1975 Act in deciding whether to make an award and if so what it should be.

---

[37] Inheritance (Provision for Family and Dependants) Act 1975, s 3. In all cases, the court must have regard to the financial resources and financial needs of any applicant for an order or of any beneficiary of the estate; any obligations and responsibilities of the deceased towards any applicants or beneficiaries; the size and nature of the deceased's net estate; any physical or mental disability of any applicant or beneficiary; and any other matter including the conduct of the applicant or any other person, which the court may consider relevant. In cohabitants' applications, the court must in addition have regard to the age of the applicant; the duration of the cohabitation; and any contribution made by the applicant to the welfare of the deceased's family, including any contribution made by looking after the home or caring for the family.

[38] CP, para 8.50(3).

[39] CP, para 8.32 and following.

[40] Indeed, in the case of a claim by a surviving spouse or civil partner the court is not restricted to meeting that applicant's needs in view of the more generous definition of reasonable financial provision which applies to such applicants: Inheritance (Provision for Family and Dependants) Act 1975, ss 1(2)(a) and 3(2).

6.37   At the same time, we believe that the court should be required to have regard to the award the applicant might reasonably have expected to receive in proceedings for financial relief on separation.[41]

6.38   We do not think that it would be possible to achieve these twin objectives if the current 1975 Act test of financial provision that is reasonable for the applicant's maintenance were retained. This would result in an undesirable conflict between that test and the factors to which the court should have regard in making an award. Our view is that the current limitation of financial provision to what is reasonable for the applicant's maintenance should be removed. The court should instead be expected to consider what is reasonable in all the circumstances of the case, having regard to the matters which are listed in the statute[42] and to the separation analogy.

Additional criteria for cohabitants who separate shortly before death

6.39   As we have explained above, we consider it is necessary to accommodate claims for family provision by those who cohabited with the deceased but whose relationship ended by separation shortly before the death. We have recommended, in paragraph 6.31, the circumstances in which such persons should be entitled to claim.

6.40   There is, of course, one important respect in which these claims differ from those by cohabitants who were still living with the deceased when he or she died. Adopting our previous reasoning, a relationship ended by separation is qualitatively different from one that was continuing at the time of the deceased's death. It seems to us that this difference should be reflected in some way by the court when it determines an application for family provision in these cases.

6.41   Reference to the "separation analogy" would allow this difference to be recognised. The claim would be being made under the 1975 Act for the simple reason that it was no longer possible for a claim to be made for financial relief under our recommended scheme. That being the case, the court should be required to consider what the applicant might reasonably have expected to receive had the claim proceeded under the separation scheme.

6.42   It would be possible to make express provision that the likely award on separation should be the maximum amount which the applicant could obtain on death, in other words that it should be a "ceiling" to the award of relief under the 1975 Act. However, we have concluded that this would not be the best way of dealing with such cases. To introduce a notional ceiling would be to break new ground as no such provision currently applies to any claims under the 1975 Act. We consider that a better solution would be simply to require the court to have regard to the fact that the applicant and the deceased were no longer living together at the time of the deceased's death as one of the factors in determining the claim.

---

[41]   We discuss the potential relevance of an opt-out agreement applicable on separation at para 6.48.

[42]   See n 37.

6.43 **We recommend that in the case of an application for family provision by a cohabitant under the 1975 Act:**

(1) **"reasonable financial provision" should mean such financial provision as it would be reasonable in all the circumstances of the case for the applicant to receive, whether or not that provision is required for the applicant's maintenance;**

(2) **in addition to the matters to which the court is currently required to have regard, the court should be required to have regard to:**

(a) **the provision which the applicant might reasonably have expected to receive in proceedings for financial relief on separation if the applicant and the deceased had separated on the day on which the deceased had died;**

(b) **if relevant, the fact that the applicant was no longer cohabiting with the deceased immediately before his or her death.**

Orders and agreements restricting future applications under the 1975 Act

Orders in separation proceedings restricting 1975 Act applications

6.44 The court has the power, on granting a decree of divorce,[43] to order that one or both parties shall not be entitled to apply for family provision under the 1975 Act on the death of the other.[44] We provisionally proposed in the CP that the court should have a similar power on making an order for financial relief on separation under our scheme.[45] Given the very limited circumstances in which we are now recommending that an individual no longer cohabiting with the deceased immediately before death should be able to bring a claim under the 1975 Act, it is in fact very unlikely that such a claim could be brought.[46] Most of those consultees addressing the issue supported our provisional proposal, and we consider that the court should have the power when making an award under our recommended scheme to restrict the recipient of that award from subsequently making any application for family provision.[47]

---

[43] And in equivalent proceedings on the dissolution of a civil partnership.

[44] Inheritance (Provision for Family and Dependants) Act 1975, s 15; see also s 15ZA in relation to civil partners.

[45] CP, para 8.50(4).

[46] It may only be possible where the applicant was a "dependant" of the deceased on death: Inheritance (Provision for Family and Dependants) Act 1975, s 1(1)(e). It would not be possible to claim at all as a former cohabitant, because we do not recommend the introduction of such a class of applicant (contrast the position of a former spouse or civil partner). Provision would therefore only be needed to prevent the theoretical possibility of a claim being brought under another category, albeit one that is essentially based on the cohabitation and its consequences.

[47] Orders under ss 15 and 15ZA in relation to spouses and civil partners similarly bar any claim from being brought; see n 46.

Agreements restricting 1975 Act applications

6.45 We invited consultees' views as to whether it should be possible for a cohabiting couple to enter into a private agreement whereby each party undertook not to make a claim against the other's estate under the 1975 Act.[48] Although most consultees considered that such agreements should be capable of being binding, subject to appropriate safeguards, we have decided not to make a recommendation to such effect.

6.46 We accept that to recognise and enforce private agreements not to claim family provision would be entirely consistent with our recommended approach with regard to opt-out agreements. In principle, parties should be free to negotiate and to enforce their own terms. For that reason, we do not find persuasive some of the reasons put forward by the minority of consultees who opposed the enforceability of these particular agreements: for example, that safeguards would be necessary in order to protect the vulnerable, or that a considerable time might elapse between the date of the agreement and the death.

6.47 We are more concerned by the importance of maintaining the coherence of the 1975 Act jurisdiction. We raised this issue in the CP, and both the Chancery Bar Association and the Law Society expressed the need for caution in giving rights to cohabitants which are not available to any other class of applicants under the 1975 Act. It is indeed the case that no other class of applicant may "opt out" of the 1975 Act by private agreement, and it is not obvious why cohabitants should, uniquely, be permitted to do so. A review of the position of other classes of applicant would be outside our terms of reference and would be better undertaken as part of a general review of the operation of the 1975 Act. We believe that in the interests of retaining the coherence and integrity of the family provision jurisdiction it should not be possible for cohabitants to agree to oust the jurisdiction of the 1975 Act.

6.48 But that is not to say that the existence of private agreements between the cohabitant and the deceased would be of no relevance to the exercise of the court's discretion in considering a claim by a surviving cohabitant under the 1975 Act.[49] If the parties had entered into an opt-out agreement, denying the right to apply for financial relief on separation, the court hearing a 1975 Act claim would be obliged to have regard to that agreement. As the agreement would affect what the applicant might have reasonably expected to receive in proceedings for financial relief on separation, it would form part of the "separation analogy". Indeed, assuming that the agreement was one that would be upheld on a claim on separation, we think it unlikely that the court would consider it reasonable in such circumstances to make provision for the survivor on an application under the 1975 Act. This conclusion would be further reinforced if the deceased had made a will, especially one made during the cohabitation, which made no provision for the applicant.

---

[48] CP, para 8.51.

[49] Contrast with the case of cohabitants who separate shortly before death: see para 6.39.

6.49 **We recommend that:**

(1) **when it makes an order for financial relief on separation, the court should be entitled, on the application of either party, to order that the other party should not on the death of the applicant be entitled to apply for family provision under the 1975 Act; but**

(2) **where cohabitants have entered into an agreement purporting to restrict application under the 1975 Act, that agreement should not be effective to bar entitlement to make such a claim.**

"Children of the family"

6.50 The 1975 Act currently permits an application by a "child of the family", that is to say by "any person (not being a child of the deceased) who, in the case of any marriage or civil partnership to which the deceased was at any time a party, was treated by the deceased as a child of the family in relation to that marriage or civil partnership".[50] We invited views in the CP on whether the definition of "child of the family" should be amended so that those treated as children of the family by cohabiting partners (for example, a child of one of the parties who lives or lived with them in their household) should be able to apply for reasonable financial provision on the death of whichever partner was not the applicant's parent.[51]

6.51 The few reported decisions on "child of the family" applications under the 1975 Act have indicated that the courts are prepared to look favourably on those applicants who can show that they have "lost their inheritance" from their parent because that parent married and then died before his or her spouse.[52] In those cases, the courts have adopted an interpretation of "reasonable financial provision" which is arguably more generous than the test imposed by statute for such claims, that is such provision which it would be reasonable for the applicant to receive for his or her maintenance.[53]

6.52 Most of the consultees who addressed this question felt that the definition should be amended. Moreover, it is entirely logical to suggest, as did the Law Society, that, where the applicant is a step-child of the deceased, he or she should only be eligible to apply for family provision if his or her parent would be, or would have been, eligible to apply as the surviving cohabitant. However, in exploring the possible consequences of such a recommendation, we have encountered significant difficulties, and we do not consider that we should recommend any amendment in the course of this project.

6.53 If applications were to be possible in such cases, the merits of the claim would largely depend upon the applicant's own financial circumstances, and (according to the "lost inheritance" cases) the source of the assets contained in the deceased's estate. Assuming that the applicant had financial needs, the question would be whether a substantial proportion of the estate was attributable to gifts,

---

[50] Inheritance (Provision for Family and Dependants) Act 1975, s 1(1)(d), as amended by Civil Partnership Act 2004, sch 4, para 15(4).

[51] CP, para 8.61.

[52] CP, paras 8.56 to 8.59.

[53] Inheritance (Provision for Family and Dependants) Act 1975, s 1(2)(b).

by the applicant's parent to the deceased, whether made when the parent was still living or in the parent's will.

6.54 The problem with adopting the logical suggestion that the applicant's parent must have been an eligible cohabitant in relation to the deceased is that it would not ensure that the applicant had a meritorious claim. Moreover, there would be a very real risk that some with meritorious claims might nevertheless fail to establish that they had a right to advance them. Assuming that the applicant's parent and the deceased did not have children together, they would have to have been living together for a minimum duration before they become eligible cohabitants. Yet the length of their relationship should not, in strict logic, make any difference to the merits of the applicant's claim. Indeed, where the applicant's parent lived with a new partner for a very short time, but in the course of that relationship executed a will making that partner the sole beneficiary of his or her estate (thereby "disinheriting" the applicant), the applicant's claim might seem very strong on the merits.

6.55 This is a difficult area. As we have observed, the very concept of "lost inheritance" which underpins these claims,[54] and is currently deployed in favour of step-children where their parent married the deceased, is problematic. It is a creation of case law, and sits uneasily alongside the statutory "maintenance" ceiling on awards to such applicants.[55] We are not presently convinced that these are firm foundations on which to build.

6.56 STEP remarked that it was not clear why the existence of a marriage or civil partnership to a third party should have any significance in determining whether the deceased had treated the applicant as his or her child. But if we take that observation to its logical conclusion, the concept of "child of the family" should be extended beyond even cohabiting relationships. Any individual, whether or not he or she has a relationship with another adult, could be said to treat someone as a child of his family.[56]

6.57 We are not, therefore, convinced that the case for reform has yet been made out. Indeed, the issues that arise in these cases would be better dealt with in the course of a comprehensive review of the law of family provision. It should be noted, as we observed in the CP, that where the applicant was in fact dependent on the deceased immediately prior to death, a claim may be made as a "dependant", irrespective of the duration, or the status, of the relevant relationships.[57]

6.58 Accordingly, we do not recommend that the definition of "child of the family" should be amended so that those treated as children of the family in relation to a cohabiting couple would qualify as applicants under the 1975 Act.

---

[54] *Re Leach* [1986] Ch 226 and *Re Callaghan* [1985] Fam 1.

[55] Inheritance (Provision for Family and Dependants) Act 1975, s 1(1)(d), (2)(b).

[56] As Scottish law recognises: eg Family Law Act 1985, s 1(1)(d).

[57] Inheritance (Provision for Family and Dependants) Act 1975, s 1(1)(e).

THE LAW RELATING TO WILLS

6.59 The Wills Act 1837 provides that a will is revoked by the testator's subsequent marriage or civil partnership.[58] This can have unintended consequences. It may be thought particularly disadvantageous where the will purported to benefit the individual who married the testator, who had previously been cohabiting with him or her. In the event that no new will is made, the spouse or civil partner is protected, to some extent, by the intestacy rules. But that protection may be less generous than the provision made by the revoked will.

6.60 We briefly raised this issue in the CP,[59] but provisionally concluded that this was not the appropriate context in which to review the operation of this rule. The application of the rule goes beyond wills purporting to benefit a spouse or civil partner with whom the testator had been cohabiting. Most consultees who answered the question agreed.

6.61 There is no doubt that the issue is an important one. STEP, arguing the case for reform, considered that marriage or civil partnership should no longer revoke a testamentary gift to the testator's new spouse or civil partner. But such a rule, which would clearly be capable of applying to cases where the parties had not cohabited prior to the marriage or civil partnership, takes us well beyond the scope of the present project. It is important that the public is aware of the effect of marriage or civil partnership on prior wills. Clear information should be provided to all those who give notice of their intention to marry or form a civil partnership. They may then review their wills accordingly.[60]

6.62 The Wills Act 1837 also presumes that, on the dissolution or annulment of a marriage or civil partnership, any appointment of the former spouse or civil partner as executor or conferment of a power of appointment shall take effect as if that individual had died on the date of the dissolution or annulment.[61] Similarly, any property devised or bequeathed to that individual shall pass as if he or she had died.

6.63 We considered in the CP whether some equivalent rule should be introduced to deal with the effect of separation between cohabitants,[62] and concluded that it should not. Nearly all of those consultees who responded to this question agreed,[63] endorsing our concerns about the serious difficulties of proof that would be involved. We also remain concerned about the possible adverse effect that

---

[58] Wills Act 1837, ss 18 and 18B. There are important exceptions to this rule in relation to a will made when the testator was expecting to be married to, or to enter into a civil partnership with, a particular person: see ss 18(3), (4) and 18B(3) to (6).

[59] CP, para 8.63 to 8.69.

[60] Such a rule might also face considerable forensic problems in practice, particularly if confined to wills made during pre-marital cohabitation: see CP, paras 8.63 to 8.66.

[61] Wills Act 1837, ss 18A and 18C.

[62] CP, paras 8.67 to 8.74.

[63] The Chancery Bar Association did not, suggesting that it is odd that an ex-cohabitant should potentially be able to take both under the will and pursuant to an application under the 1975 Act, where an ex-spouse cannot. But the provision made for the former cohabitant under the will could be taken into account by a court hearing a 1975 Act application, whether made at the instigation of that individual or some other disappointed party.

such a rule might have upon the expeditious administration of estates. It would be more appropriate, as we suggested in the CP, to leave testators to review their wills in the event of separation.

6.64 We therefore make no recommendations for reform of the Wills Act 1837.

PART 7
JURISDICTION AND APPLICABLE LAW

INTRODUCTION

7.1 In the CP we discussed the issues of jurisdiction and applicable law in cases with an international element. In an era of global mobility, and a Europe committed to the free movement of persons, there is an increasing number of "international couples": couples who do not share a nationality, or who live (temporarily or permanently) in or hold property in jurisdictions other than their country of origin. Such couples may be married or unmarried; if unmarried, they may or may not have entered a registered partnership in a jurisdiction where such an option is available.

7.2 This wide range of possibilities opens up a very broad area for discussion. However, we are concerned here only with the issue of the extent of the jurisdiction of the courts of England and Wales to operate our recommended scheme in cases with an international dimension.

JURISDICTION

7.3 In the CP, we discussed the different rules of jurisdiction in various family law matters. Jurisdiction to grant a decree of divorce or to dissolve a civil partnership[1] is governed by section 5 of the Domicile and Matrimonial Proceedings Act 1973 as amended following the introduction into domestic law of the EC Regulation known as "Brussels II revised" or "Brussels II *Bis*".[2] The court has jurisdiction when one or more of the following applies:

(1) the parties are both habitually resident in England and Wales;

(2) the parties were last habitually resident in England and Wales and one of them still resides here;

(3) the respondent is habitually resident in England and Wales;

(4) in the event of a joint application, either party is habitually resident in England and Wales;

(5) the applicant is habitually resident in England and Wales and he or she has resided here for at least a year immediately before the application was made;

---

[1] In the discussion that follows, where reference is made to a decree of divorce it is to be understood that the same can be said of the dissolution of a civil partnership; and the term "ancillary relief" includes financial relief for former civil partners as well as for divorcing couples. The private international law considerations relevant to both statuses are, for the present purposes, identical; the jurisdiction rules concerning civil partnerships are contained in the Civil Partnership (Jurisdiction and Recognition of Judgments) Regulations, SI 2005/3334.

[2] Regulation (EC) No 2201/2003, which replaced the regulation known as "Brussels II" (Regulation (EC) No 1347/2000).

(6)   the applicant is habitually resident in England and Wales and he or she has resided here for at least six months immediately before the application was made and is domiciled here; or

(7)   both parties are domiciled in England and Wales.

If no court of a Contracting State has jurisdiction under the Council Regulation and either of the parties to the marriage is domiciled in England and Wales on the date when the proceedings are begun, the English court has jurisdiction.

7.4   In addition, Brussels II *Bis* provides that where the courts of one or more Contracting States have jurisdiction pursuant to these rules, the court first seised of the matter shall determine it, and proceedings commenced elsewhere must therefore be stayed.[3] This has had some unfortunate effects, leading to a "rush to court" whereby each party hastens to issue proceedings in the jurisdiction which, of those available, is the most favourable to him or her. Where proceedings are pending in a state which is not a contracting state, the English courts' approach has been to stay proceedings where appropriate under the *forum non conveniens* doctrine.[4]

7.5   Jurisdiction to grant ancillary relief is complex. In so far as ancillary relief can be characterised as a matter of maintenance, jurisdiction is determined by the EC regulation known as "Brussels I",[5] the effect of which is that the court with jurisdiction in divorce can also make an award of maintenance. Of course, ancillary relief awards do not always deal exclusively with the parties' needs, particularly in high value cases;[6] and in so far as the award is not a grant of maintenance but a division of property arising from the marital relationship, it is not governed by Brussels I. But, in practice, the English courts' approach to the issue of applicable law on divorce – namely their exclusive application of domestic law in accordance with the *lex fori* principle[7] – means that when granting a decree of divorce the courts will do so under the MCA and they will, therefore, also make an award of ancillary relief under that Act.

7.6   Jurisdiction to make an award under Schedule 1 to the Children Act 1989 is also subject to Brussels I. The Matrimonial and Family Proceedings Act 1984 determines when the English court has jurisdiction to grant ancillary relief when a divorce has been obtained overseas.

7.7   Jurisdiction to make an award under the Inheritance (Provision for Family and Dependants) Act 1975 depends upon the deceased having been domiciled in England and Wales at the time of death.[8] This rule has been the subject of

---

[3]   Brussels II *Bis*, art 19.

[4]   See C Clarkson and J Hill, *The Conflict of Laws* (2006) p 332 and following.

[5]   Regulation (EC) No 44/2001

[6]   See *Van den Boogard v Laumen* [1997] ECR 1 to 1147, C220-95.

[7]   See para 7.18.

[8]   Inheritance (Provision for Family and Dependants) Act 1975, s 1(1).

criticism[9] because it is inconsistent with most other family law matters, where jurisdiction depends principally upon habitual residence.[10] We noted in the CP that the time might be ripe for reconsideration of this rule, but that it falls outside the scope of our present project.

7.8 In the CP, we suggested[11] that jurisdiction to make an order between cohabitants pursuant to a new scheme for financial relief on separation should be framed by analogy with the rules for divorce in Brussels II *Bis*. We noted the imperfection of the analogy with divorce, which is a matter of personal status. But the use of the concept of habitual residence is appropriate, and consistent with the criteria used in other family law matters. And the adoption of criteria matching those used – in effect, as explained above at paragraph 7.5 – for the grant of ancillary relief on divorce might be preferable to the creation of yet another set of rules.[12]

7.9 Only a handful of consultees addressed this issue, and their responses were mixed. Resolution observed that it might be inappropriate to bring within the ambit of our recommended scheme couples who had not lived together here and so could not be expected to be aware of English law. We agree that some of the Brussels II *Bis* criteria are too wide. It would be inappropriate, for example, to include a couple who had never lived together here and where one party only was habitually resident here. It could also be inappropriate to apply English law to a couple whose cohabitation had taken place for the most part in another jurisdiction, which might have no scheme of statutory relief for separating cohabitants.

7.10 We consider it particularly important that couples who move to this country from elsewhere should have a realistic opportunity to opt out of our legislation if they so wish, and that the parties' cohabiting relationship should have sufficient connection with this jurisdiction to warrant proceedings being brought here.[13] We have therefore framed our recommendations so as to ensure that in cases where most of a couple's cohabitation has taken place in another country, they should have lived as couple in a joint household in this country for a substantial period of time, even if they have a child together, before the court in England and Wales should have jurisdiction. For simplicity, we suggest that that period should correspond with the minimum duration requirement (whatever that might be).[14]

7.11 For similar reasons, we do not think that domicile should be one of the criteria for jurisdiction, despite the analogy with Brussels II. Domicile may be retained in circumstances where the individual has very little connection with England and Wales, and might have very little information about the legislative scheme. It is

---

[9] *Cyganik v Agulian* [2006] EWCA Civ 129, [2006] 1 FCR 406, at [58], Longmore LJ. The point was raised by the Society of Trust and Estate Practitioners in response to the CP; it would like to see the domicile jurisdiction rule for the Inheritance (Provision for Family and Dependants) Act 1975 replaced by habitual residence.

[10] See para 7.3.

[11] CP, paras 11.59 and following.

[12] Family Law (Scotland) Act 2006, s 28(9), takes this approach.

[13] Particularly in view of the applicable law, discussed below.

[14] Part 3.

fundamental to our scheme that cohabitants should have full opportunity to opt out of it following informed discussion.

7.12   The "rush to court" arising from the "first seised" rule is unfortunate in the matrimonial context. The rule would not be so relevant in the present context because very few European jurisdictions have legislative schemes for unregistered cohabitation. We are persuaded by Resolution's observation to the effect that it would be more appropriate for the English court simply to have a discretion to stay any application if there were foreign proceedings pending.

7.13   We remarked in the CP[15] that one of the criteria in the Matrimonial Proceedings and Property Act 1984 might provide a helpful analogy, namely the fact that either party had a beneficial interest in a dwelling house situated in England and Wales which had at some time during the marriage been the parties' matrimonial home. Would it be appropriate to add to criteria drawn from Brussels II *Bis* the fact that either party had at the time of the application a property in this jurisdiction in which the parties had shared a household at some point?

7.14   We have concluded that this would not be appropriate. Our recommended scheme would create personal obligations between the parties and would not generate proprietary rights independently of a court order. We do not think that it would be appropriate for our scheme to operate where this was the only connecting factor, in the absence of the other factors listed in Brussels II *Bis.*

7.15   **We recommend that jurisdictional rules for our recommended scheme be drawn from those contained in Brussels II *Bis,* but restricted to actions where:**

    (1)   **the parties are both habitually resident in England and Wales; or**

    (2)   **the parties were last habitually resident in England and Wales and one of them still resides here; or**

    (3)   **in the event of a joint application, either party is habitually resident in England and Wales;**

    provided, in cases (1) and (2) above, that over half of the cohabitation took place in England and Wales or that immediately prior to their separation the parties had cohabited here for a period equivalent to the minimum duration requirement.[16]

7.16   **We recommend that where an action is brought under our recommended scheme, the English court should have a discretion to stay proceedings if there are proceedings pending in another jurisdiction in relation to financial relief for cohabitants following separation.**

---

[15] CP, para 11.53.

[16] See para 3.63.

APPLICABLE LAW

7.17 Once jurisdiction is determined, there is an issue as to which law the court will apply. We are here concerned only with the question of the applicable law in the courts of England and Wales.

7.18 As we pointed out in the CP, the law of England and Wales consistently applies the *lex fori* (that is, the law of the forum, here English law) in ancillary relief proceedings. Accordingly, in the event that, say, an English husband and a French wife divorce in England, their divorce is governed by the MCA regardless of where they were married; and ancillary relief is awarded under that statute.

7.19 We suggested in the CP[17] that the same approach should be taken in cases arising from the separation of cohabitants, and the consultees who answered this question agreed.

7.20 However, we noted in the CP that cohabitation contracts are characterised for the purposes of private international law as contracts rather than as family matters. This leads to their being adjudicated in accordance with the proper law of the contract; and this has been the subject of criticism.[18] In the CP[19] we asked for consultees' views as to whether cohabitation contracts, and opt-out agreements, should be regarded as part of the court's family law jurisdiction and should be adjudicated under English law. Of the very few consultees who answered this question, most thought that they should; and we take the view that it would be particularly important for opt-out agreements to be regarded as an integral part of our recommended scheme and subject to the safeguards that we have recommended.[20]

7.21 We are not making a recommendation here regarding cohabitation contracts as such. As we noted in the CP, the characterisation of such contracts for private international law purposes is not certain. Provided that the parties had validly opted out under the law of England and Wales, there would be a case for allowing the proper law of the contract to apply thereafter.

7.22 **We recommend that the law of England and Wales should be the governing law in all cases arising in an English or Welsh court concerning:**

    (1)   **financial relief on separation; and**

    (2)   **opt-out agreements.**

REFORM PROPOSALS FROM EUROPE

7.23 Since the publication of the CP, the European Commission has proposed two major reforms in the field of private international law which would have a bearing on the private international law aspects of our recommended scheme. One is a

[17] CP, para 11.71.

[18] CP, paras 11.64 to 11.70.

[19] CP, para 11.71.

[20] See Part 5.

proposal for an instrument (known as "Rome III") amending Brussels II *Bis*[21] to reduce complexity and confusion in divorce cases with an international element. The proposed instrument would:

(1) enable the parties to choose, within a range of connecting factors, which court should have jurisdiction to grant a decree and the applicable law; and

(2) in default of such choice,

   (a) create an ordered list of connecting factors to determine jurisdiction and eliminate the notorious "first seised" rule; and

   (b) create a unified set of rules as to applicable law, to be applied consistently throughout Europe.

7.24 The object of these changes would be to enable international couples to predict with certainty which court would have jurisdiction in their divorce and which law that court would apply.

7.25 The other proposal, published on the same date, is a Green Paper on matrimonial property regimes ("the Green Paper").[22] This is a consultation document asking a series of questions about the private international law rules regarding matrimonial property regimes. Again, the aim is predictability and certainty; the European Commission is concerned about the difficulties that international couples may encounter in connection with their property, both during the relationship and on its ending, and it seeks views as to how to make both jurisdiction and applicable law predictable. The paper is concerned primarily with the property of married couples but it also asks questions about the property consequences of registered partnership and of unregistered cohabitation.

7.26 The approach of the European Commission differs markedly from the approach of the law of England and Wales, in so far as the latter invariably applies the *lex fori* to divorce and ancillary relief proceedings. We noted above[23] the problems that may be felt to arise from application of domestic English law to international couples whose cohabitation had mostly taken place outside England and Wales. Some would argue that it would be preferable if the courts of this jurisdiction were able to adopt a more flexible choice of law rule in such cases, as many other European jurisdictions do. It might be felt appropriate, for example, to apply Swedish law to a Swedish couple who had lived together and separated in Sweden and then had both taken up habitual residence in this country. We express no concluded view on this matter, and in any event do not think it feasible to recommend broader choice of law rules for cohabitation than are currently applied in ancillary relief cases. But we would expect that if the position

---

[21] Draft Council Regulation amending Regulation (EC) No 2201/2003 as regards jurisdiction and introducing rules concerning applicable law in matrimonial matters.

[22] EU Commission Green Paper on Conflict of Laws in Matters concerning matrimonial Property Regimes, including the Question of Jurisdiction and Mutual Recognition, published 17 July 2006, COM (2006) 400 final (SEC (2006) 952).

[23] Paras 7.10 and 7.11.

changed for ancillary relief, then the position for cohabitation cases would be re-examined.

7.27   The extent to which the UK will participate in possible reforms following the Green Paper is as yet unclear. The UK Government did not opt into the Rome III proposal;[24] it may choose to do so at a later date. The UK Government's response to the Green Paper[25] is cautious, counselling a proportionate and possibly non-legislative response to the difficulties that the European Commission seeks to address.

7.28   Accordingly, it is possible that there may be amendments to Brussels II *Bis,* and reform relating to property disputes between international couples, which might have an impact on the recommendations we make in this Report. But it is not possible at this stage to say what reform, if any, will take place. We make no further recommendation in respect of that possibility.

---

[24]   The deadline for doing so was 30 November 2006.

[25]   This can be seen on the European Commission's website: http://ec.europa.eu/index_en.htm (last visited 3 July 2007).

PART 8
LIST OF RECOMMENDATIONS

PART 2 – SHOULD THERE BE REFORM?

8.1 We recommend that legislation should create a scheme of general application, whereby cohabiting couples would be entitled to apply for financial relief on separation:

    (1)   provided they satisfy statutory eligibility criteria;

    (2)   but not where they had reached an agreement disapplying the statutory scheme ("an opt-out agreement"), in which case the parties' own financial arrangements (if any) would apply.

[Paragraph 2.94]

PART 3 – ELIGIBILITY FOR REMEDIES ON SEPARATION

8.2 We recommend that persons should be cohabitants for the purposes of being eligible to apply for financial relief on separation where:

    (1)   they are living as a couple in a joint household; and

    (2)   they are neither married to each other nor civil partners.

For these purposes, references to marriage and civil partnership should be taken to denote relationships recognised as such for the purposes of the law of England and Wales.

[Paragraph 3.13]

8.3 We recommend that cohabitants who are by law the parents of a child born before, during or following their cohabitation ("cohabitants who have a child together") ought to be eligible to apply for financial relief on separation.

[Paragraph 3.31]

8.4 We recommend that:

    (1)   save where cohabitants have a child together, they should not be eligible to apply for financial relief on separation unless they have lived as a couple in a joint household for a duration specified by statute (the "minimum duration requirement");

    (2)   any such minimum duration requirement should be set by statute within a range of two to five years;

    (3)   if the minimum duration requirement is set at two years, then the court should have no discretion to dispense with the requirement; but

    (4)   if the requirement is set at a period longer than two years, then consideration should be given to allowing the court to dispense with the

requirement, including in particular cases where, although cohabitants do not have a child together, they treated a child who was living with them in their joint household as a child of their family; and

(5) any minimum duration requirement should be satisfied only by a continuous period of cohabitation.

[Paragraph 3.63]

8.5 We recommend that persons should not be eligible as "cohabitants" where sexual activity between them would constitute a criminal offence owing to the age of either party or to the fact that the parties are relatives.

[Paragraph 3.70]

8.6 We recommend that cohabitants should not be disqualified from claiming financial relief on separation on the grounds that one or both of them are or were at any relevant time married to, or civil partners of, or cohabiting with, another party.

[Paragraph 3.71]

8.7 We recommend that:

(1) the scheme

(a) should not apply to any relationship which ended prior to implementing legislation coming into force; but

(b) should be capable of applying to any relationship which exists at that date; and

(2) in seeking to establish that they satisfy the eligibility criteria, parties to such relationships should be able to rely on periods of cohabitation and the birth of children prior to implementation.

[Paragraph 3.84]

PART 4 – FINANCIAL RELIEF ON SEPARATION

8.8 We recommend that the courts should be given a discretion structured by principles which determine the basis on which any financial relief is to be granted on separation.

[Paragraph 4.17]

8.9 We recommend that financial relief on separation should be granted in accordance with a statutory scheme based upon the economic impact of cohabitation, to the following effect.

8.10 An eligible cohabitant applying for relief following separation ("the applicant") must prove that:

(1) the respondent has a retained benefit; or

(2)   the applicant has an economic disadvantage.

as a result of qualifying contributions the applicant has made

8.11   A qualifying contribution is any contribution arising from the cohabiting relationship which is made to the parties' shared lives or to the welfare of members of their families. Contributions are not limited to financial contributions, and include future contributions, in particular to the care of the parties' children following separation.

8.12   A retained benefit may take the form of capital, income or earning capacity that has been acquired, retained or enhanced.

8.13   An economic disadvantage is a present or future loss. It may include a diminution in current savings as a result of expenditure or of earnings lost during the relationship, lost future earnings, or the future cost of paid child-care.

8.14   The court may make an order to adjust the retained benefit, if any, by reversing it in so far as that is reasonable and practicable having regard to the discretionary factors listed below. If, after the reversal of any retained benefit, the applicant would still bear an economic disadvantage, the court may make an order sharing that loss equally between the parties, in so far as it is reasonable and practicable to do so, having regard to the discretionary factors.

8.15   The discretionary factors are:

(1)   the welfare while a minor of any child of both parties who has not attained the age of eighteen;

(2)   the financial needs and obligations of both parties;

(3)   the extent and nature of the financial resources which each party has or is likely to have in the foreseeable future;

(4)   the welfare of any children who live with, or might reasonably be expected to live with, either party; and

(5)   the conduct of each party, defined restrictively but so as to include cases where a qualifying contribution can be shown to have been made despite the express disagreement of the other party.

Of these discretionary factors, item (1) above shall be the court's first consideration.

8.16   In making an order to share economic disadvantage, the court shall not place the applicant, for the foreseeable future, in a stronger economic position than the respondent.

8.17   The following range of orders should be available to the court:

(1)   lump sums, including payment by instalment, secured lump sums, lump sums paid by way of pensions attachment, and interim payments;

(2)   property transfers;

(3)   property settlements;

(4)   orders for sale; and

(5)   pension sharing.

Unlike on divorce, periodical payments should not generally be available.

8.18   In so far as the scheme is engaged, it should apply between the parties to the exclusion of the general law of implied trusts, estoppel and contract.

8.19   Procedural and costs rules must be carefully framed to protect the parties from oppressive litigation and to preserve court time and resources. In particular, the rules must prevent parties who are eligible cohabitants from bringing claims under the general law of implied trusts, estoppel and contract on the basis of facts which constitute qualifying contributions under the scheme.

[Paragraphs 4.32 to 4.42]

8.20   We recommend that goods given to one party by the other should not comprise a retained benefit, nor should it be possible to mount a claim for economic disadvantage on the basis of making such gifts, unless it can be proved by the donor that the gift was conditional upon the cohabiting relationship continuing.

[Paragraph 4.59]

8.21   We recommend that the promotion of mediation as an alternative to court proceedings be facilitated wherever possible by the rules.

[Paragraph 4.127]

8.22   We recommend that the scheme should include anti-avoidance provisions modelled upon section 37 of the Matrimonial Causes Act 1973, and similar provisions for the enforcement of orders.

[Paragraph 4.129]

8.23   We recommend that claims for financial relief should be brought within two years of the parties' separation.

[Paragraph 4.151]

8.24   We recommend that there be a general discretion vested in the court to extend the two-year limitation period for making a claim, to be exercised in exceptional circumstances only.

[Paragraph 4.155]

PART 5 – COHABITATION CONTRACTS AND OPT-OUT AGREEMENTS

8.25 We recommend that legislation should provide, for the avoidance of doubt, that, in so far as a contract ("a cohabitation contract") governs the financial arrangements of a cohabiting couple during their cohabitation or following their separation, it should not be regarded as contrary to public policy.

[Paragraph 5.8]

8.26 We recommend that statute provide that opt-out agreements shall be taken to have been made for valuable consideration.

[Paragraph 5.34]

8.27 We recommend that an agreement which is in writing, is signed by the parties, and makes clear the parties' intention to disapply the statute, should be enforceable as an opt-out agreement in place of our recommended scheme.

[Paragraph 5.56]

8.28 We recommend that agreements that purport to disapply the statute but do not comply with these qualifying criteria should be of no effect when the statutory scheme is invoked.

[Paragraph 5.57]

8.29 We recommend that pro forma agreements be made available for the use of cohabitants who wish to make opt-out agreements.

[Paragraph 5.58]

8.30 We recommend that parties should be able to enter into an opt-out agreement whether or not they are eligible cohabitants at the time that the agreement is made.

[Paragraph 5.59]

8.31 We recommend that minors should be capable of entering into opt-out agreements, but that such contracts should be voidable (in accordance with the general principles of contract law) at the instance of a party who was a minor at the time that the agreement was made.

[Paragraph 5.60]

8.32 We recommend that a court should be entitled to set aside an opt-out agreement if its enforcement would cause manifest unfairness having regard to:

(1) the circumstances at the time the agreement was made; or

(2) circumstances at the time the agreement comes to be enforced which were unforeseen when the agreement was made.

[Paragraph 5.61]

8.33　We recommend that there should be a period between the legislation being enacted and implementation of the scheme for financial relief during which cohabitants should be able to make an opt-out agreement.

[Paragraph 5.72]

PART 6 – SUCCESSION ON DEATH: INTESTACY AND FAMILY PROVISION

All recommendations for reform of the Inheritance (Provision for Family and Dependants) Act 1975 are contingent upon the implementation of our recommended scheme of financial relief on separation.

8.34　We recommend that the Inheritance (Provision for Family and Dependants) Act 1975 ("the 1975 Act") be amended so as to provide the same definition of "cohabitant" as that used to define eligibility to apply under the statutory scheme for financial relief on separation.

[Paragraph 6.16]

8.35　We recommend that a person ("the applicant") should be entitled to apply for provision under the 1975 Act as a cohabitant where the applicant was living in the same household as the deceased immediately before the deceased's death and:

(1)　either:

(a)　the applicant and the deceased had so lived for a period of two years immediately before the deceased's death,

or

(b)　the applicant and the deceased had a child together; and

(2)　that the court should not have discretion to dispense with these requirements.

[Paragraph 6.26]

8.36　We recommend that a person ("the applicant") who was no longer cohabiting with the deceased immediately before his or her death should nevertheless be entitled to apply for provision as a cohabitant under the 1975 Act:

(1)　if at that date the applicant had made a valid application for financial relief on separation which had not yet been determined; or

(2)　although no such application had been made, the applicant was still entitled to make one (if necessary, subject to the court granting permission to extend time for such an application to be made or setting aside an opt-out agreement).

[Paragraph 6.31]

8.37 We recommend that in the case of an application for family provision by a cohabitant under the 1975 Act:

(1) "reasonable financial provision" should mean such financial provision as it would be reasonable in all the circumstances of the case for the applicant to receive, whether or not that provision is required for the applicant's maintenance;

(2) in addition to the matters to which the court is currently required to have regard, the court should be required to have regard to:

(a) the provision which the applicant might reasonably have expected to receive in proceedings for financial relief on separation if the applicant and the deceased had separated on the day on which the deceased had died;

(b) if relevant, the fact that the applicant was no longer cohabiting with the deceased immediately before his or her death.

[Paragraph 6.43]

8.38 We recommend that:

(1) when it makes an order for financial relief on separation, the court should be entitled, on the application of either party, to order that the other party should not on the death of the applicant be entitled to apply for family provision under the 1975 Act; but

(2) where cohabitants have entered into an agreement purporting to restrict application under the 1975 Act, that agreement should not be effective to bar entitlement to make such a claim.

[Paragraph 6.49]

PART 7 – JURISDICTION AND APPLICABLE LAW

8.39 We recommend that jurisdictional rules for our recommended scheme be drawn from those contained in Brussels II *Bis,* but restricted to actions where:

(1) the parties are both habitually resident in England and Wales;

(2) the parties were last habitually resident in England and Wales and one of them still resides here; or

(3) in the event of a joint application, either party is habitually resident in England and Wales;

provided, in cases (1) and (2) above, that over half of the cohabitation took place in England and Wales or that immediately prior to their separation the parties had cohabited here for a period equivalent to the minimum duration requirement.

[Paragraph 7.15]

8.40 We recommend that where an action is brought under our recommended scheme, the English court should have a discretion to stay proceedings if there are proceedings pending in another jurisdiction in relation to financial relief for cohabitants following separation.

[Paragraph 7.16]

8.41 We recommend that the law of England and Wales should be the governing law in all cases arising in an English or Welsh court concerning:

(1) financial relief on separation; and

(2) opt-out agreements.

[Paragraph 7.22]

(Signed) TERENCE ETHERTON, *Chairman*
STUART BRIDGE
DAVID HERTZELL[1]
JEREMY HORDER
KENNETH PARKER

STEVE HUMPHREYS, *Chief Executive*
3 July 2007

---

[1] Mr David Hertzell was appointed a Law Commissioner with effect from 1 July 2007, in succession to Professor Hugh Beale QC, FBA. The terms of this report were agreed on 3 July 2007.

APPENDIX A
THE CURRENT LAW

INTRODUCTION

A.1 Part 3 of the CP was an explanation of the current law. That background is important for this Report, and accordingly this Appendix reproduces Part 3 of the CP, with some updating. The updating largely relates to the House of Lords' decision in *Stack v Dowden*,[1] which has had a profound effect upon the law relating to implied trusts of the family home.

A.2 It is worth beginning with a clear statement of what the current law does not provide. There is a widespread belief that English law recognises cohabitants as "common law spouses" once they have lived together for some period of time[2] and that they are thereafter treated for legal purposes as if they were married.[3] Fifty-six per cent of British Social Attitudes survey respondents in 2000 believed in the "common law marriage myth", and the prevalence of this misconception was slightly higher (at 59%) amongst cohabitants as a group.[4] More than six in ten respondents from the general population recently surveyed for the Living Together Campaign, which is seeking to dispel the myth, subscribed to this error.[5] Sixty-nine per cent of a survey of engaged couples – who were therefore on the way to acquire the legal rights and duties unique to marriage[6] – were similarly mistaken, some 41% further believing that marriage would have no effect at all on their legal status.[7]

A.3 In some legal contexts, it is true that a period of cohabitation can give rise to treatment analogous to that of married couples.[8] But for many purposes – not

---

[1]　[2007] UKHL 17, [2007] 2 WLR 831.

[2]　Views regarding the duration of this mythical period vary: the deceased in *Churchill v Roach* [2002] EWHC 3230 (Ch), [2004] 2 FLR 989 apparently believed that after six months' cohabitation, seven days a week, his partner would become his common law wife and acquire an interest in the property: [2004] 2 FLR 989, 991.

[3]　It would seem that failure to appreciate the legal distinctions between marriage and cohabitation is not unique to this jurisdiction. Evidence from Germany and the Netherlands suggests that there is a similar problem there: W Schrama, *De niet-huwelijkse samenleving in het Nederlandse en het Duitse recht* (2004) pp 375 and 378.

[4]　A Barlow, S Duncan, G James and A Park, "Just a piece of paper? Marriage and cohabitation", in A Park, J Curtice, K Thomson, L Jarvis and C Bromley (eds), *British Social Attitudes: the 18th Report* (2001) pp 45 to 46. Questions in the follow-up qualitative interviews about particular areas of the law found that respondents were less wrong in their perceptions about cohabitants' (lack of) rights to maintenance on separation and to provision on death, though there was still a substantial minority that were mistaken: A Barlow, S Duncan, G James and A Park, *Cohabitation, Marriage and the Law* (2005) pp 39 to 41.

[5]　http://www.advicenow.org.uk/go/livingtogether/feature_236.html (last visited 3 July 2007).

[6]　And now, in almost all respects, civil partnership.

[7]　M Hibbs, C Barton and J Beswick, "Why marry? – Perceptions of the Affianced" (2001) 31 *Family Law* 197.

[8]　For example, in relation to means-testing for welfare benefits, tax credits and access to non-molestation orders.

least financial relief on separation and death – cohabitants and spouses are treated quite differently.

A.4   On the dissolution of marriage and civil partnership, the courts have a wide-ranging discretion to adjust the couple's property and finances in accordance with what they judge to be a fair outcome in all the circumstances.[9] By contrast, when cohabitants separate, the courts use a patchwork of statutory and non-statutory rules to determine what should happen to the couple's property. The courts have few adjustive powers in these cases, so, for the most part, the focus is on determining who owns what as a strict matter of property law, rather than to whom it should in fairness be given.[10] In the case of household contents and other items of personal property, the basic position is that whoever happened to pay for the property owns it.[11] However, the home in which the parties live will often be the most valuable asset falling within the joint property pool of a cohabiting couple. Ascertaining whether one or both parties own it and in what shares, and then deciding whether it should be sold immediately or made available for occupation by one of them for a period, are often the key issues arising on separation, and the law on this issue is complicated.

A.5   In cases where one partner dies, the question of who owns what remains important, as it is necessary to identify what property falls within the deceased's estate: the general law discussed below for ascertaining ownership is therefore as relevant in death cases as it is on separation. However, there is also an adjustive statutory remedy available to the surviving cohabitant which is far more substantial than any of the remedies currently available between cohabitants on separation. The survivor will often be eligible to make an application to court to seek reasonable financial provision where the deceased's will or the intestacy rules do not adequately cater for the survivor's maintenance.

A.6   In this Appendix, we set out the current law governing the distribution of cohabitants' property and finances on separation and death, focusing particularly on ownership of the home. First, we explain how the parties may seek to regulate their property relationship by means of express trust or contract. We then consider how the question of beneficial entitlement to property is determined where no express declaration of trust has been made. We go on to explain the current statutory remedies that may be applicable on relationship breakdown. Finally, we consider the distribution of property on the death of a cohabitant.

EXPRESS REGULATION BY THE PARTIES

A.7   Cohabiting couples can seek to regulate the property and financial aspects of their relationship in several ways. The legal consequences of their arrangements may differ according to the method chosen.

---

[9]   Matrimonial Causes Act 1973 ("MCA"), Part 2; Civil Partnership Act 2004, sch 5; *Miller v Miller; McFarlane v McFarlane* [2006] UKHL 24, [2006] 2 AC 618.

[10]   *Pettitt v Pettitt* [1970] AC 777, 798, Lord Morris.

[11]   For a discussion of the law in this area in the matrimonial context (where the general law is the same as it is for cohabitants), see Matrimonial Property (1988) Law Com No 175, paras 2.1 to 2.5.

A.8 Cohabitants can make outright gifts to each other.[12] They may confer beneficial interests in property on each other by way of express trusts; depending on the nature of the property involved, certain formalities may have to be completed before such a trust will be binding. Where the home is owned by one cohabitant, the owner may confer a right to occupy on a cohabiting partner by way of contractual licence.[13] However, lingering questions remain in relation to contracts between cohabitants which are designed generally to govern their property and financial relations during their relationship and/or in the event of separation.

A.9 We shall discuss private regulation involving wills, pensions and life assurance later in this Appendix when we examine the current law applying specifically on death.

Express declarations of trust in respect of land

A.10 A couple may come to an agreement as to their respective shares (in legal terms, their respective beneficial entitlements) in the house they occupy, or indeed in any property the title to which vests in one or both of them.

A.11 Where a couple purchase a house together, they will usually instruct a solicitor. If it is intended that each should obtain a share in the house, the solicitor should draw up a declaration of trust indicating their respective shares. This must be evidenced in writing and signed by the legal owner or owners of the property who, in the majority of cases, will be the cohabitants themselves.[14]

A.12 The courts have in recent years emphasised the importance of express declarations of beneficial entitlement.[15] Such a declaration is conclusive of the entitlements of those who are party to the transaction,[16] subject only to challenge

---

[12] A promise to make a gift is unenforceable for want of consideration unless it is made by deed, but this does not apply to a completed gift: *Ayerst v Jenkins* (1873) LR 16 Eq 275.

[13] *Chandler v Kerley* [1978] 1 WLR 693.

[14] Law of Property Act 1925, s 53(1)(b).

[15] Judges have been beseeching solicitors to take the instructions of transferees as to beneficial interests in property for many years – see *Cowcher v Cowcher* [1972] 1 WLR 425, 440, Bagnall J. The most famous of these remarks is that of Ward LJ in *Carlton v Goodman* [2002] EWCA Civ 545, [2002] 2 FLR 259, at [44]. "I ask in despair how often this court has to remind conveyancers that they would save their clients a great deal of later difficulty if only they would sit the purchasers down, explain the difference between a joint tenancy and tenancy in common, ascertain what they want and then expressly declare in the conveyance or transfer how the beneficial interest is to be held because that will be conclusive and save all argument. When are conveyancers going to do this as a matter of invariable standard practice? This court has urged that time after time. Perhaps conveyancers do not read the law reports. I will try one more time: ALWAYS TRY TO AGREE ON AND THEN RECORD HOW THE BENEFICIAL INTEREST IS TO BE HELD. It is not very difficult to do." (The use of the upper case for emphasis is that of the judge.) Sir Peter Gibson recently made a similar comment in *Crossley v Crossley* [2005] EWCA Civ 1581, [2006] 1 FCR 655, at [5].

[16] "No-one now doubts that such an express declaration of trust is conclusive unless varied by subsequent agreement or affected by proprietary estoppel." *Stack v Dowden* [2007] UKHL 17, [2007] 2 WLR 831, at [49], Baroness Hale, citing *Goodman v Gallant* [1986] Fam 106.

on grounds such as fraud,[17] mistake[18] and undue influence.[19] It avoids any need to rely on the difficult law relating to implied trusts, which we discuss below.

A.13   Where land is to vest in persons as joint proprietors,[20] Land Registry transfer forms TR1 and FR1 now make provision for joint legal owners to execute a declaration of trust so as to determine their beneficial interests in the property. These forms enable the intending proprietors to state whether they hold on trust for themselves beneficially (a) as joint tenants, (b) as tenants in common in equal shares, or (c) as tenants in common in unequal shares or as regulated by a separate trust deed.[21] Where a declaration has been made, that will be conclusive as to the beneficial entitlement in that property. In the event of the relationship breaking down, the proceeds of sale of the property should be divided in accordance with the parties' beneficial shares.[22] Although the declaration is not always executed, it is the practice of Land Registry to register the transfer nonetheless in such cases.[23]

A.14   The transfer in *Stack v Dowden*, which pre-dated the introduction of Form TR1, simply stated that the survivor of the joint proprietors could "give a valid receipt for capital money arising on a disposition of the land". This was unanimously held by the House of Lords not to amount to an express declaration of a beneficial joint tenancy. It may well be that the parties' legal adviser thought at the time that it was, and that in many transfers from that era the intention was thereby to make a declaration of trust. We now know that such intentions have not been realised.

A.15   Moreover, it is unlikely that a declaration of trust will have been made if the property was not jointly purchased. There is no obvious reason why legal advice would be sought where one person owns a house into which another comes to live. Even if a house is purchased at a time when the couple are living together, Land Registry documentation does not make provision for any beneficial interests to be declared if the legal title is transferred into the name of one party only.

A.16   Where there is no express declaration of trust, a cohabitant who wishes to assert a beneficial interest in the property must resort to the doctrines of implied trust and proprietary estoppel, discussed below.

---

[17]   *Pettitt v Pettitt* [1970] AC 777, 813, Lord Upjohn; see also *Goodman v Gallant* [1986] Fam 106.

[18]   *Pettitt v Pettitt* [1970] AC 777, 813, Lord Upjohn; see also *Goodman v Gallant* [1986] Fam 106.

[19]   *Bullock v Lloyds Bank Ltd* [1955] Ch 317.

[20]   Whether on an application for first registration, on a transfer of land with registered title, or on an assent to the vesting of land in persons entitled under a deceased's estate.

[21]   Under option (c), the parties may specify their unequal shares, or they may state that the land is held on trust for the members of an unincorporated association or in accordance with a separate trust deed.

[22]   Disputes about whether the property should be sold so as to realise the parties' shares may be determined by application under the Trusts of Land and Appointment of Trustees Act 1996 ("TOLATA"), s 14.

[23]   We have discussed at para 2.17 and following the difficulties arising from this practice and the pertinent observations of Baroness Hale in *Stack v Dowden* [2007] UKHL 17, [2007] 2 WLR 831, at [52].

Express trusts of personal property

A.17 Express trusts in relation to personal property, including funds in bank accounts in the sole name of one party, do not depend on the execution of any formalities, and so may be declared orally.[24] The use of oral declarations in this context is significant and should be compared with the relevance of oral statements made in relation to land, discussed below from paragraph A.30. There is no need in the context of personal property for the beneficiary of the trust to have relied to his or her detriment on the oral declaration of trust before it will be enforceable.

"Cohabitation contracts"

A.18 Private regulation by cohabitants has been problematic owing to the historical illegality of contracts which could be said to promote extra-marital sexual relations. Contemporary case law for the most part clearly distinguishes "meretricious" contracts (where sexual relations form part of the consideration and so the contract may be regarded as contrary to public policy) from those regulating the financial and property relationships of cohabitants.[25]

A.19 Cohabitation contracts may cover various issues and be concluded at various times. They may regulate the financial affairs of the parties during the currency of the relationship, or make provision for the parties' financial affairs (including the division of their assets) on separation. They may be concluded before the parties' cohabitation, during the parties' cohabitation or following the parties' separation.

A.20 The validity of such contracts depends on the impact, if any, of the illegality rule. It seems that contracts made following separation have never been void for illegality, and so will be binding, provided that they are executed in a deed or otherwise supported by lawful consideration.[26] Difficulties arguably remain in relation to contracts made before or during the relationship, owing to the lack of clear case law upholding such contracts. Judicial comments in some of the older case law indicate that contracts between cohabitants may be unlawful or unenforceable on the ground of public policy.[27] However, the better view is that such contracts are only liable to be struck down if they comprise contracts for prostitution.[28] The modern law was recently stated by Mr Justice Hart to the effect that:

> There is nothing contrary to public policy in a cohabitation agreement governing the property relationship between adults who intend to

---

[24] *Rowe v Prance* [1999] 2 FLR 787; *Paul v Constance* [1977] 1 WLR 527.

[25] See G Treitel, *The Law of Contract* (11th ed 2003) pp 443 to 444.

[26] See G Treitel, *The Law of Contract* (11th ed 2003) p 443, n 56.

[27] *Upfill v Wright* [1911] 1 KB 506.

[28] Treitel, *The Law of Contract* (11th ed 2003) p 443; R Probert, *"Sutton v Mishcon de Reya and Gawor & Co* – Cohabitation contracts and Swedish sex slaves" (2004) 16 *Child and Family Law Quarterly* 453. In *Tanner v Tanner (No 1)* [1975] 1 WLR 1346, the court implied a contractual licence between an unmarried couple, so it seems unlikely that the courts would hold an express contract to be void for illegality.

cohabit or who are cohabiting for the purposes of enjoying a sexual relationship.[29]

A.21 On this basis, there seems no distinction as far as public policy is concerned as between the types of cohabitation contract described above. The leading textbooks are confident that contracts regulating the financial affairs of cohabitants would be enforced,[30] and books of legal precedents exist to aid cohabitants and legal advisers in drafting cohabitation contracts.[31] The current law therefore appears to allow parties to enter into all such kinds of contract and to permit enforcement by the courts in the event of breach. However, it could be argued that the statement of Mr Justice Hart above was not strictly necessary for the decision in the case. While we would expect it to be followed in subsequent cases, it cannot be conclusively said that it represents the current state of English law.

A.22 In so far as they are lawful, cohabitation contracts are governed by the ordinary rules of contract law. So, for example, there must be an intention to create legal relations and lawful consideration (or use of a deed), and a contract between cohabitants may be susceptible to challenge on grounds such as fraud, duress, undue influence, misrepresentation, mistake, duress or illegality on some other ground.

IMPLIED TRUSTS AND PROPRIETARY ESTOPPEL

A.23 Where no express declaration of trust has been made on or after the acquisition of property, the laws of implied trusts and proprietary estoppel may be called upon in order to determine the respective entitlements of cohabitants to any property which they own or occupy.[32] They can operate whether the legal title is

---

[29] *Sutton v Mishcon de Reya and Gawor & Co* [2003] EWHC 3166 (Ch), [2004] 1 FLR 837, at [22].

[30] See, for example, S Cretney, J Masson and R Bailey-Harris, *Principles of Family Law* (7th ed 2003) pp 135 to 136; G Treitel, *The Law of Contract* (11th ed 2003) p 444; *Chitty on Contracts* (29th ed 2004) paras 16-067 and 16-068; and C Barton, *Cohabitation Contracts: Extra-Marital Partnerships and Law Reform* (1985) p 48 to 49. Note also that the Committee of Ministers of the Council of Europe has recommended that cohabitation contracts should be enforceable: Committee of Ministers of the Council of Europe, *The validity of contracts between persons living together as an unmarried couple and their testamentary dispositions,* Recommendation No R (88) 3 of 7 March 1988: "contracts relating to property between persons living together as an unmarried couple, or which regulate matters concerning their property either during their relationship or when their relationship has ceased, should not be considered invalid solely because they have been concluded under these conditions".

[31] For example, H Wood, D Lush and D Bishop, *Cohabitation: Law, Practice and Precedents* (3rd ed 2005).

[32] Cases regarding beneficial ownership, most between cohabitants, constitute around 50% of the caseload of the Adjudicator to HM Land Registry. In a study of legally-aided cases, 61% of land-related cases involved current or former cohabitants or spouses: T Goriely and P Das Gupta, *Breaking the Code: The impact of legal aid reforms on general civil litigation* (2001) ch 11. This study pre-dated major legal aid reforms in April 2000. Data received from the Legal Services Commission for 2004-05 and 2005-06 show that around 80% of cases receiving General Family Help or Legal Representation in relation to trusts of land involved ex-cohabitants.

in the name of one or of both parties.[33] The significance of these principles is that they allow beneficial interests to be created despite failure to comply with the formalities that are required to create express trusts. They are particularly important in relation to the shared home, but can also apply to all other kinds of property. The ownership of funds in a joint bank account and property purchased from that source are discussed separately below.[34]

A.24 The important decision of the House of Lords in *Stack v Dowden* now requires the courts to adopt a new approach when they address the question of beneficial entitlements to the shared home of a couple who have not made any express declaration of trust. We discuss that new approach below.

Resulting trusts

A.25 Following *Stack v Dowden*, resulting trusts would appear to have limited or no application in determining the beneficial interests of cohabiting couples (or married couples, or civil partners) in the home which they occupy. But it may still be relevant in determining beneficial interests of cohabitants in other property, such as personal property or real property which does not comprise the couple's shared home.

A.26 Where the legal title to property vests in one party, but another party has paid some (or all) of the purchase price, the presumption of resulting trust holds that beneficial ownership "results" to the parties in proportion to the share of the purchase price that each provided. So if one party contributes £10,000 towards the purchase of property worth £100,000, that party will acquire a 10% share in the value of the property. The presumption of resulting trust may, however, be rebutted by evidence that the contributor did not intend to acquire a beneficial interest in the property purchased. For example, the money may have been provided by way of gift or loan.[35]

A.27 Most importantly, a resulting trust will only be presumed at all on the making of particular types of contribution. Direct financial contributions to the purchase price, payment of the deposit and contribution of a "right to buy" discount[36] have all been regarded by the courts as contributions.

A.28 Not all financial contributions are sufficient to give rise to a resulting trust. Whether making mortgage payments will give rise to a beneficial interest under a resulting trust depends on the nature of the mortgage and the intention of the payer in making the payments.[37] Crucially, "indirect" financial contributions have

---

[33] Though the new Land Registry forms, which appear to require express declarations of the beneficial shares, should mean that, in cases of joint title, the law of implied trusts need no longer be relied on: see para 2.18.

[34] See paras A.46 to A.48; and S Cretney, J Masson and R Bailey-Harris, *Principles of Family Law* (7th ed 2003) pp 159 to 160.

[35] *Fowkes v Pascoe* (1874-75) LR 10 Ch App 343; *Walker v Walker*, judgment of 12 April 1984, CA (unreported); *Re Sharpe (A Bankrupt)* [1980] 1 WLR 219.

[36] *Springette v Defoe* [1992] 2 FLR 388.

[37] See for example *Curley v Parkes* [2004] EWCA Civ 1515, [2005] 1 P & CR DG15 (payer not party to mortgage); *McKenzie v McKenzie* [2003] 2 P & CR DG6, at [77] of the full judgment (payer party to mortgage); for comment, M Dixon, "Resulting and Constructive

not been regarded as giving rise to a resulting trust: for example, where one party pays the household bills,[38] while the other pays the mortgage. Even payments into a common pool from which the mortgage is paid may not suffice.[39] Domestic contributions count for nothing.[40]

A.29 However, the significance of these limitations on the applicability of the resulting trust presumption is diminished as a result of the developing law of constructive trusts. The forms of contribution from which a resulting trust would be presumed may also generate a constructive trust, which potentially offers contributors a more substantial share than the *pro rata* value of their contributions. The constructive trust is therefore likely to be preferred by applicants; and certainly constructive trust reasoning, as developed in *Stack v Dowden*,[41] will now be employed in relation to a couple's shared home.

Constructive trusts

A.30 The common intention constructive trust is the creation of case law in the 1970s.[42] A cohabitant who wishes to claim a beneficial interest in property held in the other's sole name can argue that the legal title is held upon trust for both parties.[43] Equally where property is in joint names, as it was in *Stack v Dowden*,[44] the principles of the common intention constructive trust can be used to show that beneficial ownership does not reflect legal ownership, in that context, that there is not a beneficial joint tenancy.

Proving a common intention constructive trust

A.31 Cases of constructive trust fall into two categories:

(1) express common intention cases, arising from an express (though informal) agreement, arrangement or understanding between the parties; and

(2) inferred common intention cases, which will arise where one party has engaged in conduct referable to the acquisition of an interest in the property.[45]

Trusts of Land: the Mist Descends and Rises" (2005) *Conveyancer and Property Lawyer* 79.

[38] *Gissing v Gissing* [1971] AC 886.

[39] *Buggs v Buggs* [2003] EWHC 1538 (Ch), [2004] WTLR 799.

[40] *Burns v Burns* [1984] Ch 317.

[41] Though that fact sometimes appears to be curiously overlooked: for example, no constructive trust argument was considered in *Curley v Parkes* [2004] EWCA Civ 1515, [2005] 1 P & CR DG15.

[42] *Gissing v Gissing* [1971] AC 886.

[43] It has been the practice to claim resulting and constructive trust in the alternative; but as we noted above, it appears that the role of the resulting trust in determining ownership of the shared home may have been eliminated following *Stack v Dowden* [2007] UKHL 17, [2007] 2 WLR 831.

[44] [2007] UKHL 17, [2007] 2 WLR 831.

[45] *Lloyds Bank Plc v Rosset* [1991] 1 AC 107.

EXPRESS COMMON INTENTION CONSTRUCTIVE TRUSTS

A.32   The courts have been generous in their interpretation of the common intention requirement. They have been prepared to treat excuses for not putting one party on the title documents as evidence of an express common intention to share, even though it is clear that the private intention of the legal owner is that no such share should arise.[46]

INFERRED COMMON INTENTION CONSTRUCTIVE TRUSTS

A.33   In *Lloyds Bank Plc v Rosset*, Lord Bridge stated that a common intention would be inferred from direct financial contributions to the initial purchase price of a house or from mortgage payments, but "it is at least extremely doubtful whether anything less will do".[47] It has been suggested that these words may set the first hurdle "rather too high in certain respects",[48] and that a somewhat broader view should taken of what contributions are to be taken into account.[49]

A.34   We explained in the CP the crucial ambiguity in the case law on the issue of whether a court may infer a common intention from financial contributions if the parties confess to having never considered the matter of ownership. The clear lack of any actual intention might be expected to rebut an inference of common intention to share beneficial ownership. Some judicial remarks have suggested that this is not necessarily the case, though those remarks themselves are ambiguous.[50] If, and in so far as, actual intention need not exist, it may be more accurate to say that the intention is "imputed" to the parties than its existence inferred. But it does seem to be necessary at least that the other party was aware of the conduct from which the common intention arises.[51]

A.35   However, whether or not actual intention is required, the inference (or imputation) of common intention will only arise from certain sorts of conduct. It is clear that direct financial contributions to the purchase of the property, including the making of mortgage payments, will suffice.[52] More difficult is the question of indirect financial contributions. Some decisions and judicial comments appear to accept that, at least in circumstances where the owner paying the mortgage could not have afforded to do so had the applicant not been paying other bills, payment of those bills will count for these purposes.[53] But other cases and judicial comments

---

[46]   *Grant v Edwards* [1986] Ch 638; *Eves v Eves* [1975] 1 WLR 1338.

[47]   *Lloyds Bank Plc v Rosset* [1991] 1 AC 107, 133.

[48]   *Stack v Dowden* [2007] UKHL 17, [2007] 2 WLR 831, at [63], Baroness Hale, referring to Sharing Homes: A Discussion Paper (2002) Law Com No 278, para 4.23.

[49]   *Stack v Dowden* [2007] UKHL 17, [2007] 2 WLR 831, at [34], Lord Walker.

[50]   CP, para 3.29 and n 44. See also para A.39 and n 62 regarding the discussion of this issue in *Stack v Dowden* [2007] UKHL 17, [2007] 2 WLR 831, at least in the context of the quantification of beneficial interests.

[51]   *Lightfoot v Lightfoot-Brown* [2005] EWCA Civ 201, [2005] 2 P & CR 22.

[52]   Though, as in the case of resulting trusts, the evidence might sometimes indicate that those payments were intended for some purpose other than the creation of a beneficial share: *McKenzie v McKenzie* [2003] 2 P & CR DG6.

[53]   *Gissing v Gissing* [1971] AC 886; *Le Foe v Le Foe and Woolwich Building Society plc* [2001] 2 FLR 970.

do not support the inference of common intention on this basis.[54] It is clear that domestic contributions will not give rise to an inferred common intention to share.[55]

DETRIMENTAL RELIANCE

A.36 It is the applicant's detrimental reliance on the common intention which makes it unconscionable for the legal owner to deny the applicant's beneficial interest. In cases of express common intention, the range of conduct and contributions that will count as detrimental reliance is wider than that which will give rise to an inferred common intention. In cases of inferred common intention, the conduct from which the common intention is inferred will also constitute detrimental reliance.

A.37 However, there remain limitations on which types of conduct the courts will classify as detrimental reliance. In the case of inferred common intention, those limitations derive from the narrow view of what conduct will generate the intention in the first place. In the case of express common intention, although in theory a wider range of conduct is relevant, it seems necessary to demonstrate that the conduct in question is "referable to" the common intention, and not conduct in which the applicant would have engaged anyway had there been no such intention. The case law is particularly ambiguous about conduct which might equally be attributable to the relationship between the parties: setting up home together, raising a family, sharing household bills and so on may not be regarded as detrimental reliance. If the applicant oversteps the boundary of what might be "expected" of a partner, particularly perhaps in light of the applicant's gender,[56] a finding of detrimental reliance is more likely.[57]

Quantifying the beneficial entitlement in the shared home

A.38 Once it has been established that the property is held upon trust it is then necessary to quantify the parties' respective shares.[58] We know that the applicant

---

[54] *Lloyds Bank v Rosset* [1991] 1 AC 107, 132H to 133B, Lord Bridge; *Buggs v Buggs* [2003] EWHC 1538 (Ch), [2004] WTLR 799; *Mollo v Mollo* [2000] WTLR 227; *Mehra v Shah* [2004] EWCA Civ 632; the point was not even considered in *Curley v Parkes* [2004] EWCA Civ 1515, [2005] 1 P & CR DG15; see n 62 on the observations in *Stack v Dowden* [2007] UKHL 17, [2007] 2 WLR 831.

[55] *Burns v Burns* [1984] Ch 317; *Lloyds Bank v Rosset* [1991] 1 AC 107. At least in relation to indirect financial contributions, note the observations of Lord Walker in *Stack v Dowden* [2007] UKHL 17, [2007] 2 WLR 831, at [26] to the effect that "the law has moved on" from Lord Bridge's remarks in *Rosset*, and at [34] as to the desirability of the law "taking a wide view of what is capable of counting as a contribution towards the acquisition of a residence".

[56] See K Gray and S F Gray, *Elements of Land Law* (4th ed 2005) para 10.123.

[57] Contrast *Grant v Edwards* [1986] Ch 638, 657A to 657B, Browne-Wilkinson V-C and 648G to 648H, Nourse LJ; *Hammond v Mitchell* [1991] 1 WLR 1127; *Eves v Eves* [1975] 1 WLR 1338; *Cox v Jones* [2004] EWHC 1486 (Ch), [2004] 2 FLR 1010.

[58] In *Hurst v Supperstone* [2005] EWHC 1309 (Ch), [2005] 1 FCR 352, at [11], Mr Michael Briggs QC, sitting as a deputy High Court judge, pointed out that once the court has found a common intention to share beneficial ownership, it should ask whether the parties intended to share as beneficial joint tenants or tenants in common. As joint tenants are equally entitled to the property, the parties can only hold the property in unequal shares if they intended (or the court imputes an intention) to hold the property as tenants in common. Only at this point does the question of quantifying the parties' interests arise

has a proprietary interest in the property, but we must now determine its extent. In some cases, this is the only relevance of constructive trust reasoning because the legal title to the property is held jointly. As we explained in Part 2 of this Report, the House of Lords in *Stack v Dowden*[59] has confirmed that there is a strong presumption that where the legal title to the shared home is held jointly, the parties will be beneficial joint tenants. A cohabitant who wants to claim more than a half share will have to employ constructive trust reasoning to do so.

A.39   How, then, does the court approach the quantification exercise? The House of Lords in *Stack v Dowden* has stated that this a matter of ascertaining the parties' intentions. Prior to *Stack v Dowden*, it was understood that the court's function was to determine what would be a fair share, in the light of the parties' whole course of dealing in relation to the property.[60] This is now no longer the case. The House of Lords has preferred the "holistic" approach to quantification advocated by the Law Commission in Sharing Homes. This involves the court undertaking a survey of the parties' course of dealing and taking account of their conduct in so far as it throws light on the question what shares were intended.[61] Baroness Hale preferred this exposition of the function for two reasons:

> First, it emphasises that the search is still for the result which reflects what the parties must, in light of their conduct, be taken to have intended. Secondly, therefore, it does not enable the court to abandon that search in favour of the result which the court itself considers fair.[62]

A.40   It is clear from *Stack v Dowden* that in ascertaining the parties' intentions, the court is now required to take account of a wide range of factors.[63] At the same time, the majority were at pains to emphasise the substantial task faced by a claimant who seeks to challenge the presumption that, in the absence of an express trust, joint legal owners have joint beneficial entitlement of the shared home.[64]

A.41   As it happened, *Stack v Dowden* was itself "a very unusual case",[65] justifying departure from the starting point of joint beneficial entitlement on the grounds that:

---

where the parties are joint owners at law, see now *Stack v Dowden* [2007] UKHL 17, [2007] 2 WLR 831, discussed in the text above.

[59] [2007] UKHL 17, [2007] 2 WLR 831.

[60] *Midland Bank Plc v Cooke* [1995] 4 All ER 562, 574C to 574E; *Oxley v Hiscock* [2004] EWCA Civ 546, [2005] Fam 211, at [69].

[61] Sharing Homes: A Discussion Paper (2002) Law Com No 278, para 4.27.

[62] *Stack v Dowden* [2007] UKHL 17, [2007] 2 WLR 831, at [61]. The majority does not squarely address the issue of whether the court may impute to the parties intentions that they did not in fact have; the language of imputation is used, without comment, several times. Lord Neuberger clearly excludes imputed intentions, [125] to [127] and [144].

[63] See para 2.11.

[64] *Stack v Dowden* [2007] UKHL 17, [2007] 2 WLR 831, at [69], Baroness Hale, at [34], Lord Walker.

[65] *Stack v Dowden* [2007] UKHL 17, [2007] 2 WLR 831, at [92], Baroness Hale.

(1)   Ms Dowden contributed far more to the acquisition of the home than Mr Stack did;

(2)   they did not pool their separate resources, even notionally, for the common good; and

(3)   they undertook separate responsibility for each part of the expenditure which each had agreed to pay.

Proprietary estoppel

A.42   Proprietary estoppel and constructive trusts share common ground and may often be pleaded in the alternative.[66] For an applicant to establish an interest in the owner's property under the law of proprietary estoppel, it is necessary to show that:

(1)   a representation or assurance that the applicant has or will have an interest in property has been made or given;

(2)   the applicant relied upon that representation or assurance; and

(3)   the owner then sought to deny the applicant an interest in a way that would result in unconscionable detriment to the applicant.

Recent decisions emphasise the need to take a broad approach, looking at the matter "in the round", in deciding whether the necessary unconscionability is present.[67]

The representation or assurance

A.43   In order to give rise to an estoppel, there must be a sufficiently specific representation made, or assurance given, by the owner[68] that the applicant is to have some interest or entitlement in property. The practice of inferring or imputing a common intention in order to found a constructive trust is therefore not mirrored in a proprietary estoppel claim. For the purposes of estoppel, the representation or assurance must actually exist; it cannot be inferred or imputed. It is not necessary that any specific asset or interest in it should be identified, but it must be possible ultimately to interpret the representation as applying to a particular asset or pool of assets.[69] What will not suffice is a general promise that the

---

[66]   The precise relationship between the two doctrines has long been a matter of judicial and academic debate: Sharing Homes: A Discussion Paper (2002) Law Com No 278, paras 2.101 to 2.104; and see now *Stack v Dowden* [2007] UKHL 17, [2007] 2 WLR 831, at [37], Lord Walker.

[67]   *Gillett v Holt* [2001] Ch 210; *Jennings v Rice* [2002] EWCA Civ 159, [2003] 1 FCR 501.

[68]   This may involve the owner standing by while the applicant makes a unilateral mistake about his or her entitlement in relation to the property: *Ward v Kirkland* [1967] Ch 194, 239A to 239B, Ungoed-Thomas J; *Taylor Fashions Ltd v Liverpool Victoria Trustees Co Ltd* [1982] QB 133, 148E to 148F, Oliver J.

[69]   *Jennings v Rice* [2002] EWCA Civ 159, [2003] 1 FCR 501.

respondent will support the applicant or that the applicant will be "financially secure" in the future.[70]

Detrimental reliance

A.44 Detrimental reliance in the estoppel context poses demands on applicants that are similar to the law of constructive trust. Applicants must show that the conduct engaged in was to some extent caused by the representation. While it need not have been the sole cause of the applicant's behaviour, it must have been a factor influencing it.[71] It is clear that non-financial contributions, including "domestic" activities and associated sacrifices of paid employment, may constitute detrimental reliance for the purposes of proprietary estoppel.[72] However, as in constructive trust cases, some applicants may find it difficult to satisfy the court that such activities were made in reliance on the representation, rather than pursuant to the parties' relationship.[73]

The remedy: "satisfying the equity"

A.45 Where these requirements are satisfied, the applicant has an "equity" which can be enforced against the owner, and the court may be called on to decide what remedy is necessary to satisfy it. The courts adopt a broad approach in deciding how to satisfy the applicant's equity. Recent case law emphasises the need for the remedy to be proportionate in light of the detriment sustained and the expectation held.[74] In some cases, they will give effect to the applicant's expectation. In others, they will simply compensate the applicant for the loss suffered in relying on the assurance, rather than giving the applicant what was promised. The remedy will frequently involve conferring on the applicant some sort of proprietary interest, although not necessarily a beneficial share;[75] or it may entail monetary compensation.[76] In some cases, the court may conclude that no remedy is necessary at all in view of benefits enjoyed by the applicant which cancel out the disadvantage he or she sustained.[77]

---

[70] *Lissimore v Downing* [2003] 2 FLR 308; *Layton v Martin* [1986] 2 FLR 227.

[71] *Wayling v Jones* [1995] 2 FLR 1029.

[72] *Greasley v Cooke* [1980] 1 WLR 1306; *Campbell v Griffin* [2001] EWCA Civ 990, [2001] WTLR 981.

[73] *Coombes v Smith* [1986] 1 WLR 808; *Lissimore v Downing* [2003] 2 FLR 308; compare *Grant v Edwards* [1986] Ch 638, 656, Browne-Wilkinson V-C.

[74] *Jennings v Rice* [2002] EWCA Civ 159, [2003] 1 FCR 501; *Gillett v Holt* [2001] Ch 210.

[75] For example, a freehold in *Pascoe v Turner* [1979] 1 WLR 431; a life interest in *Greasley v Cooke* [1980] 1 WLR 1306; leases in *Griffiths v Williams* [1977] 248 EG 947 and *J T Developments Ltd v Quinn* (1991) 62 P & CR 33; and an easement in *Crabb v Arun DC* [1976] Ch 179.

[76] *Dodsworth v Dodsworth* (1973) 228 EG 1115; *Jennings v Rice* [2002] EWCA Civ 159, [2003] 1 FCR 501.

[77] *Sledmore v Dalby* (1996) 72 P & CR 196. Roch LJ, with whom Butler-Sloss LJ agreed, said (at 205) that an equity had arisen by virtue of proprietary estoppel, but that the minimum necessary to satisfy that equity had already been received by the claimant. However, Hobhouse LJ considered (at 209) that the claimant had not even established an equity in her favour by virtue of proprietary estoppel; the issue of the minimum necessary remedy therefore did not arise.

Ownership of funds in bank accounts

A.46 The ownership of funds in bank accounts merits brief separate discussion. As we have seen, where an account is held in the sole name of one party, an express trust may arise by oral declaration.[78] The mere fact that a bank account is in joint names does not mean that the account holders have a joint beneficial interest in the funds in that account. Whether they do or not depends on their intentions. If the account is fed from the resources of one party, A, but is held in joint names with B merely for convenience – for example, to give B access to funds – B has no beneficial interest in the money in the account until he or she actually exercises the right to draw funds from it. While it remains in the account, the money will belong, under resulting trust principles, to A as the party who fed the account. If B has made no contribution to the account, A will be entitled to terminate B's access to the funds at any time.[79]

A.47 Where both parties contribute to the account, pooling their resources, they will at least be found to own the funds on a resulting trust basis in accordance with their contributions. However, both in pooling cases and in cases where A has provided all the funds, the presumption of resulting trust might be displaced, for example, where there is an express declaration of trust[80] or common intention to the effect that the parties should share the account in some other proportions. Indeed, the court might find that the parties intended to be joint tenants of the beneficial interest, each equally entitled to the whole of the fund.[81]

A.48 Property purchased with funds from a joint account will ordinarily belong to whoever acquires title to that property, even if that person had no or only a part-share in the funds when they were in the account.[82] If, unusually, there is evidence that the assets acquired were intended to be held in the same way as the funds in the account, then that property will be held accordingly.[83]

RESOLVING DISPUTES OVER THE HOME CO-OWNED BY COHABITANTS

A.49 Under the general law, if one party has no beneficial interest in the property, he or she is vulnerable to being excluded by the legal owner as a trespasser.[84] Where both parties are found to have a beneficial share in the property and they are separating, dispute may arise about whether the property should be sold and the proceeds divided (in accordance with their shares) or retained for the occupation of one party and sold at a later date. Either party may apply to the court under the Trusts of Land and Appointment of Trustees Act 1996

---

[78] *Paul v Constance* [1977] 1 WLR 527.

[79] *Stoeckert v Geddes (No 2)* [2004] UKPC 54, (2004-05) 7 ITELR 506, from the Court of Appeal of Jamaica.

[80] Compare *Paul v Constance* [1977] 1 WLR 527 in relation to an account in the name of one party.

[81] For a discussion of joint tenancy and tenancy in common, see Sharing Homes: A Discussion Paper (2002) Law Com No 278, paras 2.10 to 2.22.

[82] *Stoeckert v Geddes (No 2)* [2004] UKPC 54, (2004-05) 7 ITELR 506.

[83] *Jones v Maynard* [1951] Ch 572.

[84] Subject to the finding of a contractual licence for a determinate period or that might require reasonable notice be given: *Chandler v Kerley* [1978] 1 WLR 693.

("TOLATA") for orders resolving the questions of sale and occupation. In considering such an application, the court is required to have regard to:

(1) the intentions of the person(s) creating the trust;

(2) the purposes for which the property is held on trust;

(3) the welfare of any minor who occupies or might reasonably be expected to occupy the property as his home; and

(4) the interests of any secured creditors of any beneficial owner.[85]

A.50 Where one purpose of the trust is to provide a home for the parties' children, the court may be inclined to postpone sale until the home is no longer required for the children (and their primary carer).

A.51 If the court orders that sale should be postponed and one partner granted occupation in the meantime, the occupier may be required to pay the excluded party occupation rent during that period.[86] The provisions of TOLATA have replaced the old doctrine of equitable accounting.[87] Where the couple have separated, but the property was intended to provide a family home and is still required for that purpose for the couple's children and whichever party the children are to live with, the court might decide against an order for occupation rent.[88]

A.52 In the exercise of its TOLATA jurisdiction, the court has no power to adjust the parties' beneficial shares in the property. On any sale, the proceeds will therefore be split according to the parties' beneficial entitlements, whether express or implied by the court under a resulting or constructive trust.

A.53 We consider below the statutory remedies available to non-owning cohabitants which might result in a limited right of occupation being granted in relation to the property under Part 4 of the Family Law Act 1996 or, where the couple have children, under Schedule 1 to the Children Act 1989. The latter might also be invoked between co-owning cohabitants,[89] in which case any applications under the Children Act 1989 and the TOLATA should be joined. In such cases, the Children Act application would probably be considered before the TOLATA

---

[85] TOLATA, s 15. For the application of this provision, see *Mortgage Corporation v Shaire* [2001] Ch 743; *Bank of Ireland Home Mortgages v Bell* [2001] 2 All ER (Comm) 920; *First National Bank plc v Achampong* [2003] EWCA Civ 487, [2004] 1 FCR 18; and *Chan Pui Chun v Leung Kam Ho* [2002] EWCA Civ 1075, [2003] 1 FLR 23.

[86] TOLATA, ss 13 to 14.

[87] *Stack v Dowden* [2007] UKHL 17, [2007] 2 WLR 831, at [94]. For recent use of this remedy in contexts other than occupation rent, see *Young v Lauretani* [2007] EWHC 1244 (Ch); *Wilcox v Tait* [2006] EWCA Civ 1867, [2007] BPIR 262.

[88] *Stack v Dowden* [2005] EWCA Civ 857, [2006] 1 FLR 254, affirmed by the House of Lords [2007] UKHL 17, [2007] 2 WLR 831, at [94].

[89] Especially if it is unclear whether or not the parties share the beneficial interest.

application, owing to the wider powers enjoyed by the court under the former Act.[90]

FAMILY LAW REMEDIES ON RELATIONSHIP BREAKDOWN

A.54 The court has very wide powers to deal with the property of married couples on their divorce in order to ensure a broadly fair outcome between the parties. These powers are contained in Part 2 of the Matrimonial Causes Act 1973.[91] The court may make orders for periodical payments secured or unsecured, lump sum orders, orders for settlement of property or for variation of existing settlements, pension sharing orders, orders transferring property and orders for sale.

A.55 There is no analogous, wide-ranging jurisdiction applicable when cohabiting couples separate. Most cohabitants therefore have to rely heavily on the general law of trusts and estoppel. There are, however, three statutory regimes which they may invoke.

Protection of occupation

A.56 Part 4 of the Family Law Act 1996 (titled "Family Homes and Domestic Violence") allows the court to make occupation orders in relation to a dwelling-house in which cohabitants live, lived, or intended to live together. The concept of "cohabitant" is not defined in the Act, save by analogy with marriage and civil partnership,[92] and there is no requirement that the parties' relationship should have lasted any minimum duration to qualify for protection under the Act.

A.57 While this jurisdiction is principally used in cases of domestic violence, it is not so restricted and it may in theory be employed to facilitate the separation of cohabitants by making orders for the short-term exclusion of one party from the property. However, the courts regard occupation orders as "draconian", and so without evidence of abuse that would render continued cohabitation potentially harmful, they are reluctant to make orders excluding cohabitants who are otherwise entitled to occupy the property.[93] Occupation orders may nevertheless provide a very effective short-term remedy. In practice, the long-term resolution of their occupation dispute will be resolved under TOLATA[94] (where both parties are co-owners) or Schedule 1 to the Children Act 1989 (where they have children).

Applicants who are entitled to occupy

A.58 The best protection is offered by the Family Law Act to applicants who are "entitled to occupy" the property under the general law of property, trusts or contract, or by statute. Spouses and civil partners are included in this category of

---

[90] *White v White* [2003] EWCA Civ 924, [2004] 2 FLR 321.

[91] Equivalent provision is made for civil partners under the Civil Partnership Act 2004, sch 5.

[92] Family Law Act 1996, s 62(1); for judicial application of the concept, see *G v F* [2000] Fam 186.

[93] *Chalmers v Johns* [1999] 1 FLR 392, a case arising at the end of a twenty-year long cohabiting relationship, where an interim occupation order was withheld despite a history of assaults by each party against the other, in preference for use of non-molestation orders.

[94] TOLATA, ss 12 to 15.

applicants by virtue of their statutory "home rights".[95] Where a cohabitant is "entitled to occupy" the property, the court may make an order allowing him or her to occupy the property to the exclusion of the other party for an unlimited period.[96] The court is required to make an order in certain cases where the "balance of harm" demands it.[97] Otherwise, in deciding whether to make an order and (if making an order) in what terms, the court is required to have regard to all the circumstances, including:[98]

(1) the housing needs and housing resources of each of the parties and of any relevant child;[99]

(2) the financial resources of each of the parties;

(3) the likely effect of any order, or any decision not to make an order, on the health, safety or well-being of the parties and of any relevant child; and

(4) the conduct of the parties in relation to each other and otherwise.

Applicants who are not entitled to occupy

A.59 Applications by cohabitants who are not entitled to occupy property which the other is entitled to occupy are more complicated.[100] The court must first decide whether to give that cohabitant the right to occupy against the wishes of the other (entitled) partner. In making that decision, the court is required to have regard to all the circumstances, including those listed in paragraph A.58, and also:[101]

(1) the nature of the parties' relationship and in particular the level of commitment involved in it;

(2) the length of time during which they have cohabited;

(3) whether there are or have been any children who are the children of both parties or for whom both parties have or have had parental responsibility;

(4) (where relevant) the length of time that has elapsed since the parties ceased to live together; and

---

[95] Family Law Act 1996, s 30.

[96] Family Law Act 1996, s 33.

[97] See Family Law Act 1996, s 33(7): this complicated test in broad terms entails weighing (i) the harm that might be suffered by the applicant or any relevant child attributable to the conduct of the respondent if an order were not made against (ii) the harm that might be suffered by the respondent or any relevant child if an order were made. If the harm under (i) is greater than that under (ii), an order must be made. If not, the court has a discretion to make an order.

[98] Family Law Act 1996, s 33(6).

[99] Defined broadly by s 62(2) to include any child who lives with or who might reasonably be expected to live with either party and whose interests the court considers relevant.

[100] Family Law Act 1996, s 36; contrast s 38, which applies where neither party is entitled to occupy.

[101] Family Law Act 1996, s 36(6).

(5)   the existence of any pending proceedings between the parties under Schedule 1 to the Children Act 1989 for a property settlement or transfer for the benefit of a child, or relating to the legal or beneficial ownership of the dwelling.

A.60   If the court decides to allow the non-entitled party to occupy, it then considers whether to restrict the entitled partner's occupation of the property. In making that decision, it is directed to have regard in particular to the factors listed in paragraph A.58, and the "balance of harm" arising to the parties from making or not making an order.[102]

A.61   Where the party seeking the order is not entitled to occupy the property under the general law, the duration of the order is strictly limited in the first instance to a maximum of six months. It may be extended for only one further six-month period, offering at most twelve months' protection.[103] We shall see below that considerably longer occupation protection can be obtained indirectly by a non-owning cohabitant with whom the parties' children live, by virtue of Schedule 1 to the Children Act 1989.

A.62   The court has the power to attach various supplementary provisions to an order made under the Family Law Act.[104] These may deal with repair and maintenance obligations, possession and the use of furniture and other contents. They may require the party in occupation to pay occupation rent to the excluded, entitled party. Finally, and most importantly, they may impose obligations on one party to fund the rent, mortgage payments or other outgoings affecting the property. However, owing to apparent legislative oversight, orders requiring payment of rent, mortgage instalments or outgoings are effectively unenforceable.[105] This is a serious problem, which may effectively deprive this otherwise useful order of much of its utility (not only in non-entitled cohabitants' cases, but more widely).[106]

Transfer of tenancies

A.63   Under Schedule 7 to the Family Law Act 1996, the court may order the transfer of certain types of residential tenancy when cohabitants have "ceased to cohabit".[107] In order to qualify for this remedy, the parties' relationship need not have lasted any minimum duration.

[102] Family Law Act 1996, s 36(7)(8): see n 97, but note that in cases brought by non-entitled cohabitants, the balance of harm test never requires the court to make an order; it retains complete discretion.

[103] Family Law Act 1996, s 36(10) and s 38(6).

[104] Family Law Act 1996, s 40(1).

[105] See *Nwogbe v Nwogbe* [2000] 2 FLR 744.

[106] TOLATA contains no provisions that could be used to plug the gap. There might be indirect means of enforcing an obligation to pay in matrimonial cases, for example, by spouse A undertaking to pay the mortgage. The court can encourage A to meet that undertaking by making a nominal periodical payment order in favour of spouse B, who is in possession of the property. B in turn undertakes not to seek a variation of the periodical payments order unless A fails to pay the mortgage, in which case the order will be increased so that B can pay the mortgage directly. This mechanism involves certain complexities and potential economic disadvantage to B.

[107] This provision originates in Domestic Violence and Occupation of the Family Home (1992) Law Com No 207, Part 6.

A.64 The legislation directs the courts to have regard to all the circumstances when considering the exercise of this power, including:

(1) the circumstances in which the tenancy was granted to either or both of the cohabitants, or in which either or both became the tenant;

(2) the suitability of the parties as tenants;

(3) factors (1) to (3) from the list of considerations relevant to the making of occupation orders for applicants who are entitled to occupy the property (see paragraph A.58); and

(4) where only one of the cohabitants is entitled to occupy the dwelling under the tenancy, factors (1) to (4) from the list of additional considerations relevant to the making of occupation orders for applicants who are not entitled to occupy the property (see paragraph A.59).

A.65 The party to whom the transfer is made may be required to pay compensation to the other.[108]

A.66 There is little reported case law to show how the courts are exercising this power[109] and no centrally collected court statistics record the number of Schedule 7 applications or orders made.[110] It may be the case that local authorities are often co-operative and prepared to transfer the tenancy without the need for a court application, assuming that both parties agree to the transfer. The case law does indicate that the courts may be reluctant to make transfer orders in respect of social housing, save in cases of domestic violence or impending homelessness, where to do so may hamper housing authorities' policies.[111]

A.67 Conversely, in making such an order, care also needs to be taken to ensure that the party against whom it is sought is not therefore liable to be treated as "intentionally homeless" and so prejudiced in his or her attempts to find new social housing.[112] It seems that this may effectively require respondents to oppose the application for a tenancy transfer, expending time and resources in the process.

A.68 In some circumstances, notably where the tenant has the right to buy, an application for tenancy transfer might be bitterly contested. However, in other

---

[108] Family Law Act 1996, sch 7, para 10.

[109] The tenancy in *Gay v Sheeran* [2000] 1 WLR 673 was not of a relevant type; for a recent example in a case between spouses, see *Lake v Lake* [2006] EWCA Civ 1250, [2007] 1 FLR 427.

[110] Figures obtained from the Legal Services Commission for the year from April 2005 up to March 2006 (financial year ongoing) reveal only a very small number of cases involving tenancy transfer between cohabitants receiving General Family Help and Legal Representation; Legal Help, Family Mediation or Help with Mediation cases are not included, as the codes for these are not specific enough to identify cases involving cohabitants.

[111] *Vuong v Huang*, judgment of 11 January 1999, Family Division (unreported), [1999] CLY 3734; contrast *Jones v Jones* [1997] Fam 59; *Akintola v Akintola* [2001] EWCA Civ 1989, [2002] 1 FLR 701.

[112] See Housing Act 1996, s 191.

cases the power to obtain a tenancy transfer may be of only limited value. Much depends on the security represented by the tenancy. In the private sector, the tenant is likely to hold an assured shorthold tenancy which is easily terminable by the landlord serving notice.[113]

A.69 Where the tenancy is held jointly, it may be vulnerable to one party serving notice to quit on the landlord before an application can be made.[114] Questions have been raised about the compatibility of the rule permitting unilateral notice to quit with the other party's rights under Article 8 of the European Convention for the Protection of Human Rights and Fundamental Freedoms ("ECHR").[115] The courts currently have no statutory anti-avoidance or other powers to rectify this problem once the tenancy has been terminated,[116] although it has been suggested that, in cases involving children, an injunction to prevent notice being given could be sought under Schedule 1 to the Children Act 1989 or the inherent jurisdiction.[117] We have already recommended in the course of our project on Renting Homes that all tenants should agree to the service of a notice to quit in order for it to be effective.[118]

Provision for children

Maintenance and the Child Support Act 1991

A.70 Where the Child Support Agency has jurisdiction over a case under the Child Support Act 1991,[119] income payments for the child's maintenance will usually be

---

[113] Housing Act 1988, s 21(1): the landlord can serve a notice under s 21(1)(b) at any point which must give the tenant a minimum of two months' notice. However, the court may not make an order for possession during the first six months of the tenancy.

[114] *Hammersmith and Fulham LBC v Monk* [1992] 1 AC 478; *Newlon Housing Trust v Al-Sulaimen* [1999] 1 AC 313.

[115] *Harrow London Borough Council v Qazi* [2003] UKHL 43, [2004] 1 AC 983, held that the consequent possession proceedings brought by the public sector landlord were compatible with the Convention (this finding seems to survive *Kay v Lambeth LBC* [2006] UKHL 10, [2006] 2 AC 465); the case did not consider the compatibility of the underlying notice to quit rule as it operates between the tenants. In relation to the latter, see S Bright, "Ending tenancies by notice to quit: the human rights challenge" (2004) 120 *Law Quarterly Review* 398; and I Loveland, "After *Qazi*: Part 1: Sole tenant termination of joint tenancies and Article 8 ECHR" (2005) *Conveyancer and Property Lawyer* 123.

[116] In the case of spouses, see H Conway, "Protecting Tenancies on Marriage Breakdown" (2001) 31 *Family Law* 208; for arguments based on the European Convention for the Protection of Human Rights and Fundamental Freedoms, see I Loveland, "After *Qazi*: Part 1: Sole tenant termination of joint tenancies and Article 8 ECHR" (2005) *Conveyancer and Property Lawyer* 123.

[117] *Bater v Greenwich LBC* [1999] 4 All ER 944, Thorpe LJ. The court may also have inherent powers to bar the frustration of an application under Schedule 7 before notice to quit has been given: S Bridge, "Transferring Tenancies of the Family Home" (1998) 28 *Family Law* 26, at 29.

[118] Renting Homes: The Final Report, Volume 1: Report (2006) Law Com No 297, paras 4.9 to 4.12 (available at: http://www.lawcom.gov.uk/docs/lc297_vol1.pdf (last visited 3 July 2007).

[119] Generally, where the child is a "qualifying child" (Child Support Act 1991, ss 3(1) and 55), maintenance is sought by a "person with care" (s 3(3)) from a "non-resident parent" (s 3(2)), and all parties are habitually resident in the United Kingdom (s 44); see also restrictions in s 4(10). See para 1.44 on the current Bill.

exclusively a matter for the Agency. In such cases the courts are ordinarily unable to award periodical payments.[120]

Capital provision under Schedule 1 to the Children Act 1989

A.71 However, in all cases, the court has exclusive jurisdiction to make orders against the child's parent for lump sums,[121] property transfers and settlements for the benefit of the child, regardless of the nature of the relationship between the parents.[122] The relevant provisions are contained in Schedule 1 to the Children Act 1989. These powers, focused entirely on the child's needs, are potentially of very great importance to all parents, even if they never cohabited.

A.72 The legislation sets out a checklist of factors to be considered by a court exercising its jurisdiction under Schedule 1. These factors are very similar to those contained in matrimonial legislation for the benefit of children of spouses.[123] The welfare principle contained in section 1 of the Children Act does not apply to this jurisdiction,[124] but the welfare of the child is nevertheless an important factor.[125] In addition, the court must consider, amongst all the circumstances of the case:

(1) the income, earning capacity, property and other financial resources which each parent[126] has or is likely to have in the foreseeable future;

(2) the financial needs, obligations and responsibilities which each parent has or is likely to have in the foreseeable future;

(3) the financial needs of the child;

---

[120] The cases where the court will have the power to order periodical payments alongside the Agency's maintenance calculation are listed in Child Support Act 1991, s 8: orders made by consent (which only preclude an application to the Agency for one year (s 4(10)(aa)) or until the parent with care claims relevant means-tested benefits, whichever is sooner); orders in respect of education expenses (such as school fees) or expenses attributable to the child's disability; and orders dealing with any net income of the non-resident parent which exceeds the jurisdictional limit of the Agency (£2,000 per week).

[121] Lump sum orders must not be used as a vehicle for evading the limits on the court's jurisdiction to make maintenance provision. Capitalised maintenance in the form of a lump sum therefore cannot be ordered where the Agency has exclusive jurisdiction over maintenance: *Phillips v Peace* [1996] 2 FLR 230.

[122] Regardless of whether the parents ever cohabited. The Act can only be used to make orders against an individual who is not the child's parent where that individual is married (or in a civil partnership) and both parties to the marriage (or civil partnership) treat the child as a child of the family. This is the case regardless of whether the child is related to either party. Cohabitant "step-parents" and other non-parents are therefore not liable for their partners' children: Children Act 1989, s 105 and sch 1, para 16. See further para 4.108.

[123] See, for example, MCA, s 25(3) to (4); and, for civil partners, Civil Partnership Act 2004, sch 5, para 22. Where the parents have been married and divorce proceedings are pending, the court will almost always make orders under its MCA jurisdiction rather than under the Children Act 1989, sch 1.

[124] Children Act 1989, s 1 and s 105, definition of "upbringing".

[125] *Re P (A Child) (Financial Provision)* [2003] EWCA Civ 837, [2003] 2 FLR 865.

[126] The legislation also allows applications to be made by various non-parents: Children Act 1989, sch 1, para 1(1) and in limited cases by the child, para 2(1), in which cases see para 4(4).

(4)   the income, earning capacity (if any), property and other financial resources of the child;

(5)   any physical or mental disability of the child; and

(6)   the manner in which the child was being, or was expected to be, educated or trained.

A.73   Where the parties have been cohabiting, the standard of living enjoyed by the family is also a relevant consideration.[127]

A.74   Orders made under this legislation can, in theory, provide children with very substantial protection, for example, the provision of accommodation in the family home with the primary carer.

A.75   There are, however, important limitations to orders under the Children Act. They may ordinarily be directed only to meeting the children's needs during minority, or until the completion of their education.[128] They cannot be used to require the paying parent to support or house children into adulthood when the children are capable of supporting themselves.[129] The courts are therefore reluctant to order transfers of capital where that capital will not be exhausted in meeting the child's needs during minority. So, for example, the court will not transfer a house outright.[130] Once the child reaches majority or completes education, the home will revert to the parent (or parents), in accordance with their property law entitlements, as is appropriate for a remedy designed to protect the children.

A.76   The parent caring for the children is likely to benefit indirectly from orders made for the children, not least by being permitted to occupy the property reserved for them. However, any benefit enjoyed will be in that individual's capacity as the children's primary carer, and only to the extent necessary to enable him or her to perform that role.[131] The Act confers no power to adjust the adult parties' property rights in order to achieve a fair outcome between them, as opposed to providing for the children. The courts cannot, therefore, give parents with care any beneficial share in the house or an interest in the other party's pension fund or other property. Again, this is appropriate in the context of a remedy designed to protect the children.

---

[127] *F v G (A Child: Financial Provision)* [2004] EWHC 1848 (Fam), [2005] 1 FLR 261.

[128] In *A v A (A Minor: Financial Provision)* [1994] 1 FLR 657, the house was settled on trust for the child until six months after she reached the age of 18, or six months after she finished her full-time education (which included her tertiary education), whichever was latest. See also *Re P (A Child)(Financial Provision)* [2003] EWCA Civ 837, [2003] 2 FLR 865.

[129] *A v A (A Minor: Financial Provision)* [1994] 1 FLR 657; contrast where the child is disabled and so "special circumstances" apply: Children Act 1989, sch 1, para 3(2)(b); *C v F (Disabled Child: Maintenance Orders)* [1998] 2 FLR 1.

[130] The property will instead be held on trust by the parents (or other individuals) as trustees for the child for the duration of the order: *K v K (Minors: Property Transfer)* [1992] 1 WLR 530.

[131] *Re P (A Child)(Financial Provision)* [2003] EWCA Civ 837, [2003] 2 FLR 865.

A.77   In the unusual cases where the court has jurisdiction to make periodical payments for the child,[132] that order can include a carer's allowance. But such an allowance is designed to provide the child with a carer and to meet that person's consequent needs in that capacity. The parent with care cannot be awarded periodical payments for his or her own personal benefit, even while the children are pre-school and may be inhibiting that parent from re-training or returning to full-time work. The adult parties have no independent personal claims against each other, so, for example, the amount awarded by way of carer's allowance will not permit the parent with care to make savings or invest in a pension.[133] However, in one recent case a carer's allowance was awarded on the basis that the mother should have a choice between using it: (i) to buy in child-care, enabling her to retain full-time employment and to accrue earnings of her own from which investments could be made; or (ii) to reduce her working hours so that she could spend more time with the child, but thus forgo her chance to earn and so to save.[134]

PROPERTY ENTITLEMENT ON THE DEATH OF A COHABITANT

A.78   In general terms, English law confers full powers of testamentary disposition on competent individuals, whether married or unmarried. Individuals with capacity to do so may therefore dispose of their estate as they wish by making a will, provided that the disposition complies with the relevant statutory formalities and is otherwise valid. Where a person dies having failed to dispose of the whole, or some part, of his or her estate, the intestacy rules will govern its destination.

A.79   However, the court has an important statutory discretion to make awards for reasonable financial provision to defined classes of applicant under the Inheritance (Provision for Family and Dependants) Act 1975 ("the 1975 Act"). The effect of a court order made under this legislation will be to vary or even to overturn the testator's dispositions by will (or the devolution of such of the estate that is not disposed of by will pursuant to the intestacy rules).

A.80   It is also important to remember that whenever someone dies, the first task must be to ascertain what property falls within the deceased's estate. For these purposes, the general law of property and trusts, outlined above from paragraphs A.7 to A.17 and from A.23 to A.48, will apply.

Property passing otherwise than by probate

A.81   The property of a deceased person may pass by other means than by will or by operation of the intestacy rules. Certain items of property (typically a house, or a bank account) may be held by cohabitants beneficially as joint tenants at the time of the death, in which case the doctrine of survivorship will apply.[135] On death the property in question vests automatically in the survivor without any need for further legal formality. This can be an effective and efficient means of transmitting important items of property, and in some cases (where the cohabitants have only

---

[132] See n 120.

[133] See *Re P (A Child)(Financial Provision)* [2003] EWCA Civ 837, [2003] 2 FLR 865.

[134] *F v G (Child: Financial Provision)* [2004] EWHC 1848 (Fam), [2005] 1 FLR 261.

[135] K Gray and S F Gray, *Elements of Land Law* (4th ed 2005) paras 11.8 to 11.21.

one major asset, such as their home) may mean that it is unnecessary to make a will.

A.82 Provision may also be made for a cohabitant by exercising a power of nomination in relation to small investments held by industrial and provident societies.[136] Or a cohabitant may receive a death-in-service payment in relation to a partner who has nominated him or her to receive it.[137]

A.83 Certain residential tenancies (that is, of houses or flats) are transmitted on death by the operation of the Housing Act 1985, the Housing Act 1988, the Housing Act 1996 and (now relatively rarely) the Rent Act 1977.[138]

A.84 The Life Assurance Act 1774 renders void and illegal any policy of insurance where the applicant for the policy did not have an "insurable interest" in the life to be insured. A person has an insurable interest in the life of his or her spouse or civil partner, regardless of whether the death would cause any financial loss. However, there is no such automatic interest in the case of cohabitants. The subject of life assurance falls outside the scope of this project, but in a separate project on insurance contract law we are considering whether these rules should be reviewed to establish whether reform is desirable.[139]

Intestacy

Entitlement on intestacy

A.85 Under current law, a cohabitant has no entitlement on the intestacy of his or her partner. Entitlement under the intestacy rules is strictly confined to those who are related by blood or by marriage to the deceased.

Bona vacantia

A.86 There is, however, one instance where the operation of the intestacy rules themselves may, albeit indirectly, result in benefit to a cohabitant. Where an intestate dies without leaving any relatives qualifying under the intestacy rules, his or her estate will devolve upon the Crown (or, if the intestate dies resident there, upon the Royal Duchies of Cornwall or Lancaster) as *bona vacantia*.[140]

---

[136] J G Miller, *The Machinery of Succession* (2nd ed 1996) p 111.

[137] Such nominations are usually not binding on pension trustees but are rarely departed from in practice.

[138] We have recommended changes to cohabitants' succession rights in Renting Homes: The Final Report, Volume 1: Report (2006) Law Com No 297, Part 7. Under our recommendations, the criteria for succession would be essentially the same, but survivorship would not constitute a succession, and a second succession would be possible in some circumstances.

[139] Insurance Contract Law: A Joint Scoping Paper (2006) Law Commission and Scottish Law Commission, para 2.2. This issue will be considered in detail in a consultation paper to be published in 2008: see Insurance Contract Law: Misrepresentation, Non-Disclosure and Breach of Warranty by the Insured (2007) Law Commission Consultation Paper No 182, Scottish Law Commission Discussion Paper No 134, paras 1.3 and 6.55.

[140] If the estate is small (consisting of a net cash residue not exceeding £500) the case need not be referred to the Treasury Solicitor. There is a special procedure for estates over £500 but under £2,000. See The Treasury Solicitor Bona Vacantia Division, *Guidelines for*

A.87   The Crown has power (historically derived from the Royal prerogative) to make discretionary provision for "dependants" of the intestate and for other persons for whom the intestate might reasonably have been expected to make provision.[141] The policy and the criteria applied by the Treasury Solicitor in making discretionary grants have been published since December 2002. In exercise of this power, it is relatively common for grants to be made to cohabitants, as indicated in the published guidelines:[142]

> If the deceased was married at the time of his or her death then, in general, the estate will not pass to the Crown. However, discretionary grants have often been made in cases where the applicant and the deceased, although unmarried, lived together in an established relationship. For example, the deceased may have lived with his or her partner as man and wife. Alternatively, the deceased may have lived with his or her partner in an established same-sex relationship.

A.88   When deciding whether to make a discretionary grant, and deciding upon its value, the factors which the Treasury Solicitor considers are:

(1)   the size and nature of the estate;

(2)   the length and nature of the relationship between the deceased and the applicant;

(3)   any legal or moral obligations the deceased had towards the applicant;

(4)   the way in which the applicant behaved towards the deceased (including the contribution, if any, made by the applicant to the deceased's welfare); and

(5)   any other matter which in the particular circumstances the Treasury Solicitor considers relevant.[143]

These factors are similar to, but not the same as, the considerations to which the court must have regard in exercising its jurisdiction under the 1975 Act.[144]

A.89   There is substantial overlap between the making of discretionary grants and the law of family provision. Where the applicant for a grant is entitled to make a claim under the 1975 Act, it is the Treasury Solicitor's policy to require the applicant to bring proceedings under the Act.[145] This enables the Crown to ensure that all

referring estates to the Treasury Solicitor (2005), available at http://www.bonavacantia.gov.uk/default.asp?PageId=1345 (last visited 3 July 2007).

[141]   Administration of Estates Act 1925, s 46(1(vi)).

[142]   The Treasury Solicitor Bona Vacantia Division, Guide to discretionary grants in estates cases (2005) para 31(a). Available at http://www.bonavacantia.gov.uk/default.asp?PageId=1347 (last visited 3 July 2007).

[143]   The Treasury Solicitor Bona Vacantia Division, Guide to discretionary grants in estates cases (2005) para 10.

[144]   See paras A..101 to A.103.

[145]   The Treasury Solicitor Bona Vacantia Division, Guide to discretionary grants in estates cases (2005) para 21. See, for example, Re Watson [1999] 1 FLR 878.

those entitled to claim are party to any compromise that is reached and thereby to minimise the risk of a late and unanticipated claim being made once the estate has been administered. The requirement may, however, be waived. If the estate is modest in size (below £20,000), or if it would not be reasonable to expect the applicant to pursue an application under the 1975 Act (typically on grounds of frailty due to old age or ill health), the Crown may make grants without requiring prior commencement of action.[146] It may also be the case that the applicant is not entitled to claim under the 1975 Act.[147] This will not, of course, preclude an application for a discretionary grant.

A.90   In theory, at least, there may be advantages to claiming under *bona vacantia* rather than under the 1975 Act, although, in practice, much will depend on the size of the estate. If a cohabitant claims reasonable financial provision under the 1975 Act, the claim is confined to that which is reasonable for his or her maintenance.[148] If a cohabitant claims a discretionary grant under the *bona vacantia* jurisdiction, there is no such ceiling to the claim.

Family provision

A.91   The Inheritance (Provision for Family and Dependants) Act 1975 (as amended) provides a scheme for those who claim that the disposition of an estate (whether effected by will or the intestacy rules or the combination of the two) has failed to make them reasonable financial provision.

A.92   The scope and extent of family provision legislation has expanded since its introduction in 1938. Initially, the only persons who could apply were the deceased's spouse, infant son, unmarried daughter, and adult sons and married daughters who by reason of some mental or physical disability were incapable of maintaining themselves.[149] Consistent with its objective to deal with "unjust wills", claims could only be brought if the deceased died testate, and the only order available to the court was one for periodical payments, save where the estate was below £2,000.

A.93   The current statute was enacted following a review of the family provision laws by the Law Commission.[150] The 1975 Act originally set out five qualifying classes of applicant;[151] a sixth was added in 1995.[152] A surviving cohabitant may now have a claim under one or both of two classes: as a dependant or as a cohabitant of the deceased.

---

[146] The Treasury Solicitor Bona Vacantia Division, *Guide to discretionary grants in estates cases* (2005) para 22.

[147] In particular, if the cohabitant lived with the deceased for less than two years, and is unable to establish dependency immediately before the death.

[148] See paras A.98 and following.

[149] Inheritance (Family Provision) Act 1938, s 1(1).

[150] Second Report on Family Property: Family Provision on Death (1974) Law Com No 61.

[151] Spouses, former spouses, children, children of the family and dependants of the deceased.

[152] Cohabitants: Inheritance (Provision for Family and Dependants) Act 1975, s 1(1)(ba), inserted by the Law Reform (Succession) Act 1995, s 2.

Claim as a dependant

A.94   A dependant is defined as "any person [not otherwise qualifying as an applicant] who immediately before the death of the deceased was being maintained, either wholly or partly, by the deceased".[153] The applicant must be able to establish an assumption of responsibility by the deceased for the applicant during their life-times.[154] This can, however, be implied from the fact of maintenance.[155]

A.95   Further clarification is provided by section 1(3) of the 1975 Act:

> ... a person shall be treated as being maintained by the deceased, either wholly or partly, as the case may be, if the deceased, otherwise than for full valuable consideration, was making a substantial contribution in money or money's worth towards the reasonable needs of that person.

A.96   In order to determine whether the applicant is eligible to apply as a dependant, the court must therefore value the contributions made by the deceased, and any valuable consideration given by the applicant, and conduct a balancing exercise to determine whether the former exceeds the latter.[156] If it does, then a claim can be made. If it does not, then the applicant will not be eligible to apply under this category. The courts are expected to approach this balancing exercise with common sense: it "cannot be an exact exercise of evaluating services in pounds and pence".[157] Accordingly, the financial relationship between the deceased and the applicant must be looked at "in the round", avoiding "fine balancing computations involving the value of normal exchanges of support in the domestic sense".[158]

A.97   The effect of these limitations is that it is not always the most deserving of applicants who qualifies and that those who have given more than they have taken (for example by devoting many years of care and possibly financial support to an ailing partner) may not be able to claim.

Claim as a cohabitant

A.98   It was partly as a consequence of the limitations of the class of dependants that the Law Commission recommended the addition of cohabitants in their own right as a sixth class of applicant to the 1975 Act.[159] This recommendation was implemented by the Law Reform (Succession) Act 1995, which amended the 1975 Act in its application to deaths on or after 1 January 1996. The legislation does not use the word "cohabitant", but instead describes the class of applicant in the language used by the Fatal Accidents Act 1976. To be eligible to apply under this category, the applicant must have been living:

---

[153] Inheritance (Provision for Family and Dependants) Act 1975, s 1(1)(e).

[154] *Re Beaumont* [1980] Ch 444.

[155] *Jelley v Iliffe* [1981] Fam 128.

[156] *Re Wilkinson* [1978] Fam 22; *Jelley v Iliffe* [1981] Fam 128; *Tyler's Family Provision* (3rd ed 1997) p 88.

[157] *Jelley v Iliffe* [1981] Fam 128, 141, Griffiths LJ.

[158] *Bishop v Plumley* [1991] 1 WLR 582, 587, Butler-Sloss LJ.

[159] Distribution on Intestacy (1989) Law Com No 187.

during the whole of the period of two years ending immediately before the date when the deceased died…

(a)   in the same household as the deceased; and

(b)   as the husband, wife or civil partner, of the deceased (although not in fact married to or a civil partner of him or her).[160]

Reasonable financial provision

A.99   Whether the claim is made as dependant or as cohabitant, the applicant has to establish that the disposition of the deceased's estate effected by his or her will or by the law relating to intestacy (or by the combination of the two) is not such as to make the applicant "reasonable financial provision". If the claimant crosses that hurdle, the court then has to consider what, if any, order is required so as to make such "reasonable financial provision".

A.100   Reasonable financial provision in both cases is statutorily defined as "such financial provision as it would be reasonable in all the circumstances of the case for the applicant to receive for his maintenance".[161] This has been judicially explained as meaning "such financial provision as would be reasonable in all the circumstances of the case to enable the applicant to maintain himself in a manner suitable to those circumstances".[162]

A.101   Whether the claim is made as cohabitant or dependant, in considering whether the disposition of the deceased's estate makes reasonable financial provision for the applicant, and in determining whether and in what manner to exercise its powers to make such provision, the court must have regard to:

(1)   the financial resources and financial needs which the applicant has or is likely to have in the foreseeable future;

(2)   the financial resources and financial needs which any other applicant for an order has or is likely to have in the foreseeable future;

(3)   the financial resources and financial needs which any beneficiary of the deceased's estate has or is likely to have in the foreseeable future;

(4)   any obligations and responsibilities which the deceased had towards any applicant for an order or any beneficiary of the deceased's estate;

(5)   the size and nature of the net estate of the deceased;

(6)   any physical or mental disability of any applicant for an order or of any beneficiary of the deceased's estate; and

---

[160] Inheritance (Provision for Family and Dependants) Act 1975, ss 1(1)(ba), (1A) and (1B); *Re Watson* [1999] 1 FLR 878; *Gully v Dix* [2004] 1 WLR 1399; *Churchill v Roach* [2002] EWHC 3230 (Ch), [2004] 2 FLR 989. On the requirement of a joint household, see *Kotke v Saffarini* [2005] EWCA Civ 221, [2005] 2 FLR 517 (considering the equivalent provision in the Fatal Accidents Act 1976).

[161] Inheritance (Provision for Family and Dependants) Act 1975, s 1(2)(b).

[162] *Re Coventry* [1980] Ch 461, 494, Buckley LJ.

(7)   any other matter, including the conduct of the applicant or any other person, which in the circumstances of the case the court may consider relevant.

A.102   If the claim is made as a dependant, the court must have regard to "the extent to which and the basis upon which the deceased assumed responsibility for the maintenance of the applicant and to the length of time for which the deceased discharged that responsibility".[163]

A.103   If the claim is made as a cohabitant, the court must also have regard to:

(1)   the age of the applicant and the duration of the cohabitation; and

(2)   the contribution made by the applicant to the welfare of the deceased's family, including any contribution made by looking after the home or caring for the family.[164]

A.104   If the court finds that the applicant has not received "reasonable financial provision", as defined, from the deceased's estate, and concludes that some provision should be made, it has a wide range of orders at its disposal. Those orders, similar to those available under the MCA on divorce and Schedule 1 to the Children Act 1989, include periodical payments, lump sum, property transfer, and property settlement orders.[165]

CONCLUSION

A.105   It will be clear from the foregoing survey that cohabitants and their children are not ignored by the law. Both statute law and the general law may be used to resolve some of the disputes that arise on separation or on death of one party. Cohabitants can regulate their affairs through express trusts or contracts. If they have not taken these steps, they may seek to claim a beneficial interest in a specific asset using the law of implied trusts or proprietary estoppel. Certain statutory remedies are available; cohabitants may claim orders for the occupation of the home, tenancy transfer and financial provision for their children. Cohabitants may be entitled to claim financial provision from the estate of their deceased partner.

A.106   However, the resolution of cohabitants' financial and property affairs on the termination of their relationships is largely driven by strict property law entitlements. The current law has been subjected to heavy criticism. In Part 4 of the CP we discussed those criticisms at some length. In Part 2 of this report we revisit those concerns in light of *Stack v Dowden*[166] and consultees' responses.

---

[163] Inheritance (Provision for Family and Dependants) Act 1975, s 3(4).

[164] Inheritance (Provision for Family and Dependants) Act 1975, s 3(2A).

[165] Inheritance (Provision for Family and Dependants) Act 1975, s 2.

[166] [2007] UKHL 17, [2007] 2 WLR 831.

APPENDIX B
FINANCIAL RELIEF ON SEPARATION: HOW WOULD IT WORK?

HOW IS ECONOMIC DISADVANTAGE TO BE QUANTIFIED?

B.1 In Part 4, we noted that recommending a scheme designed specifically for cohabitants and based on a principled discretion, rather than simply recommending the extension or adaptation of Part 2 of the MCA or the introduction of a rule-based system, brings with it certain consequences. In particular, the courts would have to quantify the value of applicants' claims in accordance with those principles, rather than exercising a wide discretion to adjust the parties' property rights in accordance with its view of what is fair. We appreciate that this would involve some potentially difficult factual questions but nevertheless take the view that our recommended scheme is the preferable option for cohabitants.[1]

The nature and limits of the exercise

B.2 The economic disadvantage principle would pose some relatively new questions for the family courts. Quantification of economic disadvantage would involve, to some extent, proof of the impact of the applicant's contributions to the relationship on his or her economic position. This would involve proving "what would have happened" on the balance of probabilities.[2]

B.3 This sort of quantification exercise has not commonly been undertaken under the MCA discretion. However, in *Miller v Miller; McFarlane v McFarlane*,[3] the House of Lords identified "compensation for relationship-generated disadvantage" as one of the three strands underpinning the exercise of the MCA discretion. It is therefore to be expected that the courts will increasingly be invited to consider "what would have happened" in the matrimonial context.

B.4 However, it is important to bear in mind that the quantification of economic disadvantage, while an important step in the reasoning process when our scheme is being applied, would not itself determine the value of any award ultimately made. There would be other matters to be taken into account:

(1) the economic equality ceiling – the principle that the court's award must not put the applicant in a stronger economic position for the foreseeable future, in terms of income and living standards, than the respondent; and

(2) the discretionary factors bearing on the value of the award and the particular orders which are to be made.

---

[1] In Appendix C we explain in more detail why we have rejected various alternative schemes that were promoted by some consultees.

[2] It would not be akin to the "loss of a chance" encountered in personal injury litigation: see para 4.62.

[3] [2006] UKHL 24, [2006] 2 AC 618.

B.5 The operation of the economic equality ceiling and the discretionary factors might often mean that precise quantification of economic disadvantage was unnecessary. Where, for example, an award would inevitably be "capped" by the economic equality ceiling or by the respondent's available resources, the court should take a proportionate approach to the proof and quantification of economic disadvantage claims.

B.6 Awards under our recommended scheme would be made on a clean-break basis, periodical payments being limited to very narrow purposes (unlike those awarded under the MCA). Where relief was granted by means of a lump sum or property transfer, as would usually be the case, a discount would be made for accelerated receipt.

Potential sources of assistance

B.7 We have already identified some potential sources of assistance with quantification.[4] We now discuss those sources further. In doing so, we refer again to our recommendation[5] that procedural and costs rules be designed to minimise litigation costs and, in particular, to discourage excessive use of expert evidence.

B.8 There are several potential sources of guidance to be found in the operation of other family law statutory schemes in England and Wales,[6] Scotland[7] and New Zealand.[8] Practitioners and courts in all of these jurisdictions have experience of applying principles similar to that of economic disadvantage in determining financial relief following relationship breakdown.

B.9 However, care is needed when examining approaches taken by courts in applying statutory regimes whose overall shape and purpose are different from that of our recommended scheme. Only the recent Scottish legislation, making provision for financial relief between cohabitants on separation, entails a relatively freestanding inquiry into the economic impact of the cohabitation on the parties.[9] So while "economic disadvantage"[10] may provide the sole basis for relief in such cases, in others, inquiries about economic disadvantage (or its equivalent) are conducted alongside the application of a fair or equal sharing principle or rule, and include separate consideration of the applicant's needs.[11] In many cases, application of these other principles, without any reference to economic disadvantage, will result in the applicant obtaining a substantial award which may, in particular, meet the applicant's accommodation needs and offer

---

[4] Para 4.66.

[5] Para 4.42.

[6] MCA.

[7] Family Law (Scotland) Acts 1985 and 2006.

[8] Property (Relationships) Act 1976, s 15.

[9] Claims may be made in relation to economic advantage, economic disadvantage and the continuing economic burden of caring for children following separation. However, as we observe in Part 4, at n 33, we have developed the principles of retained benefit and economic disadvantage independently, so judicial interpretation of the Scottish legislation ought not to be assumed to be applicable to our recommended scheme.

[10] Family Law (Scotland) Act 2006, s 28(3).

some pension security. That being so, such cases may take a rather narrower view of economic disadvantage than we would expect to be taken under our recommended scheme.

B.10 There is, as yet, little guidance from reported cases in relation to the operation of the "compensation" principle of *Miller; McFarlane*.[12] Case law in Scotland considering the quantification of "economic disadvantage" is limited, but provides some guidance about how the task can be undertaken.[13] Scottish courts hearing economic disadvantage claims in the context of financial provision on divorce have allowed various methods of proof, including expert evidence[14] and evidence of colleagues whose career progress had not been inhibited by family responsibilities of the sort experienced by the applicant.[15] Where the applicant has been out of work for many years, the courts have been willing to take into account economic disadvantage in a rough and ready way when fashioning the final award despite the lack of concrete evidence indicating what the applicant's position would otherwise have been.[16]

B.11 The growing body of New Zealand case law reveals various approaches being taken to the quantification of economic disadvantage relating to loss of earning capacity. Reported cases have tended to involve relatively large asset pools. Given the sums at stake in these cases, it is not surprising that evidence has been adduced, as it has been in some Scottish cases, from experts such as chartered accountants, actuaries, employment or human resources consultants and recruitment agencies, together with affidavit evidence from the applicant's previous employers and work colleagues.[17]

[11] See the regimes applicable to ancillary relief on divorce in England and Wales and Scotland, and that contained in the New Zealand statute at n 8.

[12] Further general observations about the compensation principle in the MCA context are given by the Court of Appeal in *Charman v Charman* [2007] EWCA Civ 503, [2007] 2 FCR 217, at [71], and by Coleridge J in *RP v RP* [2006] EWHC 3409 (Fam) at [59] to [64]; see also *Lauder v Lauder* [2007] EWHC 1227 (Fam), at [65] to [69], Baron J.

[13] For example, *Coyle v Coyle* 2004 FamLR 2; *Ali v Ali (no 3)* 2003 SLT 641; *Wilson v Wilson* 1999 SLT 249; *Cunliff v Cunliff* 1999 SLT 992; *Adams v Adams (no 1)* 1997 SLT 144; *Loudon v Loudon* 1994 SLT 381. There are, as yet, no reported cases under the Family Law (Scotland) Act 2006, which introduced financial relief for cohabitants on separation. But the results of a small-scale survey of practitioners indicate that a "relatively simple approach" is being adopted to quantifying economic disadvantage claims under the 2006 Act, directly addressing loss of earning capacity and pension rights where the applicant has given up paid employment to care for children: K Malcolm, "Fair split?" (2007) Spring/Summer *Family Law Bulletin* 6 (journal of the Family Law Association in Scotland). These early indications apparently suggest that an approach akin to assessing compensation for personal injuries may be being taken by some practitioners; compare our view, at paras B.13 to B.14.

[14] *Wilson v Wilson* 1999 SLT 249.

[15] *Adams v Adams (No 1)* 1997 SLT 144; *Coyle v Coyle* 2004 FamLR 2.

[16] *Loudon v Loudon* 1994 SLT 381.

[17] For example, *Smith v Smith* [2007] NZFLR 32; *Allen v Allen* [2006] NZFLR 735; *M v B* [2006] NZFLR 641; *L v L* [2005] NZFLR 1145; *B v B* [2004] NZFLR 653.

B.12   Even where the available assets are extensive, expert evidence may be costly and unduly complex.[18] Where the cost is disproportionate to the value of the claim it should not be allowed under the procedural rules to be developed for our recommended scheme.[19] Anecdotal evidence suggests that most cases in New Zealand involve much smaller asset pools where parties are deterred by costs factors from adducing expert evidence.

B.13   The assessment of damages in tort may provide some assistance, although the analogy should not be pushed too far. In the CP, we quoted from a recent Scottish case in which Lady Smith had rejected counsel's attempt to apply the Ogden tables (used in personal injury cases to calculate future earnings losses) as a basis for quantifying economic disadvantage. It is worth repeating her words here:

> I do not accept that it is appropriate to approach the application of the economic disadvantage principle … as though an award were being made in a personal injuries case. The inappropriateness of doing so is highlighted by the fact that, in applying the statutory provisions, the question arises as to whether any economic disadvantage suffered by the pursuer has been balanced by economic disadvantage suffered by the defender … Moreover, the court is directed to take "fair account" which clearly involves an exercise of discretion. These requirements underline that … an overall view of the fairness and reasonableness of the outcome must be looked at.

B.14   While tort law provides an obvious source of guidance about how impairment to earning capacity and loss of future earnings may be measured, we endorse the view of Lady Smith. Her invocation of the Scottish statutory language of "fair account" corresponds with our discretionary factors, which are an important feature of our recommended scheme, as a principled but discretionary exercise, which clearly contrasts with the hard-edged nature of a tort claim.

B.15   In most cases the production of expert evidence would be disproportionately costly. We would therefore expect that disputes would normally be resolved (whether by agreement or by the courts) without its assistance. Information in the public domain could be used to assess in broad terms the economic disadvantage sustained in an individual case. For example, published tables of standard salaries, such as those contained in *At A Glance* and official statistics from sources such as the Labour Force Survey and the Annual Survey of Hours and Earnings might prove useful. These provide data about mean and median

---

[18]   B Atkin, "Harmonising Family Law" (2006) 37 *Victoria University of Wellington Law Review* 465, at 473.

[19]   In *RP v RP* [2006] EWHC 3409 (Fam), an MCA case, Coleridge J discusses (at [59] to [64]) the dangers of speculative use of expert evidence, and indeed of speculative "what if?" exercises. Because it is founded not upon needs in general, but upon loss arising from the cohabitation, our recommended scheme would have to take some steps in the direction of assessing what would have happened but for the cohabitation or, put another way, assessing what had been the impact of the applicant's contributions on his or her economic position.

earnings by reference to type of occupation, highest educational qualification, region, age and gender.[20]

B.16 Where the applicant had given up an occupation in which seniority for pay purposes is acquired simply by virtue of length of service, it would be relatively straightforward to calculate, by reference to the pay-scale, the earnings that the applicant would otherwise have had when the relationship broke down. The court would then need to assess the time it would take for the applicant to re-establish him- or herself in that occupation and reach the level that he or she would probably have attained but for having given up work.[21] The calculation of pension entitlement forgone would be similarly straightforward where the applicant had been a member of an occupational, final-salary pension scheme; in more complex cases, expert valuations might be needed.

SOME WORKED EXAMPLES

B.17 The scheme we recommend in this Report has been developed and, where possible, simplified since the CP and so we think it useful to provide some worked examples to illustrate its effect.

B.18 While our recommended scheme would allow claims to be made on separation, and confer jurisdiction on the court to make orders for financial relief, we would expect that most claims would be resolved by the parties without recourse to the court. We have specifically recommended that the promotion of mediation as an alternative to court proceedings be facilitated wherever possible by procedural rules.[22] However, for the purpose of explaining how our scheme would operate, we assume that attempts to resolve the parties' dispute privately have not been successful and that the court would therefore have to deal with the claim that has been made.

Example 1

A and B, who are both in their twenties, have been living together for two years. They have both worked full-time throughout the relationship and have kept their finances separate. They have shared the cooking and cleaning, and shared all outgoings related to the household equally. They are now separating.

B.19 Let us first assume that the property is rented by A and B from a private landlord. This is an example of a case which is highly unlikely to engage the scheme. Depending on the length of the minimum duration requirement settled on by

---

[20] The Labour Force Survey is based on household interviews of individuals and covers a wider range of variables, including educational qualification; some of the information is obtained by proxy: http://www.statistics.gov.uk/about/data/guides/LabourMarket/ and http://www.statistics.gov.uk/onlineproducts/default.asp#labour (last visited 3 July 2007). The Annual Survey of Hours and Earnings covers fewer variables, but is based on information provided by employers: http://www.statistics.gov.uk/StatBase/Product.asp?vlnk=13101 (last visited 3 July 2007).

[21] Compare the observations made in *Nathan v Nathan* [2007] NZFLR 32.

[22] Para 4.126.

Parliament, it may be that the parties are simply ineligible to claim at all.[23] Even if they did satisfy the eligibility test, the scheme would not provide either party with a remedy, as on separation neither is left with a retained benefit or an economic disadvantage. Neither has retained any benefit in the property, as it is rented, and the relationship has been economically neutral for each of them in terms of earnings and earning capacity. If either party were to apply under the scheme they would achieve nothing other than to incur legal fees and to risk cost penalties.

B.20 Exactly the same analysis would apply if the couple had been living together in property bought by A before the relationship began, where A had paid the mortgage during the relationship. The fact that only A would leave the relationship owning a property would not, in itself, provide any basis for a claim under the scheme.

B.21 The position would not be altered if B had paid rent to A or had assumed liability for all the household bills, unless B could show that A would not have been able to meet the mortgage instalments without B's payments. This would be difficult to do if A had been able to pay both the mortgage and the bills before B moved in.

B.22 The position would, however, be substantially different if B had contributed to A's mortgage payments or made a capital contribution to A's property which was not reflected in the legal ownership. In such circumstances, A would have a retained benefit which, provided the eligibility requirements were satisfied, B could reclaim under the scheme.[24]

B.23 Even if the couple had been living together for a longer (even a substantially longer) period, the same analysis would apply. The length of the cohabitation would, in itself, be irrelevant, save that it might affect eligibility under the scheme. A or B would only succeed in claiming a remedy if they could show that there was a retained benefit or continuing economic disadvantage.

Example 2

> C and D, both in their thirties, had been living together for three years in C's house when they started a family. C's salary was sufficient to support the family and, as they both wanted the baby (E) to be looked after at home by D, they agreed that D should not return to work after E was born. Their relationship has now foundered and they are separating, after five years together. E, who is now two, is going to live with D.

B.24 Our recommended scheme:

(1) would not affect C's obligation to pay child support and to make other provision for the benefit of E under Schedule 1 to the Children Act 1989;

---

[23] Two years is the shortest period of cohabitation that we have indicated to Government that we consider appropriate as a minimum duration requirement.

[24] If the couple were not eligible under the scheme B would have to proceed under existing property and trust law.

(2) would not enable D to make any claim against the value of C's home just because D had been living there; D's claim would be based upon the economic impact of having given up work to look after E and the need to care for E after the separation; and

(3) would require C to share the economic disadvantage caused by D's contributions.

B.25 As the law stands, C is obliged to provide for E but not for D. The couple share the basic cost of caring for E, because C will pay child support;[25] but even so, most of the practical consequences of care, in terms of earning loss and career disadvantage, will fall solely on D's shoulders. This in turn could lead to hardship for E, who is closely affected by D's financial circumstances. It is very unlikely that D will be able to establish any beneficial share in the family home.[26]

B.26 A court operating our recommended scheme would start by considering the possibility of retained benefit. On these facts there is none. C owned the house before the cohabitation began, and there is no suggestion that C had difficulty making the mortgage payments. It might be that D's moving in meant that there was more money to spare in the household and, for example, D might have helped to pay the bills. But that does not amount to the conferral of a retained benefit. If D had not moved in, C would nevertheless still have owned the house and have met the mortgage payments.

B.27 Nor could we say that D had a retained benefit. C supported D after E's birth; but we cannot point to funds that D retained as a result.

B.28 The court should then turn to economic disadvantage. It is likely that D would be able to establish an economic disadvantage claim. D made a career sacrifice in order to look after E. This was a rational decision while the family was together but it is one that left D vulnerable when the couple separated.

B.29 D would not be able to claim for the earnings forgone during the cohabitation. Economic disadvantage refers to a lasting economic impact arising from contributions to the relationship. D has made such contributions, in particular, in giving up work to look after E. D might be able to point to the following disadvantages caused by D's contributions:

(1) loss of future earnings, or earning capacity, arising from D's inability to return immediately or in the near future to the sort of paid employment D would have had, had D not given up work to care for E;

---

[25] Child support payments are designed to cover half the cost of caring for the child Part 4, n 89. As we explain at para 4.102, neither the payment nor receipt of child support would give rise to any claim under our scheme. But the fact that D was receiving child support would mean that D could not make any claim for economic disadvantage in relation to the basic costs of providing for E's needs; and the fact that C was making those payments would be relevant under the discretionary factors (see para 4.38), as an existing financial obligation of A's.

[26] See discussion of implied trusts and proprietary estoppel in Appendix A.

(2)   savings that would otherwise have been made during the relationship;[27]

(3)   pension and National Insurance payments that would otherwise have been paid during the relationship and following separation had D remained in paid employment;[28] and

(4)   any child-care costs that might be necessary to enable D to return to work (in so far as not covered by tax credits).

B.30   The court should assess in a broad-brush manner how far D was likely to have reduced future earnings as a result of any loss of earning capacity suffered during D's time out of the employment market during the relationship. It would expect D to mitigate any economic impact in so far as it was reasonable and possible to do so. It would also have to think about D's future child-care responsibilities; as the parent with care, if D returned to full-time work D would require paid child-care, particularly before E starts school and then, later, outside school hours. Alternatively, D could look after E, but that would limit D's earning potential. Much would depend upon the nature of D's employment and its future opportunities, and any tax credit entitlements in relation to child-care. The court should consider what D would have earned if D had continued in employment, and take a view on how long it would be before D could catch up. It may well be that for the next, say, three to five years D would have no earnings; and that for another five years D might be able to work part-time, or full-time but incurring child-care expenses.

B.31   It is unlikely that C would be able to establish an economic disadvantage claim. C had, of course, supported D and the baby but it is likely that C did so out of income that would otherwise have been spent in other ways. It might be possible to show that C failed to make savings that would otherwise have been made, for example, by pointing to a regular savings pattern that was interrupted when D stopped earning. But, in any event, C's claim would be subject to the operation of the economic equality ceiling. If C is in a stronger economic position than D on separation, D could not be ordered to make a payment that would put D in an economically weaker position than C.

B.32   The value of the award C had to pay to D, and the form the relief took, would depend upon both the discretionary factors and the economic equality ceiling. The court's first consideration would be E's welfare, and its main concern would be to ensure that E has a home. We have highlighted the current difficulty in making orders for the benefit of the children of separated cohabitants under Schedule 1 to the Children Act 1989.[29] Under the current law, unless someone in C's position is wealthy enough to provide a home outright (subject to its return to C when the children grow up), it may not be practicable to make a Schedule 1

---

[27]   Such a claim must be based on evidence, and be more than a hypothetical possibility.

[28]   B may currently be entitled to a Home Responsibilities Payment: see Social Security Contributions and Benefits Act 1992, sch 3, para 5; and see Pensions Bill 2007, cl 3. But (subject to that) the loss of National Insurance Payments is one of the costs of giving up work to look after a child.

[29]   See para 2.66 and following, and, in more detail, CP, para 4.34 to 4.46.

order at all, as the house must remain entirely C's.[30] Moreover, there is no power to order C to make mortgage payments, and while C might nevertheless undertake to do so, it might be unrealistic to expect C to maintain a mortgage, voluntarily, on the house for the years of E's minority.

B.33 But under our recommended scheme D would have access to capital as a result of D's claim for financial relief against C. C's liability to D could be satisfied in one of a number of alternative ways, depending in part on the amount of equity in the property and other resources available to each party. For example, it might be realistic to sell the house (or for C to borrow against some of the equity in it) and to make a payment to D out of the proceeds. The capital thereby freed would then assist D in buying a smaller property.

B.34 Another option would be for the court to make a property adjustment order, giving D a share in C's house.[31] Depending upon the income available to C and to D, it might be practicable for such an order to be combined with an order under Schedule 1 to the Children Act for the house to be held upon trust for D to live there with E until E reached 18 or completed further education. D would now have a stake in the property and it would be a shared asset. D might be able to fund future mortgage payments by means of D's earnings, child support payments and any lump sum paid by instalments by C.[32] Alternatively, C might undertake to pay all or part of the mortgage instalments.[33] When the court order for E's benefit expired, both C and D would have a share in the equity of the house. They may then decide that one should buy the other out; or they might choose to sell the house and share the proceeds.

B.35 Whether it was feasible to use the family home owned by C in this way would depend on the extent of C's resources (and, in particular, C's need for housing) and the extent of D's claim. In some circumstances, it would simply be impractical for D and E to continue to live in the family home. In such cases, D would either have to purchase a smaller property using whatever resources were available or, if that were impossible, use any award under the scheme (together with child support and any other income) to secure rental accommodation.

B.36 The element of the award that represents child-care costs might form part of a lump sum award, but it may well be more appropriate to share that element of D's economic disadvantage in the form of periodical payments, which could be subsequently varied as necessary.

Example 3

F and G have been living together since 1975, when they were in their late twenties. When they decided to set up home together, F

---

[30] The lack of power to order sale or divide capital under Schedule 1 to the Children Act 1989 is one of the factors that inhibits its usefulness, particularly in cases with relatively modest asset pools.

[31] The value of that share reflecting the value of D's claim under the scheme.

[32] Which would help build up the equity to which D would be entitled on sale. It would be necessary, if D was to take over the property from C and so assume liability for the mortgage for the mortgagee's agreement to be secured. As in MCA proceedings, C would make undertakings to use best endeavours to achieve this.

was a schoolteacher and G was developing a business career. They originally lived together in rental accommodation, but later moved to a substantial house held in G's name. G's business required a considerable amount of travel, and G was keen to have F's company on the frequent trips abroad. This was incompatible with F retaining a teaching job, and so on G's request, F agreed to give up work. This arrangement also meant that F could devote time to running the household and extensive garden. They had hoped to have children but they were unable to do so. They are now separating. The house is free of mortgage and G has substantial investments and pension funds.

B.37 F is in a very vulnerable position. F is probably unable to resume work, being so near retirement age, has only a very small pension from the early years as a teacher and has nowhere to live. As the law stands, G has no obligations towards F, and F probably has no interest in the home under the law of trusts.

B.38 Our recommended scheme:

(1) would enable the court to make an order sharing between the parties the economic disadvantage sustained by F during the course of their long relationship;

(2) would enable the court to make an order which would recognise the disadvantage that F inevitably faces in attempting to obtain housing, in consequence of F's contributions and their overall impact on F's economic position; but

(3) would not allow F to claim maintenance from G (because of the commitment in the scheme to a clean break).

B.39 F very probably has no claim for a retained benefit in relation to G's acquisition of the house or business career, as it is extremely unlikely that F's activities contributed to that wealth. F would not be able to claim in respect of past loss of earnings. F's claim would be based principally on the economic disadvantage relating to the loss of future earnings, and to the loss of past and future pension contributions. These would be readily calculable in this example, as teachers have a standard salary scale and a final-salary pension scheme. We can assume that F would have continued as a teacher and moved steadily up the pay scale (but without speculating that F might have become a head teacher or, indeed, that F might have moved into a different career).

B.40 F may also be able to make an economic disadvantage claim in respect of lost savings. In view of F living with G for all these years and because F had no income during the relationship, F did not enter the housing market or make other capital savings or investments. F could argue that, had it not been for giving up employment, F would have either contributed to the mortgage on the home (in which case F would have had a retained benefit claim) or made equivalent investments, leaving F with a nest-egg which F could now have been using to

---

[33] In which case C would continue to build up equity in the property.

obtain suitable housing following separation. In a case like this where F has spent much of F's adult life in the relationship, the court would be likely to accept that F would have made use of earnings in this way.

B.41 The court would be likely to make an award sharing F's economic disadvantage, subject to the economic equality ceiling. The decision that F should give up work was a joint one, and its consequences should be shared. F would not be entitled to claim periodical payments.[34] Any relief ordered to F would therefore be in the form of capital provision, which would assist F in obtaining accommodation, and could include pension sharing.

Example 4

H and J have lived together for three years in a large house which J inherited from a relative. H is a self-employed builder. H spent a year renovating the property full-time without receiving any payment from J. H then returned to business as a builder, and they shared household costs. H's substantial renovations added considerably to the market value of J's house. The relationship recently broke down.

B.42 Assuming that the parties were eligible cohabitants,[35] our recommended scheme:

(1) would not oblige H to pay J anything in respect of board and lodging during the cohabitation;

(2) would not oblige J to pay H the earnings that H lost during the year spent working on the house; but

(3) would enable H to reclaim from J the value added to J's house by the renovations.

B.43 Under the current law, H would be restricted to a claim in relation to the house based on implied trust or proprietary estoppel, and such a claim would probably fail.

B.44 Under our recommended scheme, the first issue would be retained benefit. The value of J's house has been enhanced. That value should not be difficult to quantify, and the scheme would require J to repay that value to H.

B.45 Next we would have to ask if, following repayment of that value, there would remain outstanding any economic disadvantage on the part of H. Certainly H would not be entitled to the full payment that could have been charged for the work, since that is a past earnings loss. In any event, to allow such a claim where H was to be rewarded for the fruits of that labour under the retained benefit principle would involve double-counting.

B.46 Once the value of J's retained benefit were ascertained, the discretionary factors would have to be considered before an award was made, and J's own needs and

---

[34] Such orders would be available only in respect of child-care costs: para 4.101 and following.

[35] Which, in this context, would turn on whether their relationships satisfied the minimum duration requirement.

responsibilities would come into play to shape the form of the order. J might be able to raise the sum by means of a further mortgage; or J might have to pay in instalments. The court would endeavour to frame an order that did not require J to sell the house.

APPENDIX C
FURTHER DISCUSSION OF ALTERNATIVE
SCHEMES FOR RELIEF

INTRODUCTION

C.1 In Part 4 of this Report we reject a number of possible bases for financial relief between separating cohabitants before setting out our recommended scheme. We explore those rejected options in more detail here and expand upon why we have concluded that they would not form an acceptable basis for relief.

C.2 The challenge of selecting an appropriate basis of relief between cohabitants is amply demonstrated by the huge diversity of opinion amongst our consultees. For example, while some advocated adoption of the MCA, many others strongly opposed such a move. A few advocated a presumption of equal sharing of property accumulated during the relationship; but some others would specifically exclude such a presumption. Many would base relief on needs, but others would not, either at all or in the absence of other factors.

EXTENSION OF THE MATRIMONIAL CAUSES ACT 1973 AND ITS UNDERLYING PRINCIPLES

C.3 We have already explained what we regard as the principal reasons why it would be inappropriate simply to open up the MCA to separating cohabitants.[1] We develop that discussion here, and address some variants on this option which we have seriously considered.

The suitability of the Matrimonial Causes Act 1973 for cohabitants

C.4 Two prominent aspects of the MCA scheme, as interpreted by the courts,[2] are the principles of sharing and need. We have taken the view that, whether as components of the MCA scheme, or as principles to be adopted in a new scheme devised specifically for cohabitants, neither is appropriate in this context.

Problems with the "sharing" principle

C.5 We explained in the CP why we considered that a scheme or principle that, at least as a default position, would divide any portion of the parties' assets equally would not be suitable for cohabitants as a class.[3] Cohabiting relationships vary enormously in character, especially in terms of their duration, commitment and the degree of economic interdependence between the parties.[4] Some couples

---

[1] See para 4.5 and following.

[2] Following *White v White* [2001] 1 AC 596, *Miller v Miller; McFarlane v McFarlane* [2006] UKHL 24, [2006] 2 AC 618.

[3] CP, paras 6.92 to 6.114.

[4] This issue was highlighted by Professor Gillian Douglas, Julia Pearce and Hilary Woodward in their consultation response, based on their recent research into the resolution of disputes between separating cohabitants: *A Failure of Trust: Resolving Property Disputes on Cohabitation Breakdown* (2007), available at http://www.law.cf.ac.uk/researchpapers/papers/1.pdf or http://www.bris.ac.uk/law/research/centres-themes/cohabit/cohabit-rep.pdf (last visited 3

elect to own their homes jointly and to pool their money. But evidence suggests that this is less common among cohabitants than among spouses.[5] Moreover, researchers have recently cautioned against attempts to make assumptions about the nature of parties' commitment and the nature of their relationship from the form of money management which they appear to use.[6]

C.6 It is true that marriages are not homogenous either, and the exercise of the MCA discretion may be tailored according to the circumstances of the particular parties. However, all marriages and civil partnerships at least share the feature that the parties have made an express, legal commitment to each other and so can be said to have opted in to this particular legal regime. It may therefore be appropriate to conclude, at least in the absence of clear evidence that the parties intended otherwise,[7] that it will generally be fair to apply a regime of financial relief that ordinarily entails a sharing of assets.

C.7 Several responses from members of the public strongly opposed the notion that a former cohabiting partner should be entitled to stake a claim to half of their property. Some of these concerns might be assuaged by confining sharing to property acquired during the relationship, or even further to particular categories of asset acquired during that period.[8] But it seems clear that for many of these consultees, the economic value of parties' actual contributions to the asset pool was important. Data from the British Social Attitudes survey suggest that the mere fact of a difference in personal wealth does not by itself justify requiring the wealthier individual to make financial provision to the other party, at least

July 2007); see also "Dealing with Property Issues on Cohabitation Breakdown" (2007) 37 *Family Law* 36.

[5] See sources discussed in CP, Part 6, nn 73 to 78; more recently, see A Barlow, C Burgoyne and J Smithson, *The Living Together Campaign – An investigation of its impact on legally aware cohabitants* Ministry of Justice Research Report (forthcoming, 2007); C Vogler, M Brockmann and R Wiggins, "Intimate relationships and changing patterns of money management at the beginning of the twenty-first century" (2006) 57 *The British Journal of Sociology* 455; and by the same authors, "Managing money in new heterosexual forms of intimate relationship" (2007) *Journal of Socio-Economics* (in press) doi:10.1016/j.socec.2006.12.039; for the first study of money management by same-sex couples in this jurisdiction see M Burns, C Burgoyne and V Clarke, "Financial affairs? Money management in same-sex relationships" (2007) *Journal of Socio-Economics* (in press) doi: 10.1016/j.socec.2006.12.034.

[6] See for example observations made by A Barlow, C Burgoyne and J Smithson, *The Living Together Campaign – An investigation of its impact on legally aware cohabitants* (2006), at pp 62 to 63, in light of findings from that study and recent related research; see also K Ashby and C Burgoyne, "Separate financial entities? Beyond categories of money management" (2007) *Journal of Socio-Economics* (in press), doi:10.1016/j.socec.2006.12.035. Note also the observations of Lord Neuberger in *Stack v Dowden* [2007] UKHL 17, [2007] 2 WLR 831, at [113] and [132] about the difficulties of inferring parties' intentions regarding beneficial ownership of the shared home from their money management practices and decisions about how property is held.

[7] Note, in this regard, recent judicial encouragement for a review of English law's approach to pre-nuptial agreements, at least in the context of a wider review of ancillary relief: *Charman v Charman* [2007] EWCA Civ 503, [2007] 2 FCR 217.

[8] And some research indicates strong public support for sharing regimes, at least between cohabitants with children: see para C.13.

following a short, childless relationship.[9] This would also seem to militate against sharing in such cases.

C.8 While a principle of sharing or partnership might appear suitable for some cohabitants,[10] we think that many would regard it as deeply inappropriate for others. We discuss below the possibility of bringing only cohabitants with children within the MCA or a similar regime.

Problems with a "needs" principle

C.9 As we noted in Part 4, need was a factor that featured in many consultees' suggested schemes. However, while they cited factors such as length of relationship and nature of commitment, those consultees did not develop a clear, principled justification for needs-based relief that would help to determine in particular how "need" should be measured, which "needs", if any, should be met by a former partner, in what circumstances and for how long.

C.10 While spouses and civil partners might appropriately be subjected to the sharing principle, so might they generally be taken to have assumed a responsibility for each other's needs. Some cohabitants might also have made a commitment of a sort that justifies the conclusion that they have assumed a mutual responsibility to meet each other's needs in the long term, including after the end of their relationship. But it is far from clear that this can be said for all cohabitants, even those who fall into those categories that we have suggested should be eligible for relief under our recommended scheme. Many financially independent couples without children may baulk at the suggestion that they should, by cohabiting (whether at all or for a specified period), be taken to have assumed any financial responsibility for each other. We therefore doubt that it would be suitable to confer on the courts the general power to require individuals to meet the needs of their former cohabiting partner following separation.

C.11 However, needs specifically arising from the parties' contributions to the relationship are different. Here there is a demonstrable connection between the applicant's needs and the relationship, which it can be argued would justify the grant of financial relief between the parties. Data from the British Social Attitudes survey indicate strong support for the grant of relief between cohabitants in such circumstances.[11] However, as we discussed at paragraph 4.24, our preferred approach to such needs is to respond to them by means of a principle of economic disadvantage.

C.12 It is also important to note that a scheme based on need alone would not be able to resolve the problems that arise between many cohabitants on separation. They might be aggrieved by the financial outcome of their relationship even where the assets exceeded their needs. One possible recourse in such cases, of course, could be the general law of property and trusts: the party whose needs-based claim was small but who felt that he or she had a larger claim in the law of implied

---

[9] See A Park et al, *British Social Attitudes. The 24th Report* (forthcoming, January 2008).

[10] We note the effect of the strong presumption of beneficial joint ownership in relation to the family home created by *Stack v Dowden* [2007] UKHL 17, [2007] 2 WLR 831 in cases where the parties put their home in joint names.

[11] See A Park et al, *British Social Attitudes. The 24th Report* (forthcoming, January 2008).

trusts would therefore have a clear incentive to pursue that other remedy. But as we explained in Part 4, we consider it essential to develop a scheme that would make invocation of the general law unnecessary.

Extending the Matrimonial Causes Act 1973 to cohabitants with children

C.13 It was suggested to us that the MCA regime – or something very like it – should be adopted, but only for cohabitants with children.[12] It can be said that the economic effect of having children is much the same whether the parents are married or not. Academic commentators have argued that financial remedies following relationship breakdown, and other aspects of the law, should differentiate not between spouses or civil partners and cohabitants, but between couples who have had children and couples who have not. The formal status of the parents' relationship (and possibly whether they ever shared a household) should, on this view, be irrelevant.[13] In the CP, we noted research which suggests that pooling techniques of money management are more common amongst cohabiting parents (as amongst all spouses). Regimes comprising an element of sharing may therefore be more appropriate for these couples than for those without children.[14]

C.14 There is also research evidence that a significant weight of public opinion is in favour of a functional approach to the family, treating couples with children alike when they have, or have had, children.[15] However, members of the public who have expressed a wish for cohabitants generally (or cohabitants with children specifically) to be treated "in the same way" as spouses may not appreciate how the current law deals with financial disputes between spouses on divorce. Their endorsement of equal treatment of spouses and cohabitants can therefore not safely be taken to amount to an endorsement of the MCA, specifically, for cohabitants (or for spouses). In particular, many of those individuals may be unaware of the potentially dramatic effects that the MCA regime can have on parties' property rights, given the enormous awards that can be generated in some of the "big money" cases, even after a short relationship.[16]

C.15 It is also necessary to bear in mind the criticisms and calls for a review of the MCA that have recently been made, including by members of the judiciary.[17] At a time when the MCA is coming under scrutiny in its existing sphere of operation, it is arguably inappropriate to bring further categories of relationship within its

[12] Professor Anne Barlow advocated adoption of the MCA in these cases.

[13] See generally, for example, discussion in M Maclean and J Eekelaar, *The Parental Obligation* (1997).

[14] CP, paras 6.106 to 6.110, and material referred to in n 5.

[15] This view was expressed by some of our consultees and is evident from recent research findings: eg E Cooke and A Barlow, *Community of Property: a regime for England and Wales?* (2006) p 33; and larger-scale Omnibus Survey findings from a study conducted in 1995 for the Law Commission by the Centre for Socio-Legal Studies. Data from the British Social Attitudes survey 2006 also indicate majority support for equal treatment of spouses and cohabitants, at least where the couple had had children or the relationship was not short: A Park et al, *British Social Attitudes. The 24th Report* (forthcoming, January 2008).

[16] Following *White v White* [2001] AC 596 and *Miller v Miller; McFarlane v McFarlane* [2006] UKHL 24, [2006] 2 AC 618.

[17] *Charman v Charman* [2007] EWCA Civ 503, [2007] 2 FCR 217; see also A Greensmith (National Chair, Resolution) "Let's play Ancillary Relief" (2007) 37 *Family Law* 203.

scope. Moreover, it would be difficult for us to devise a scheme for cohabitants that looked very like the MCA regime, since that would invite difficult questions about the similarity or otherwise of the two schemes and the outcomes that they should produce.

C.16 Applying the MCA regime only to cohabitants with children would, of course, leave open the issue of cohabitants without children. They could be left with the general law, or a special scheme could be devised for them alone. Neither of these options appeals to us. While the presence of children commonly influences eligibility criteria, in none of the other jurisdictions that we have examined does the presence of children determine which basic set of principles should apply to the grant of financial relief between the cohabitants themselves.[18] Few of our consultees advocated difference of treatment along these lines and some consultees emphasised that cohabitants without children may experience as great a need for remedies on separation as those cohabitants with children. Any wider review, examining the treatment of spouses and civil partners (as well as cohabitants, and even parents who have never had a co-residential relationship) by reference to whether or not they have children, is beyond the scope of this project.

ADAPTING THE MATRIMONIAL CAUSES ACT 1973

C.17 A different approach would be to adapt the MCA specifically for cohabitants. This is not a possibility on which we consulted. But it has been suggested to us[19] that the MCA regime might be used for cohabitants subject to:

(1) a proviso that there should be no presumption of equal division of the sort now applied by the courts on divorce;[20] or

(2) a proviso that the court should take into account the fact that the parties have not given each other the commitment involved in marriage (or civil partnership).[21]

C.18 The first option – in so far as it depends upon the current judicial interpretation of the MCA – would be difficult to draft: the "yardstick of equality" approach is not found in the statute. More importantly, instructing the court about what it was not to do would provide no positive guidance about what it ought to do.

---

[18] Though there may be separate provision for the children themselves; see also provisions such as Family Proceedings Act 1980 (New Zealand), ss 78 to 81, which confer power to grant maintenance between natural parents. The set of principles applicable between the adult parties may include issues clearly pertinent only to parents: eg relating to the economic burden of child-care post-separation: Family Law (Scotland) Acts 1985, s 9, and 2006, s 28.

[19] In particular at the Nuffield Foundation seminar on 18 September 2006.

[20] Following *White v White* [2001] 1 AC 596 and *Miller v Miller; McFarlane v McFarlane* [2006] UKHL 24, [2006] 2 AC 618.

[21] Contrast the repealed Family Law Act 1996, s 41 (dealing with occupation orders, used particularly in cases of domestic violence): the court was required "to have regard to the fact that [the parties] have not given each other the commitment involved in marriage"; and the words that replaced it in section 36(6) of that Act: "the nature of the parties' relationship, and in particular the level of commitment in it".

C.19 The yardstick of equality derives from the factor in the MCA checklist relating to the parties' "contributions".[22] Disapplication of that yardstick would leave parties and courts having to find some other way of valuing their contributions, or of dividing any surplus after needs had been met. As we explained in the CP, a scheme based simply on the parties' "contributions", providing no guidance about how those contributions were to be measured, would give rise to considerable problems, particularly in determining how to compare and evaluate incommensurable contributions.[23] It is at least in part for this reason[24] that the MCA discretion has moved in the direction of a presumption of equal sharing between spouses.[25] That precludes difficult argument, in particular, about the weight to be given to non-financial contributions. To rule out the sharing approach for cohabitants but to leave the courts evaluating contributions would simply be to revive all of those difficult questions while providing no answer to them.

C.20 The court would be left with a wide discretion without any clear objectives for the relief to be granted. Parties and their advisers would be left uncertain about the basis on which their case would be resolved were it litigated.

C.21 The second suggested proviso is also problematic and uncertain. Presumably, the court would have to determine what relief would have been granted had the couple been married, and then go on to consider what relief would in fact be appropriate in view of the fact that they had not been married. This would not only take time. It would also be difficult to see what effect such an exercise would have: what would be the "discount" for not being married? And should the court be encouraged to focus on ensuring that the applicant was granted less than a married applicant would have obtained, rather than on addressing the particular situation of the parties? Again, this approach would provide neither the courts nor parties and their advisers with any positive guidance about the principles by reference to which cases should be determined.

C.22 Accordingly we do not think that these options, in the form in which they were presented to us, would be workable.

SOME OTHER OPTIONS

C.23 A central plank in our arguments against the inclusion of sharing and needs principles has been that the diversity of cohabiting relationships is such that those principles are not universally appropriate. We address here two specific counter-arguments which might be made against that position.

Schemes with multiple principles

C.24 One response is to say that, if those principles would be suitable for at least some cohabitants, the courts should be given wide powers enabling them to

---

[22] MCA, s 25(2)(f).

[23] CP, paras 6.78 to 6.82 and 6.115 to 6.125.

[24] But also in recognition, regardless of any question of value, of the partnership entailed in marriage: E Cooke, "*Miller/McFarlane*: Law in Search of Discrimination" (2007) 19 *Child and Family Law Quarterly* 98.

[25] Subject to needs, compensation, and, exceptionally, arguments regarding special contributions and conduct.

grant relief on that basis in those cases, whilst taking a different approach to other cases.

C.25 We are not attracted by that sort of approach. We set considerable store on parties knowing, from the outset, what principles would determine the grant of relief in their case. Leaving cohabitants exposed to the possibility that all, or only some, of a set of principles might apply to them, depending on the judge's evaluation of the type of relationship that they had, would generate considerable uncertainty. It would require a potentially intrusive and inherently subjective inquiry into the nature of the parties' relationship. In order to avoid this prospect, our recommended scheme endeavours to articulate a set of principles that could fairly be applied to all types of cohabiting relationship.

C.26 It is for this reason that we do not feel able to adopt the scheme proposed to us by Resolution, the specialist organisation for family law solicitors which has done much to promote the case for law reform in this area and to bring the issues to public attention. They have done considerable work[26] in devising a scheme for financial relief on separation of cohabiting couples. They consider that the court's "overriding objective" should be to "take fair account" of "any economic advantage derived by either party from contributions economic or otherwise made by the other party during the cohabitation, and of any economic disadvantage suffered by the other party in the interests of the other or of any child of the family".[27] For the purposes of the economic advantage principle, "contributions" would be broadly defined, covering all sorts of direct and indirect, financial and non-financial contributions to the parties' assets and to the welfare of the family.[28] There are clear parallels here with our concepts of retained benefit and economic disadvantage. However, Resolution would apply them in a "global" way, examining advantages and disadvantages arising during the relationship, whether or not their effects were continuing at the point of separation. We have rejected this approach on the basis that it would entail too onerous an investigation, and that the focus should be on contributions whose effects were continuing at separation and so more obviously called for a remedy.

C.27 Resolution's scheme goes on to state that there should no presumption of equal sharing, and that it should be presumed that the parties will be self-supporting. Orders for maintenance would therefore only be made where the applicant was unable to support him or herself adequately owing to child-care responsibilities, or, if an order would be reasonable in all the circumstances, because his or her earning capacity was impaired by the circumstances of the relationship.[29] They also suggest that the court should be required to take into account a long list of wide-ranging factors, including the nature of the commitment and degree of

---

[26] Earlier, in conjunction with the Law Society; these organisations submitted separate consultation responses to us which differed in some respects.

[27] This language is borrowed from Scottish law: Family Law (Scotland) Acts 1985, s 9, and 2006, s 28. It also forms a central part of the scheme proposed to us by the Law Society, who consider that regard should also be had to the nature of the parties' commitment during their cohabitation.

[28] They base their proposal on the formula used in the Property (Relationships) Act 1984 (New South Wales), s 20.

[29] This too is based on the formula used in the Property (Relationships) Act 1984 (New South Wales), s 27(1).

dependency or interdependency between the parties, the duration of the cohabiting relationship, and the physical and mental ability of each parties to obtain paid employment.

C.28 The difficulty with this proposal, as we see it, lies in the relationship between the overriding objective and the wide-ranging factors in the subsequent list. Resolution envisage cases in which relief should be granted even though it could not be justified by reference to the otherwise overriding principles of economic advantage and disadvantage. For example, they have suggested that relief should be available following a long, childless relationship during which both parties had been in paid employment where shortly before separation one party sustained an injury that prevented him or her from working.

C.29 We consider that this would give rise to the problem described above: uncertainty about which principles would apply and when, and so about the potential nature and scope of liability between cohabitants on separation.[30] Where a scheme merely indicates a wide range of factors to which regard might be had, it is not immediately obvious in an individual case what the basis of any claim is, what factors the court will regard as determinative and so what the award might be. Compromise would seem difficult to attain in such circumstances, as the parties would find the task of predicting the likely outcome of litigation hazardous.

C.30 However, these concerns aside, we note that there is much common ground between our recommended scheme and that of Resolution. We support their view about the inappropriateness for cohabitants of both the MCA generally and a general principle of equal sharing, specifically. They, like us, are keen that a new scheme be devised specifically for cohabitants, focusing on the gains and losses arising from cohabitation.

Relying on opt-out agreements to accommodate diversity?

C.31 Another response to our concerns about the suitability of sharing and need might be to argue that while such principles might not suit everyone, they could nevertheless operate as a default regime. Couples who did not want to be subjected to them would remain free to opt-out of the scheme and reach their own agreement.

C.32 We believe couples should be encouraged to address the financial implications of their relationships expressly and to reach agreement about them wherever possible. At the same time, we are concerned that whatever default position is adopted for those couples who do not or cannot take that step should be appropriate for as many as possible. While some may contend that our judgement of what is most appropriate is incorrect, we remain of the view that sharing and need (in unqualified terms) are not suitable for most cohabiting couples.

RULE- OR FORMULA-BASED SCHEMES AND APPROACHES

C.33 It can be said that an important ingredient of fairness is certainty. As we have just explored, in the context of an essentially discretionary regime, a degree of certainty can be provided by clearly identifying the principles within which that

[30] See paras C.25 and 4.14 to 4.16.

discretion must operate and by excluding more wide-ranging examination of "all the circumstances". While wider examination in each case might appear to offer the potential for more individualised justice, and so fairness in that sense, it does so at the expense of certainty.

C.34 However, the concern for certainty can be taken further. There is growing interest in this jurisdiction in the possibility that ancillary relief on divorce might be reformed in order to provide parties with greater certainty than the MCA scheme appears to afford. This could be effected by the introduction of more concrete rules, presumptions, formulae or guidelines. Options of this sort include community of property regimes;[31] tariffs for recognising particular types of contribution;[32] sharing of at least some categories of property by reference to the duration of the relationship;[33] and formulaic approaches to calculating maintenance[34] and compensation-based awards.[35] Advocates of these approaches are attracted to these options not least because of the forensic difficulties entailed in an individualised approach. It is also becoming increasingly apparent[36] that the position of England and Wales, in not having a matrimonial property regime and not enforcing pre-nuptial agreements, is unusual in the European context.[37]

C.35 It may be that, in the long term, a more rule-based or formulaic approach should be considered by this jurisdiction. However, as we noted in the CP, we do not currently have a statutory regime of sharing for spouses and civil partners. Formulaic approaches to the quantification of financial relief between adult partners (as opposed to child support) are currently alien to this jurisdiction. Moreover, although there is increasing dissatisfaction with the operation of the MCA, in particular its uncertainty of outcome, our consultation exercise indicates that most family law practitioners remain keen to retain a discretionary approach to financial relief on relationship breakdown. Indeed, many may feel that our recommended scheme is itself more restricted than they would like.

C.36 In these circumstances, we do not consider that more rule-based or formulaic approaches can be recommended now for cohabitants. If we were to go down that route in this jurisdiction, the first step would have to be to remodel the system of ancillary relief following the dissolution of marriage and civil partnership.

---

[31] See E Cooke, A Barlow, T Callus, *Community of Property: a regime for England and Wales?* (2006).

[32] *Charman v Charman* [2006] EWHC 1879 (Fam), [2007] 2 FCR 217, at [133] to [136], Coleridge J.

[33] J Eekelaar, "Property and Financial Settlement on Divorce: Sharing and Compensating" (2006) 36 *Family Law* 754.

[34] D Hodson, "A Formula Will Do Nicely, Sir" (2007) 37 *Family Law* 57.

[35] J Eekelaar, "Property and Financial Settlement on Divorce: Sharing and Compensating" (2006) 36 *Family Law* 754.

[36] Note comments made by the Court of Appeal in *Charman v Charman* [2007] EWCA Civ 503, [2007] 2 FCR 217, at [123] to [125].

[37] Like England and Wales, Ireland and Scotland have discretionary systems for the equitable redistribution of wealth on divorce, rather than a matrimonial property regime combined with jurisdiction to make awards of maintenance.

APPENDIX D
ACKNOWLEDGEMENTS

D.1 We are grateful to many individuals and organisations for their invaluable assistance since the CP's publication, including:

MEMBERS OF OUR LEGAL ADVISORY GROUP

Rebecca Bailey-Harris, barrister
David Burles, barrister
Jane Craig, solicitor
Lynn Graham, Legal Services Commission
Mark Harper, solicitor
District Judge Richard Harper
Ann Lewis, Advice Services Alliance
The Honourable Mr Justice Munby
Rebecca Probert, University of Warwick
Dr Jens Scherpe, University of Cambridge
Marilyn Stowe, solicitor
District Judge Helen Wood

OTHER INDIVIDUALS AND ORGANISATIONS

District Judge Duncan Adam
Advicenow
David Allison, solicitor
Association of District Judges
Professor Bill Atkin, Victoria University of Wellington, New Zealand
Dr Samia Bano, University of Reading
Professor Anne Barlow, University of Exeter
Professor Chris Barton
Harry Benson
Dr Margareta Brattström, University of Uppsala, Sweden
Julian Buxton, Centre for Population Studies, London School of Hygiene and
    Tropical Medicine
Ray Byrne, Law Reform Commission of the Republic of Ireland
Dr Janeen Carruthers, University of Glasgow
Chancery Bar Association
Citizens Advice
Lynda Clarke, Centre for Population Studies, London School of Hygiene and
    Tropical Medicine
Liz Clery, National Centre for Social Research
Conveyancing and Land Law Committee of the Law Society
Professor Elizabeth Crawford, University of Glasgow
Michael Croker, Land Registry
Professor Antony Dnes, University of Hull
Professor Gillian Douglas, University of Cardiff
District Judge Sally Dowding
District Judge Julie Exton
Family Justice Council
Family Mediators Association

Family Law Bar Association
Family Law Committee of the Law Society
Dr Belinda Fehlberg, University of Melbourne, Australia
John Fotheringham, solicitor
Peter Hennessy, New South Wales Law Reform Commission, Australia
Judith Ingham, solicitor
Institute of Advanced Legal Studies
Professor Maarit Jänterä-Jareborg, University of Uppsala, Sweden
Mark Jitlal, Centre for Population Studies, London School of Hygiene and
  Tropical Medicine
Kent Law School cohabitation workshop
Professor Kathleen Kiernan, University of York
Law Society, East Midlands Region
Jane Lewis, National Centre for Social Research
David Lockett, actuary
Mavis Maclean, University of Oxford
Kirsty Malcolm, Faculty of Advocates, Edinburgh
Professor Werner Menski, School of Oriental and African Studies, University of
  London
Professor Jenni Millbank, University of Technology Sydney, Australia
David Nichols, Scottish Law Commission
Julie Nind, Ministry of Justice, New Zealand
District Judge Tony North
Nuffield Foundation
One Parent Families
Professor Patrick Parkinson, University of Sydney, Australia
Julia Pearce, University of Bristol
Nazia Rashid, solicitor
Resolution
Jenny Richards, Flinders University, Australia
Tony Roe, solicitor
David Salter, solicitor
Dr Prakash Shah, Queen Mary, University of London
Ian Sharman, solicitor
Steve Smallwood, Office for National Statistics
Society of Legal Scholars, Property Law and Family Law subject sections
Nerissa Steel, Legal Services Commission
Ros Tennant, National Centre for Social Research
Hajj Ahmad Thomson, barrister
Professor Nick Wikeley, University of Southampton
Cathy Williams, University of Sheffield
Wills and Equity Committee of the Law Society
Sharon Witherspoon, Nuffield Foundation
Hilary Woodward, University of Cardiff

Members of staff at the Ministry of Justice

D.2 The following responded to our consultation paper:

LEGAL ORGANISATIONS

Association of District Judges
Association of Muslim Lawyers
Association of Women Solicitors
Centre for Child and Family Law Reform
Chancery Bar Association
Charles Russell (Solicitors)
Family Division of the Supreme Court of Northern Ireland
Family Justice Council
Family Law Bar Association
Institute of Legal Executives
Law Reform Committee of the Bar Council
Law Society
Lawyers' Christian Fellowship
Resolution
Society of Trust and Estate Practitioners

OTHER ORGANISATIONS AND GROUPS

Bristol Community Family Trust
Catholic Bishops' Conference of England and Wales
Catholic Union of Great Britain
Cheltenham Group
Christian Action Research and Education ("CARE")
Evangelical Alliance
Family Education Trust
Manchester Beth Din
Marriage Resource
Men's Aid
Mission and Public Affairs Council of the Church of England
Mothers' Union
Odysseus Trust
One Parent Families
Plaid Cymru
Relate
Rights of Women
Society of Pensions Consultants
Stonewall

GOVERNMENT BODIES

Legal Services Commission
Ministry of Defence

JUDGES

Lord Justice Lloyd
Lord Justice Wall

MEMBER OF PARLIAMENT

The Right Honourable John Redwood MP

INDIVIDUAL LEGAL PRACTITIONERS

Richard Adkinson, barrister
Miranda Allardice, barrister
Simon Beccle, solicitor
Christine Dooley, barrister
Fiona Goode, solicitor
Jenny Gracie, solicitor
David Hodson, solicitor
Jennifer Horne-Roberts, barrister
Caroline Hunter, solicitor
Alison Padfield and Katharine Gollop, barristers
John Passmore, barrister
James Petts, barrister
Alec Samuels, barrister and formerly Reader in Law
Janys Scott, advocate
Emma Slessenger, solicitor
Linda Smith, solicitor
Hajj Ahmad Thomson, barrister
Andrew Turek, solicitor
Arthur Weir, solicitor
Rachel Wingert, barrister
Roy Withyman, solicitor

ACADEMICS

Professor Bill Atkin, Victoria University of Wellington, New Zealand
Professor Anne Barlow, University of Exeter
Professor Chris Barton
Professor Elizabeth Cooke, University of Reading
Dr Stephen Cretney, University of Oxford
Professor Antony Dnes, University of Hull
Professor Gillian Douglas, Julia Pearce and Hilary Woodward, Universities of
  Cardiff and Bristol
John Eekelaar, University of Oxford
Craig Lind, University of Sussex
Rebecca Probert, University of Warwick
Liz Rodgers, Nottingham Trent University
Kate Standley, University of Essex
Dr Dawn Watkins, University of Leicester
Dr Simone Wong, University of Kent

OTHER INDIVIDUALS

The Law Commission received 183 responses from other individuals. Those whom we can identify are named here, unless their response was confidential.

Lynn Alexander-Briggs
Judith Allcock
Michael Alsop

Clare Annamalai
Mary Argent
Caroline and Susan Ashley-Cooper

Terry Ashton
Jan Atkinson
Ken Atkinson
D P Atterbury
Kevin Baker
Adrian Barbour
Enid Barnett
Dudley Baker-Beall
Diane Beedle
Martin Bentham
Olivier Berlage
Barry Biggs
Sandy Blakeborough
Dr Paula Boddington
Terri Bolton
Stephanie Borowska
D Breach
Simon Brickwood
Michael Bright
Dragana Brown
Tracy Bruno
Brian Buchanan
Trish Canham
Mark Charman
A Christiansen
Rachael Churcher
George Clark
Elaine Clarke
Tony Cox
Cherie Cran
Ian Crosland
Ian Cross
Judith Cross
Michael Curtis
James Dancer
R and N Darsley
Jackie David
Dean Davies
Alan Davis
Sharon Davis
Nigel Dodd
S J Donaldson
Jean Driscoll
Morgan Ellis
Stuart Fairney
C E Fennemore
Louise Fisher
Paddy Forrest
Gillian Fox
Dr Elliot Fullwood
Stuart Fyfe
Paul Gay

A N Gallagher and Judith
   Robertson
Karen Gallant
Frank Gerschwiler
Richard Gillingham
Harold Gough
Sue Green
Dr J J Gristock
Alice Halliwell
Gavin Hampshire
M D Halliday
Michael Hardman
Tom Hargreaves
David Harkness
Tony Harmer
Monica Henderson
Dolina Hendry
Daniel Hilling-Smith
Sara Hoare
Shan Jayran
Jenny Jenkins
Christine and Michael Johnson
Gareth Jones
Paul Keane
Simon Kearney
Yasmin Khan
Angela Kilby and Ian Whitehead
David Jason King
J P King
E M Kingsley
Dennis Kirk
Robert Knight
Alan Kristensen
Dr Thomas Langley
S D Lavery
Dr J B Lawton
Peter Leckie
John Lee
Dr Terry Leigh
Andrew Lewicki
David Lloyd
Malcolm Lochhead
Neil Locke
John Jacob Lyons
Marilyn MacPherson
Charles Mahon
Marianne Maunsell
John McBride
Alexandra Merz
Maurice Millen
Paul Millsom
David Mitchell and Joan Irving

Alexandre Montagu and Michael
  Anderson
Janice Moore
Sheryl Morrell
Stanley Morton
Sara Muir
J R Neville
Reverend Nick Nicholas
Ann Palmer
M Parker
Reverend Canon Robert Paterson
David Peers
Jenet Peers
Brian Peters
Caroline Petherick
Lucas Phillips
Jo Pollock
H A Prowse
David Redman
Kim Revell
Lesley Richards
John Rigg
Faith Robertson
Lynn Rowan
Doug Rickard
Vivien Ross
M Rutherford
David Ryland
Colin and Margaret Rymill
David Ryszka

Nejla Sabberton
Marion Saunders
Christine Scales
Helen Scarlett
Paul Scott
Sue Shepherd
Susan Singleton
Jen Sjoberg
Anne Smith
John Smith
Haward Soper
Phillip Sorensen
Ruth Stanley
Jerry Suenson-Taylor
Robert Swift
Kathlyn Thomas
Steve Towbridge
J Unwin
Kevin Walden
Tony Walpole
Stuart Watson
C M Webster
Arthur Weir
Chris White
Stuart White
Paul Wilds
Janet Williams
Shaun Winter
D M Woodward

Printed in the UK for The Stationery Office Limited
on behalf of the Controller of Her Majesty's Stationery Office
ID5610370 07/07

Printed on Paper containing 75% recycled fibre content minimum.